DYNASTY

Thanks to the Boston Celtics of my youth for making basketball so much fun to watch and to my father Joseph Freedman and uncle Sidney Kristal for taking me to my first NBA games when I was too young to drive.

DYNASTY

THE RISE OF THE BOSTON CELTICS

LEW FREEDMAN

The Lyons Press
Guilford, Connecticut
An imprint of The Globe Pequot Press

The Lyons Press is an imprint of The Globe Pequot Press.

Text design by Maggie Peterson

Library of Congress Cataloging-in-Publication Data

Freedman, Lew.
Dynasty : the rise of the Boston Celtics / Lew Freedman.
    p. cm. Includes bibliographical references and index.
    ISBN 978-1-59921-124-4
 1. Boston Celtics (Basketball team)—History. I. Title.
GV885.52.B67F74 2008
796.323'640974461—dc22

2008008711

Printed in the United States of America
10 9 8 7 6 5 4 3 2 1

CONTENTS

ACKNOWLEDGMENTS

A special thank you to Mike Carey, former longtime Boston Celtics beat writer at the city's newspapers, for his encouragement with my career long ago and his beyond-the-call help with this project.

Thanks to the staff at the research library at the Naismith Basketball Hall of Fame in Springfield, Massachusetts. They provided help and direction in sorting out musty newspaper clips from a half-century ago and led me to the Bill Mokray scrapbook collection, which charts the early years of the Celtics. Reading *Boston Globe* and *Boston Herald* stories from the sports pages of the 1950s and 1960s reacquainted me with the work of Jack Barry, Joe Looney, Clif Keane, Bud Collins, and others.

Thanks to all the former Celtics and NBA players all over the country who took the time for lengthy telephone conversations, delving into their memory banks to relive the days of their playing careers.

And thanks to the Boston Celtics dynasty teams that provided me with so many fond memories, and the leader of those teams, Red Auerbach, whom I did have the pleasure of meeting some years ago at (where else?) the Boston Garden.

INTRODUCTION: ME AND THE CELTICS

My team. The Boston Celtics were the team of my youth, the team that more than any other turned me into a sports fan. The Celtics spoiled me with unprecedented success, winning with such regularity, grace, and style that they numbed the rest of the basketball world.

When you're a kid you love the sport for the sport's sake if it engages you, but you have a blind allegiance to your hometown team as well. So if the hometown team verges on perfection, if it not only wins whenever you go to a game, watch a game on television, or listen to a game on the radio, addiction comes easily. Then, as a bonus, if that team wins the world championship year after year, chances are you are hooked for life.

The Celtics Dynasty was a run of eleven championships in thirteen seasons, beginning in 1957 and concluding in 1969, when I was eighteen. As a youngster living in a Boston suburb, sometimes we attended Celtics games as a family, my father, Joseph, the planner, my mother, Phyllis, a general rooter, my sister, Barbara, involved in team sport cheering for perhaps the only time in her life, and my brother, Alan, like me a fan of the game. More than forty years later, with knees that have held up better than mine, Alan still plays hoops in two rec leagues every week.

Our most memorable Celtics family outing was being in attendance in the balcony for Bob Cousy Day at the Boston Garden, the game when the great guard was honored on March 17, 1963, prior to his retirement. I still have the game program. In adulthood I have seen only two other copies, both in museums. I still have the program from Red Auerbach Day in 1966 too, when he was making the transition from being the world's greatest basketball coach to the world's greatest basketball executive.

I also benefited from field trips to the Garden with an uncle, Sidney Kristal, who loved the NBA above all, and took me to doubleheaders regularly, even when they ran late on school nights. Yes, in those days, a league struggling for complete public acceptance might feature a preliminary game with two other league teams, or a warm-up game highlighting the Harlem Globetrotters. It was an awesome deal.

In an era when the season was shorter, the Celtics were always involved in the playoffs in April, the month of my birth, and Celtics playoff tickets became my regular birthday present. I couldn't think of anything I wanted more.

Most games I accompanied either my father or my uncle—just two of us at a time. Regardless of my companion, we had the same ritual. We stopped at the Joe and Nemo hot dog stand across from the Garden entrance in North Station. Then as we walked up one of the winding ramps into the Garden, we came upon the same peanut vendor seated in a corridor. He used crutches and, if memory serves, had lost a leg. I can hear his voice in my head still, "Peanuts a dime! Three for a quarter!" We always shelled out the two bits for unsalted nuts in their little brown bags.

In between Celtic games seen in person, I relied on the radio descriptions of harsh-voiced Johnny Most to tell me what was going on. I depended on the radio more than Joe Louis fans did during his heavyweight heyday. It wasn't until I was in college that I ever heard anyone (New York Knicks fans) say that Most was a "homer." As a kid, I just thought he was telling it like it is. Often, especially during games from other time zones, I fell asleep to Most's hectic play-by-play.

In elementary school and junior high, my best friend's dad owned a boys' clothing store in town. It was named Eric Stevens after his two sons. At a time when athletic endorsements were rare and less lucrative, Mr. Black enticed several members of the Celtics to appear at his store to sign autographs. By virtue of my status as Eric's friend, I got to schmooze with players in the back room. I still have the autographed photos. I wonder if those players made more than $50 to do the signings. It is difficult to imagine today's millionaire players making such appearances.

One way players earned extra income was by hosting summer basketball camps. A week's worth of basketball, seven hours a day, beat the heck out of day-camp whittling. In the summers after eighth and ninth grades, I attended Celtics forward Jim Loscutoff's basketball camp. Several years later, when he was coaching at Boston State, I interviewed him for a story. Decades later, I reminded Loscutoff that in my second year at his camp I was the youngest, shortest, slowest, worst player in the senior division.

"I hope we gave you a trophy," he quipped.

No trophy, but I learned some hard lessons about where I ranked in the sport's hierarchy.

Over the years, sometimes in my role as a sportswriter, sometimes not, I met almost all the prominent Celtics of the Dynasty era. I talked amiably with Bob Cousy at the NCAA Final Four in Indianapolis after he presented the Bob Cousy Point Guard Award and informed him that he sent me an autographed picture on request when I was about eleven.

In 2001, when I opened a copy of the *Chicago Tribune,* I was stunned by an advertisement heralding the appearance of Bill Russell at a Borders book store on Michigan Avenue, the Magnificent Mile, signing copies of a new book. For decades, Russell had notoriously refused to sign autographs. Now he was going to sign his name for three hours? This I had to see. I waited an hour to obtain Russell's signature on a book, and it took this long because he graciously chatted with every customer.

We briefly talked about the Celtics of the 1950s and 1960s and the Boston Garden, and his parting comment about the old building was, "Between you and me, it was a dump."

I so admired Cousy and Russell as a kid, and I rooted from the depths of my heart for Tommy Heinsohn, Frank Ramsey, Tom Sanders, Jim Loscutoff, Bill Sharman, Sam Jones, K. C. Jones, John Havlicek, and all the others in green. I knew I was watching something special, but it wasn't until I was much older, when time provided perspective, that some of their feats seemed so incredible. Just how amazing is it that the first-team backcourt of Cousy and Sharman was backed up by Sam and K. C., and that all four were elected to the Hall of Fame?

Year after year, the Celtics won, with essentially the same cast—a circumstance now impossible given the free agency of the modern era—men molded by a singularly wise master of the game, Red Auerbach. The Dynasty is a great sports story, but it is a story rooted in a transcending and tumultuous period in American history. The longevity of the championship run is boggling. But that it was constructed and played out against the backdrop of tremendous societal upheaval is even more remarkable.

When the Celtics Dynasty began, Elvis Presley was king. By the time it ended, the Beatles were princes.

When the Celtics Dynasty began, blacks across America were routinely discriminated against. By the time it ended, federal law ensuring black voting rights was in place, and Martin Luther King Jr. was an international hero. Along the way, the Celtics became the first pro basketball team to start five black players in 1965 and the first team in any sport to hire a black coach in 1966.

When the Celtics Dynasty began, the United States was just beginning to assume the failed role of the French in Vietnam. By the time it ended, the United States was trying to extricate itself from Vietnam.

When the Celtics Dynasty began, professional basketball was a niche sport still seeking its footing among American sports fans, a game that relied more on tried and true x's and o's than improvisation, a game where many players still employed the set shot. By the time it ended, pro basketball was a vertical game, and everyone used the revolutionary jump shot.

When the Celtics Dynasty began, players were contractually tied to teams until they were cut. By the time it ended, a union had been formed and grown and a rival league, the American Basketball Association, established, providing players employment options and making them rich.

The Celtics players were a diverse group of men from all corners of the country, but they had more in common than they, or anyone else, would have thought. Dramatic changes swirled about them, powerful social changes took hold in the country, the nature of basketball itself changed, but none of those developments distracted the players enough to disturb their artistry on the court. All the Celtics did between 1957 and 1969—while their nation changed forever—was win.

1

RAW BEGINNINGS

As a 1930s Depression-era kid in Hillsdale, Wyoming, with the closest neighbor a half-mile away, Kenny Sailors's pickup games were one-on-one against his brother Bud—his older brother, his bigger brother, who had six inches on him and what seemed like a mile's worth of reach advantage.

In their backyard basketball games amid the swirling dust and a Rocky Mountains backdrop, the boy counted on guile to survive. If there was ever a hope of outscoring Bud, he'd need a fresh idea. He didn't want that leather ball swatted back into his face each time he tried to throw up a shot. It took some time, and some blocked shots, before he found a way.

One day the solution came to him. When Bud stretched out to knock his rising shot into the next county, Kenny fooled him. Instead of firing a slow-to-unfold set shot, he jumped. Instead of releasing the ball in front of his jaw, he let the ball fly at the apex of his leap, hands over his head.

It was simple, really, the physics of it. Logical, too, the intuitiveness of it. But until then, it was an undiscovered weapon, the mere suggestion of a basketball player leaving his feet to pass or shoot was heresy. It was reckless behavior, not to be tolerated by a grounded coach. Only feckless, fundamentally unsound players dared attempt such plays.

Other basketball players around the country were toying with shooting innovations. They took one-hand shots instead of cradling the ball cautiously in two hands. They tried running one-handers where they threw the ball toward the hoop though they seemed unbalanced. Outside shooting morphed from many hands, but the man who invented the jump shot, the true jump shot as it is employed today by every playground player, gym rat, scholarship collegian, and moneyed pro, was Kenny Sailors.

"I don't say that I'm the first guy who ever shot a jump shot," Sailors said. "I'm sure there must be some kid somewhere who jumped in the air and shot a ball somewhere. But the old-timers credit me with it."

Sailors rode the jump shot from the Hillsdale prairie, 25 miles east of Cheyenne, to high school stardom, to the Most Valuable Player award in the 1943 NCAA championship game—when the University of Wyoming won the title—to the cover of *Life* magazine, where he was shown in mid-air demonstrating a splendid vertical leap for a 5-foot-11 guard.

The late Ray Meyer, who coached at DePaul University for forty-two years, was one of those old-timers.

"There's a lot of people who say they shot it before him," Meyer said. "Kenny was the jump shooter that we know today. He got off the floor."

Joe Lapchick, one of the original Celtics from the 1920s and a famous coach for St. John's University and the New York Knicks, called Sailors "one of the most influential players of the century."

The NBA was founded in 1946, a meshing of two predecessor leagues. One of the original coaches, with the Washington Capitols, was a young man named Red Auerbach. One of the original players, with the Cleveland Rebels, was Kenny Sailors. Sailors played professionally for the first five years of the NBA, moving on to the Providence Steamrollers, the original Denver Nuggets, and the Baltimore Bullets. For a few months during the 1950–51 season, Auerbach's first season with the Boston Celtics, Sailors was a player for the team.

Sailors's first pro coach, Dutch Dehnert, another of the original Celtics, was skeptical of the jump shot. He didn't think much of players who used it, admonishing Sailors. "Sailors," the player said the coach told him,

"Where did you get that running one-hander? You will never make it in this league with that shot."

Dehnert was wrong about Sailors, who averaged in double figures during his career, and wrong about the shot itself. Imagine Dehnert coping with the fly-through-the-air acrobatic players of today's game.

The National Basketball Association that Sailors and Auerbach joined was a second-class citizen in the sports world. Baseball reigned as the national pastime. College football was more popular than the pro game. Boxing was in its glory days, and horse racing, today reduced to sports-page prominence for the Triple Crown and Breeder's Cup only, was big news almost daily. Sports editors never sent their writers on the road for NBA games, and sometimes the only report to fans was a few paragraphs accompanied by a box score. *Dick Tracy* comics often got more space.

During its formative years the league was a crazy quilt of cities with teams coming and going. At one time franchises were located in Sheboygan, Wisconsin; Anderson, Indiana; and Waterloo, Iowa. Still, major metropolises such as New York, Boston, and Philadelphia were represented. In some cases, owners like Celtics founder Walter Brown held deed to arenas that needed more tenants. (Brown was essentially a hockey man whose Bruins occupied the Boston Garden many winter nights.)

But there were many other November-through-March dates available. Initially, Brown was less an enthusiast of professional basketball than a building manager looking for a fresh event to display on the marquee. Eventually, he fell in love with the Celtics, felt paternalistic toward the outfit, and basked in the glory attained.

As owners such as Ned Irish, whose Knicks played at Madison Square Garden, Ben Kerner of the Hawks, whose team settled into St. Louis for a long run at Kiel Auditorium, and Fred Zollner, who transferred his Pistons from Fort Wayne, Indiana, to Detroit, coped with drafty buildings at first, other franchises folded. The league's players were all white, the game's pace was stodgy, salaries were low, and outside income was virtually nonexistent for players who rated far behind baseball players in celebrity status in their home city.

Sailors, who made a peak salary of $7,500, had one endorsement opportunity in his career—prune juice. All he could drink.

"And that was a big deal," Sailors said at age eighty-six from his home in Laramie, Wyoming. "It was completely different. People always ask me why I didn't play longer than five years. I couldn't make any money. The NBA didn't amount to a whole lot then. The NBA was pretty shaky back then."

A rookie at twenty-six after twice being chosen All-American at Wyoming and spending three years as a captain in the Marines, Sailors's best season was 1949–50 when he averaged 17.3 ppg for Denver and was selected second-team all-pro. The Nuggets folded after that season, however, and the NBA conducted a dispersal draft—something common enough in those days when teams went belly-up.

"Walter Brown pulled my name out of a hat," Sailors said.

Sailors became a Celtic the same year Auerbach became coach.

The idea of the Celtics growing into the most storied basketball team in the world seemed far-fetched in the early days of the NBA. Brown clutched his forehead almost as often as his thinning wallet while attempting to transform his nonstop headache into a profitable business venture.

Their first season, 1946–47, the Celtics finished 22-38, last in the Eastern Division. The next year Boston was 20-28, the third season 25-35, the fourth season last again at 22-46. Brown's groans could be heard in St. Louis, the farthest-west outpost of the league at the time.

It was the product, not the building, keeping fans away. In its old age, critics viewed the Boston Garden as a decrepit dowager, with rats running uncontrolled under the floorboards. But in the late 1940s and early 1950s, the Garden was a sports palace. It seated 13,909 for basketball—a figure that would stick prominently in fans' minds during the title years when announcer Johnny Most repeated it on the air.

The Boston Garden opened in 1928 and besides being home to the Celtics and hockey's Bruins, it hosted political conventions, tennis matches, music personalities from Rudy Vallee to Elvis Presley, the famed Beanpot college hockey tournament, boxing title matches, the circus, and the Ice Capades.

Before the Garden closed in 1995, Joe Louis fought there, Bob Dylan and Bruce Springsteen sang there, Roy Rogers rode rodeo there, George Burns and Gracie Allen told jokes there, and Bobby Orr skated there. So did Olympian Sonja Henie. John F. Kennedy, on his way to the presidency in 1960, spoke there.

The legendary parquet floor, unlike any other, recognizable via television anywhere in the world, was always present for a basketball game. The removable floor—a puzzle of interlocking wooden panels—would be laid down over the Bruins' ice sheet. In later years, it was said in dead seriousness that Celtics players possessed a great advantage over opponents because they knew where all the dead spots on the floor were located. The implication was that visitors made dribbling errors bouncing the ball off a crack while the Celtics had a road map in their heads to avoid them.

Opponents complained of cold water in the showers, cramped visitors' locker rooms, the heat being turned up on hot days and the heat being turned down on cold days. Auerbach smirked and humored the complaints with vague replies. It was part of his psych job, seeking to gain every little advantage, real or imagined.

The phrase Celtic Mystique has leached into basketball lexicon, but John Havlicek, a member of the early title teams who stayed a Celtic long enough for the rebuilding success of the 1970s, laughed about the application of the words beyond victories. If the Celtics had a real-life leprechaun to match its winking, cartoonlike character team symbol twirling a basketball on a fingertip, it was Auerbach. Not many people called him impish; nonetheless, he seemed to share a certain number of characteristics with the mascot's image.

"Red's the one who created the mystique," Havlicek said. "It was always the result of some shenanigan. We didn't know where the dead spots were on the floor. Meanwhile, we had cold showers too."

And if anyone ventured into the home locker room in the Garden, the most favorable comparison they could make to other real estate was that it resembled a dilapidated inner-city studio apartment. No wonder Bill Russell called the entire structure "a dump." But he did say it fondly, while chuckling.

Walter Brown was a Boston Irishman and was considered a sportsman at a time when the word meant something more than a guy with deep pockets who liked athletes. He was known for his honesty and candor, and in 1946, Brown, in a tête-à-tête with Howie McHugh, later a team official, named the team the Celtics. Some other choices on the table were Unicorns and Whirlwinds, both of which got the hook faster than a lousy vaudeville performer. Brown chose Celtics because Boston was full of Irishmen, and they wore green uniforms for the same reason.

Brown fervently believed that basketball would be a hit in Boston, but poor attendance accompanied the dismal early records of his team. Meanwhile, in the first year of the NBA the best regular-season record was earned by the Washington Capitols, who finished 49-11. The Capitols were coached by a brash professional newcomer named Arnold "Red" Auerbach, who had yet to establish his fame.

After three years in Washington—his hometown—and a dispiriting season leading the Tri-Cities Hawks (the only losing season of his NBA coaching career), Auerbach was available when Brown needed a new floor general. In a partnership that outlasted tough times, that bred uncommon affection, loyalty, and respect, Auerbach joined Brown and the Celtics for the 1950–51 season. Together they molded a sorry team into champions and created the greatest basketball dynasty ever.

That year, All-American guard Bob Cousy, from nearby Holy Cross, was foisted on a kicking and screaming Auerbach, the beginning of another unique partnership that foreshadowed the authorship of history.

Kenny Sailors made his few-month cameo in Boston that season too, and described Auerbach as initially low-key.

"When he first came there, he was just feeling his way," Sailors said. "He didn't do much yelling. He had four or five tough little guards. Red didn't need me. I finally said, 'You guys drew me by luck. Why don't you sell me or trade me?' "

Sailors was shipped to the Baltimore Bullets, where he ended his career that spring and went on to a life as a big-game hunting guide, a teacher, and a coach of high school basketball in Alaska.

Sailors remains popular and visible in Wyoming. In 1990 when the NCAA Final Four was held in Denver, as part of a tribute to Rocky Mountain basketball, Sailors was the keynote speaker at a pretournament dinner. He is a member of his university's hall of fame and attends many football and basketball games. Even though he spent only a small portion of his career with the Celtics, the other teams he played for folded, so that affiliation is frequently cited in connection with his name.

"I sure was proud of the fact that I played with them," Sailors said.

Sailors, always in tremendous physical shape from guiding hunters at high altitudes and taking long walks, still occasionally visited the gym to play one-on-one and practice his jump shot until he turned eighty.

It wasn't long after his retirement that the Boston Celtics and the other teams in the NBA were loaded with jump shooters.

2

A MAN NAMED RED

When it came to managing men and building a team, Arnold "Red" Auerbach was always the smartest guy in the room. He read the NBA laws like a lawyer looking for loopholes. From the time owner Walter Brown brought him to Boston to coach the Celtics, Auerbach was the architect of the organization, the godfather of the team.

He was always protective of his team and players, whether it was with referees, other team's officials or players, fans, anyone perceived to be on the other side. A rogue, a manipulator, fiercely loyal, and ruthless in search of an edge, Auerbach was all of these things.

Never the friendliest general manager in the league, Auerbach was all about winning. And you couldn't be all about winning if you had a soft spot that someone might consider weakness. He was very basic and very complex, but above all he was a genius of the hardwood.

The most amazing—and telling—summation of Auerbach's half-century career as coach, general manager, and president of the Celtics is that he was probably the greatest professional basketball coach of all time and he was arguably the greatest professional basketball executive of all time.

Those around Auerbach would be hard-pressed to remember him expressing moments of doubt. He was the one who put the belief in others.

Even young Red Auerbach seemed to know where he wanted to go and to have a plan how to get there. Once he joined the NBA with the Capitols, he focused on getting to the playoffs and winning championships. Yet it took a decade of coaching pro basketball before Auerbach coached a title winner. Once he started, he never stopped.

The original NBA days of Auerbach were erased from the memory of others, replaced by the image of a grinning champion puffing on his big fat victory cigar, waving it in the faces of the vanquished. In the rough-and-tumble NBA of the 1950s, when fights were common, verbal abuse routine, and rivalries extraordinarily heated, Auerbach reveled in being the last man standing. As he laid the brick-and-mortar foundation of the abstract—Celtic Mystique—Auerbach proclaimed, "The Boston Celtics are not a basketball team. They are a way of life."

Walter Brown hired Red Auerbach after sitting around in a bull session with Boston sportswriters sampling their opinions. That is an unlikely modern-day scenario. Brown's previous coaches didn't win and didn't fill the Boston Garden. He believed in the eventual success of the Celtics, but he didn't want to go bankrupt from the courage of his convictions. Brown was rich compared to the average hourly worker, but he was not a Rockefeller, Vanderbilt, or Morgan. He possessed the wealth of a successful businessman, not the gilt of a tycoon. It was not impossible for the Celtics to send him to the poor house, as went the expression so often used in the 1950s.

In Auerbach, Brown discovered a man passionate to win, with a kindred philosophy of spending what it took but not a nickel more. In time Auerbach invested Brown's money as conservatively as if the two shared a joint bank account. One immediate dividend for Brown was the willingness of Auerbach's brother, Zang, a noted artist and cartoonist, to design a team logo. It was Zang who created the grinning leprechaun as the Celtics symbol.

Auerbach hustled as if a big bully was going to round the corner and steal his earnings. If there was one thing most of his prized recruits and draft picks—white and black—had in common during the glory years, it was that they did not grow up in families that placed silver spoons in their mouths. They might not all have had outhouse upbringings, but they didn't live in mansions either.

They also had winning backgrounds. Auerbach's handpicked men usually came with championship resumes from high school and college.

"Red Auerbach was a management genius," said Hall of Fame Celtics forward Tommy Heinsohn. "The teams I played on had so many players that had won a championship in their conference, or a national title, [and] they had shown evidence they knew how to win and be part of a winning team."

Auerbach was born on September 20, 1917, the son of Hymie and Marie Auerbach, who met working in a Manhattan restaurant. Hymie was an immigrant from Minsk, Russia, and his family fled from the growing hostility to Jews in the early part of the twentieth century, settling in the Williamsburg section of Brooklyn. Later, Hymie ran his own delicatessen and, by the time Auerbach turned fourteen, operated a clothes cleaning and drying plant, then a dry cleaners. Auerbach was one of four children—three boys and a girl.

Auerbach became enamored of his two favorite sports, handball and basketball, at an early age. He was the captain of his high school handball team and was selected second-team All-Brooklyn in basketball despite suffering from asthma and never growing taller than 5-foot-9. He then enrolled in Seth Low Junior College in New York. One of his classmates was Isaac Asimov, whose later fame was built on a vivid imagination expressed through science fiction. Asimov never had a great outside shot, but apparently he could see the future. Auerbach likewise.

After two years at Seth Low, Auerbach transferred to George Washington University. The school and its basketball coach, Bill Reinhart, exerted a lifelong influence on Auerbach, who maintained his home in the District of Columbia throughout his decades of affiliation with the Celtics. Reinhart believed in an up-tempo game, and Auerbach claimed that Reinhart invented fast-break basketball. If so, the Celtics certainly perfected it. Auerbach, a heretofore overactive dribbler, learned how much more efficiently a team could get the ball upcourt to attack with long passes instead of a guard's walk-it-up dribbling.

Auerbach is best remembered as a balding, gray-haired man, but as a young man he deserved the nickname Red. Years later he said Reinhart always remained calm and in control, but Auerbach attributed his own tendency to blow a gasket to having red hair. Auerbach called Reinhart a great coach who was way ahead of his time.

The future legendary coach soaked in Reinhart's methods and emphasis on rebounding, tossing the outlet pass deep, and running the ball. In his early years with the Celtics, Auerbach didn't have the personnel to operate that type of offense, but with Bob Cousy at point guard and Bill Russell at center, fast-breaking became the Celtics trademark.

Dorothy Lewis was a freshman at George Washington when Auerbach was a junior. She aspired to a career in journalism, and by the time she met Red had already obtained work writing a love-advice column for the old *Washington Times-Herald*. Auerbach wooed her at the Student Club with such innocent activities as the purchase of a Coca-Cola and a walk on campus. She was the daughter of a doctor, and Auerbach planned to become a teacher. He would do plenty of instructing in the years to come, just not in the normal classroom.

Auerbach earned a degree in physical education from George Washington in 1940 and immediately began a master's program before marrying Dorothy in 1941. He also became a high school basketball coach at nearby St. Alban's Prep School.

Years later, Auerbach amused his Celtics players by telling them a story about his brief tenure at St. Albans. Auerbach informed his high school players that basketball was a simple game. He held up a ball and said, "This is a basketball." Then he said the object of the game was to put the ball in the hole and to prevent the other team from putting the ball in the hole. "Any questions so far?" he asked.

Coming from a man who guided the Celtics to nine world championships with a playbook that was only seven basic plays thick, the reduced summary of the sport seemed completely believable. Hall of Famer John Havlicek said Auerbach just felt that "proper execution would make a play successful." That was the trump card in Auerbach's repertoire. You might know what was coming if you scouted his teams, but his teams were so superbly drilled that they could make the play work anyway.

After completing his graduate degree, Auerbach was hired by Roosevelt High School to teach history and hygiene and to coach the basketball and baseball teams. His salary was $1,800. Employing his sophisticated eye for talent, Auerbach plucked a gangly, 6-foot-5 Bowie Kuhn out of the student body and suited him up in the frontcourt. Kuhn's future would lie elsewhere. Decades later Kuhn was selected as the commissioner of Major League Baseball.

This was the crossroads of Auerbach's adult life. He sampled his future and might have spent the next forty years as an anonymous high school teacher and coach, but World War II intervened. He was summoned into the Navy and assigned to develop recreational programs for sailors. When he completed his naval service, Auerbach yearned for a bigger challenge than high school coaching. Coincidentally, there was a new professional basketball league forming with a franchise in Washington. At the age of twenty-eight, with only high school head-coaching experience, he talked his way into the job of leading the Capitols.

There were some fine players on the squad, including Bob Feerick, Fred Scolari, and Horace "Bones" McKinney. McKinney, who became a successful coach and a longtime Auerbach confidante, later recommended to his former boss an unheralded guard from North Carolina, Sam Jones, who would become a key cog in the Celtics' championship run.

A single-season interlude with the Tri-Cities Blackhawks representing Rock Island and Moline, Illinois, and Davenport, Iowa, followed Auerbach's Capitols stint. Auerbach signed on with Ben Kerner, who subsequently moved the team to St. Louis, where they became a huge Celtics rival. Kerner and Auerbach disagreed mightily over player abilities. Each thought he knew more about basketball than the other. The tension induced Auerbach to listen to other NBA offers.

In 1950, as Auerbach accepted the job to coach the Celtics, one of his early worries came true. When Auerbach decided to try professional coaching in Washington, D.C., he understood that there was little job security and that someday he might have to take a job in another city. But he chose not to uproot Dorothy and their two daughters, Nancy and Randy. Dorothy preferred living in D.C., and Nancy, like her father, had asthma. Her parents and grandparents agreed that the climate in Washington might be better for her. Throughout his great success with the Celtics, Auerbach retained his main residence in D.C. along with secondary living quarters in Boston. Somehow, his marriage endured.

Auerbach, the coach, was neither cuddly nor a big-brother figure to his players. He could be brusque. He was tough and demanding. He didn't wait for outside observers to call him a dictator, but he described himself that way.

"There is room for only one boss, and that's me," he said.

Auerbach had an open door for players who wanted to talk and he listened to their ideas about basketball. But when he issued an order, he wanted it followed. To Auerbach the dirtiest word in the English language was *Why?* He was the superior military officer in command and he wanted a salute, not a quiz, when he told players what to do.

Well before Auerbach became the Celtics coach, many of his later widely publicized habits or identifying traits were ingrained. Although he never smoked cigarettes, he smoked a pipe when he was younger. He started smoking cigars in the Navy and he first smoked a cigar on the bench while coaching when he was still with the Capitols. Other coaches smoked cigarettes, so he saw no reason why he couldn't light up a stogie. He smoked them all the time, perhaps ten a day, not just during games.

Mark Acres, a Celtic from the 1980s, once said, "You could always smell his cigar before you saw him coming." At least it was the aroma of victory.

Over the years, Auerbach gravitated from Robert Burns, Antonio Cleopatra, to Hoyo de Monterrey, or Dutch Masters cigars. It was the sight of Auerbach contentedly puffing away symbolizing that his team had the game wrapped up before the final buzzer that made opponents choke rather than the thick cloud of smoke enveloping his head. Other coaches and players who considered the maneuver to be disagreeable taunting would have been happy to smash the cigar down Auerbach's throat. Surprisingly, it never happened.

Another habit Auerbach acquired early was carrying a rolled-up program in his left hand as he marched up and down the sideline. The program wasn't for reading material in case he got bored. When Auerbach first coached the Capitols, he would pound his right fist into the palm of his left hand repeatedly during the game, regularly bruising or cutting his hand on his wedding ring. Whacking the program against his hand served the same demonstrative purpose without the same risk of injury.

Fans and other players might have figured that Auerbach shouted at his guys in practice as often as he did on the sidelines during games. There were innumerable photographs of Auerbach cupping his right hand over his mouth and yelling to be heard over the roar of arena crowds, but Auerbach didn't shout at the Celtics all of the time.

Ernie Barrett, a 6-foot-3 guard drafted No. 1 out of Kansas State in 1951, said Auerbach's skill at handling players always impressed him. "He knew which players responded well to the screaming, and he knew which ones to motivate in a more subtle way," Barrett said.

Auerbach said it was imperative that he maintain mutual respect with his players. As a coach he had to make it clear that he understood and knew the game's nuances, or the players would lose respect for him. X's and o's counted. K. C. Jones, a nine-year guard in the championship era, called Auerbach "an encyclopedia of basketball." That may be one way to say that he wrote the book.

These days, coaches in the NBA wear suits straight out of the pages of *GQ*. There seems to be a subterranean competition to see who is the best-dressed sideline mentor. Armani seems to be a bigger name to them than their power forward. Auerbach may have finished first in the standings, but he would have placed last in a fashion sweepstakes. Kids used to take umbrage at the taunt, "Your mother dresses you funny!" Auerbach would have tuned out the comment.

Auerbach seemed to shop nowhere more upscale than Goodwill. He wore so much unsightly plaid that he might as well have matched his sport coats with a kilt. He just didn't care. He wasn't on the prowl to meet women. He wasn't a night-life aficionado. No one could convince Red Auerbach that wearing a more tasteful sport jacket was going to help the Celtics win games, so it was irrelevant.

Finally, early on in his professional tenure, Auerbach developed his passion for Chinese food. He did not like to eat before games, but after the buzzer sounded he was famished. Chinese restaurants were open late, and he would often get take-out. Auerbach found it easier to digest noodles and rice than other types of cuisine.

So four elements—cigar smoking, toting the rolled-up program, dressing as if his entire wardrobe was full of hand-me-downs, and noshing on chow mein—were long established in Auerbach's routine before he ever won a championship with the Boston Celtics. The habit of winning it all came a little bit later in the 1950s.

But it was winning, more than Chinese food, that Auerbach hungered for. Bill Russell, the center who has been called the greatest winner in team sports, once said of his coach that Red "thought about winning more than I thought about eating when I was little."

Bob Cousy, the other player so closely linked with Auerbach's greatest on-court moments, said people told him throughout his life that he was "overly competitive. But I've never seen anyone like Arnold, where the commitment to winning was so absolute."

It took years, however, for the formula that percolated in Auerbach's mind and the desire that roiled his gut to take form on the court, years before anyone bestowed the appendage *World Champions* on the Boston Celtics.

3

BELOVED BOB COUSY

The Bob Cousy acquisition story is legendary in Boston. It's the first luck-of-the-Irish tale ascribed to the leprechaun.

Cousy was a 6-foot-1 guard who was an All-American at Holy Cross, a wizard with the basketball at a time when coaches believed more forcefully in fundamentals than magic. Cousy basically invented the behind-the-back pass and he was more popular in Boston than baked beans.

For a franchise struggling on the court and at the box office, the Cooz seemed to be the appropriate prescription, medicine for what ailed Walter Brown. But Red Auerbach didn't want him. He wanted a big man to build around, a reliable rebounder to clean the glass. Short guys were in plentiful supply. Tall guys were in short supply. The Celtics had enough guards.

Auerbach seemed wary of Cousy's propensity for show time, to make glitzy plays. He pictured a player who fired passes that his teammates couldn't catch. He imagined a player with an ego the size of the Empire State Building—rather like his own—and he couldn't have that. It didn't suit the dictator in him.

Presiding over the April 1950 draft of collegiate players, Auerbach, his resistance solidifying as pressure mounted for him to select Cousy, made one of the biggest personnel gaffes of his career. Perhaps because of hubris, the genius goofed. He dug in his heels against the wishes (but not orders) of Walter Brown and local newspapermen. He not only passed over Cousy in the selection process, but Auerbach famously rubbed it in, commenting with disdain about Cousy's capabilities.

The Celtics' No. 1 pick was 6-foot-10 Charlie Share from Bowling Green University in Ohio, the rebounder Auerbach sought. Only college basketball fans appreciated Share's name, though Auerbach definitely thought he was acquiring a player who would share the ball. By comparison, Cousy was a household name in Boston.

Auerbach infuriated the writers by being Auerbach. He made his choice and defended it vociferously. It was the sportswriters' introduction to the gruff, often cantankerous new coach. In one of the most famous utterances of his Celtics tenure, Auerbach declared, "I don't give a damn for sentiment or names. That goes for Cousy and everybody else. The only thing that counts with me is ability, and Cousy still hasn't proven to me that he's got that ability. I'm not interested in drafting someone just because he happens to be a local yokel."

Local yokel? That tore it. Grumbles turned to roars. It was bad enough, the writers felt, that Auerbach wasn't smart enough to pick the right player, but to insult him too? Auerbach, who had convinced Brown that he was doing the proper thing, turned to the owner and said, "Am I supposed to win, or am I supposed to please these guys?" Echoing the future declaration of Oakland Raiders owner Al Davis, Brown replied, "Just win."

Brown supported the men he hired. He did want to see Cousy in a Celtics uniform and felt the player would help the gate. But he had agreed to a hands-off stance in yielding to Auerbach's basketball wisdom. He would not pull a Ben Kerner. This was the first test of his faith in Auerbach. Many times in the coming years Auerbach would fulfill that faith, pointing to his own track record. There was no track record yet, but Brown chose not to meddle.

Cousy grew up in New York, but was an adopted son of Massachusetts. Holy Cross is located in Worcester, about 35 miles from downtown Boston, but the Crusaders played some home games at the Boston Garden. Cousy's flair and Holy Cross's 1947 NCAA championship outdrew the Celtics at the

Garden. Heck, the 10,000 fans who showed up to celebrate the title at the train station in Worcester when the Crusaders returned from Madison Square Garden outdrew the Celtics. With the NBA's early emphasis on teams selecting players who had a big name in their home territories, Cousy expected to turn pro with the Celtics. He was devastated by Auerbach's harsh assessment.

Born Robert Joseph Cousy in Manhattan in 1928, his parents, Joseph and Juliet, came from France by boat. Cousy was more immersed in French than English as a toddler. He also had a lisp. Sometimes teased as "Flenchy" by neighborhood kids, Cousy was introduced to basketball as a thirteen-year-old after the family moved to Queens.

By no measure was Cousy's a glamorous or affluent upbringing. He was an only child. His parents were more taciturn than warm, and his father drove a taxi cab for a living. Later, Cousy recalled there being little communication in the house, a place he did not associate with laughter or light-hearted times.

Like many of his future Celtics teammates, Cousy had to scrap for what he got, had to work for what he earned. He'd dabbled in stickball in Manhattan, but transferred his sports passion to basketball and was more or less discovered in high school when a coach noticed he had a facility for using either hand for dribbling. During his sophomore year at Andrew Jackson High School, Cousy played on the junior varsity. By modern standards that makes him more of a late bloomer than a prodigy. But then, Michael Jordan, whom many consider the greatest basketball player of all time, was cut from his high school team at first as an aspiring freshman.

Ironically, like so many young players today who thrive on summer AAU (Amateur Athletic Union) club teams, Cousy's development as a basketball player accelerated during his summer playground games. He gained confidence and knew he would be able to make his mark on the school's varsity team. By flunking a course in citizenship, however, a brokenhearted Cousy was ruled ineligible for the first semester of his junior year. He did not play a game until midway through the school year, but he erupted for 28 points in his debut. The kid could play.

Cousy was an overnight sensation. He improved steadily and in a place that appreciated basketball more than any other part of the country. Cousy was noticed. There were no *Parade* or McDonald's All-American teams for schoolboys in the 1940s, but New York newspapers honored the finest players in the city. Cousy led the city in scoring and was chosen as a first-team all-star.

A friend mentioned along the way that Cousy was probably good enough to earn a college scholarship. Cousy had not thought of himself that way, and the days of omniscient recruiting, with junior high prospects identified and touted, was decades in the future. A player of Cousy's skills today would receive a shoebox full of mail from panting college coaches before he completed high school.

Cousy did garner sufficient attention by the standards of the times. He knew he wanted to play college basketball, to attend a Catholic school, and to leave home. Boston College expressed interest and he was tempted. Then Holy Cross coach Doggie Julian wrote to Cousy. When a Holy Cross alumnus stopped by the Cousy home, he sold Cousy's mother on the school with the aid of a brochure noting that all students were required to attend mass every day at 7:00 a.m.

The choice changed Cousy's life. More than sixty years later, he still maintains a residence in Worcester. Fronting the Crusaders elevated his profile and lifted him into the professional basketball career that made him a legend.

Cousy was six feet tall in high school and grew just one more inch. He had disproportionately long arms and did not look as if he ran as fast as a rabbit, despite always seeming to get where he needed to go lickety-split. Cousy possessed remarkable quickness, terrific vision, and a sixth sense of knowing what was about to unfold on the court, where his teammates would be with regard to the basket. He had jet black hair and an earnest handsomeness. A proud player, to Cousy winning was the only thing. Consolation prizes were for kids' games. Give out ribbons to all for three-legged races at Fourth of July picnics.

To illustrate Cousy's prominence in Massachusetts basketball at the time Auerbach disparaged him, a 1950 Boston newspaper feature on Cousy compared him to Red Grange in football and Babe Ruth in baseball. Pretty fancy company. The story may have been hyperbolic and premature, but with hindsight, it turned out to be true.

As was common decades ago among basketball players who completed their eligibility, and baseball players who made salaries barely more lucrative than office workers, postseason teams were cobbled together for barnstorming tours. Television did not yet deliver a game per day in every sport to every household. Fans who did not get to the ballpark in person had their images shaped by radio and newspapers.

Cousy formed the Bob Cousy All-Stars. If you wanted to see the great Bob Cousy in the flesh and didn't have the opportunity to attend Holy Cross games, here was Cousy coming to you. Such baseball tours featuring Negro League stars like Satchel Paige and Major League pitchers like Dizzy Dean and Bob Feller had proven their worth. The All-Stars packed gyms in games against local semi-pro teams all over New England. Cousy pocketed a tidy sum and felt he could go on playing exhibitions like this indefinitely.

The NBA of the time was not on par with Major League Baseball, the nation's most popular sport. Neither TV nor newspaper coverage permeated most cities around the country. If your city had a team, then chances were you knew a little bit about pro basketball. But in 1950, games were played at a pedestrian pace by little-known players (unless they were local) in drafty arenas before small crowds. It was no wonder that Cousy, who had never been to a professional game, could say that his impression of the NBA was "Mickey Mouse."

Young players now dream of the day their name is called in the NBA draft. Not only is there the prestige of playing the sport in the best league in the world, the job also comes with a salary that often reaches into the millions of dollars. Being a lottery draft pick in the top echelon is not so different from winning the lottery in any state. Often it guarantees the type of riches that mean the winner never has to work again.

When Cousy was bypassed by the Celtics, he was drafted by Ben Kerner's Tri-Cities Blackhawks. Even with the head start of a map and a magnifying glass, Cousy couldn't have identified the Tri-Cities. He had little interest in relocating to Iowa or Illinois and pretty much decided if he couldn't play for the Celtics he wouldn't play in the NBA. He was angry about the Auerbach snub. But eventually, Cousy negotiated with Kerner. The owner's offer produced a fresh insult—$6,500 for the season. Cousy said he wanted $10,000 or no go.

Negotiations broke off, and Kerner shipped Cousy to the Chicago Stags.

The shaky nature of the early NBA showed itself. The financially struggling Stags folded and a dispersal draft followed. Arguments that could not be successfully mediated by Commissioner Maurice Podoloff erupted over which player would go to which team. Ultimately, three names remained from the roster and they were written on slips of paper and placed in a hat. The most coveted player, Max Zaslofsky, was the league's fourth-best scorer during the winter of 1948–49, averaging 20.6 ppg. He was one of the biggest stars in the league. Also available was Andy Phillip, another double-figure scorer, and Cousy.

The inexperienced Cousy was the least desirable commodity. Knicks owner Ned Irish reached blindly into the hat first and withdrew the paper with the name of the biggest prize—Zaslofsky. Philadelphia owner Eddie Gottlieb took his turn and grabbed Phillip (who ended up with the Celtics for two seasons later in the 1950s). One owner left, Walter Brown. One team left, the Boston Celtics. One player left, Bob Cousy. Cousy signed for $9,000. No one ever argued that Kerner was more generous than Brown.

Red Auerbach's worst mistake was rectified for him. He never paid the price for rejecting Cousy because Cousy was dropped into his arms. It was like meeting your future wife on a blind date that you didn't want to go on. Despite their mutual wariness, the two men shared a common goal of victory in every game, effectively making the relationship work. The Auerbach-Cousy connection blossomed into one of the closest and most fruitful partnerships in professional basketball history.

Auerbach did not immediately change his attitude about Cousy's fancy tactics. But he quickly came to see that when Cousy passed the ball behind his back it was for a purpose. Just as the player insisted, he threw the ball that way because it was the best way to get the ball where he wanted it to go. And Auerbach saw that when Cousy was in the lineup, the Celtics played more energetically. He made things happen. In college, area sportswriters labeled Cousy's Holy Cross team the "Fancy Pants AC" because of his slick ball handling. In the NBA, Al McGuire, later coach of NCAA champion Marquette University and a popular basketball commentator, called Cousy's passes "French Pastry." In a staid era, Cousy thought outside the box.

Early on, however, Auerbach took Cousy aside and gave him one piece of advice about his creative passes. They were worthless, he pointed out, if his teammates couldn't catch them. Auerbach told Cousy to make sure the passes were accurate. Another time Auerbach screamed at Cousy in public, away from the court, and with just as much feistiness Cousy blasted back. Cousy didn't accept gratuitous insults, and Auerbach learned to back off. Over time the men grew so close that Cousy became just about the only person in the world besides Auerbach's wife to call him Arnold, his given first name, instead of Red.

Cousy's short answer to Auerbach's predraft stubbornness was his 1950–51 rookie season performance. Cousy averaged 15.6 ppg and was named to the league all-star team. He likely would have been rookie of the year, but there was no official award until 1953. Cousy—as good as advertised by everyone except Auerbach—was on his way to making jersey No. 14 famous. The Celtics finished 39-30, the first winning record in team history.

Guard Kenny Sailors, winding up his NBA career, spent part of that season with Cousy and Auerbach on the Celtics and observed the early feeling of the duo's dynamics.

"Red wasn't too sure he wanted Cousy," Sailors said. "He was kind of a Fancy Dan. He was a great dribbler, but he pulled some stuff that the old-timers didn't go for. Oh boy, it worked out for both of them, though."

Sailors said he recognized that Cousy was a good player, but he wasn't sure Cousy yet possessed the confidence he displayed later.

"He didn't even know if he would stay in the league," Sailors said. "I tried to teach him the jump shot, but he didn't need a jump shot. He had a one-handed runner and lifted his right foot."

Old films show Cousy releasing the ball on the fly, his right hand pushing the ball toward the goal from in front of his face rather than from overhead at the top of a leap. It was sufficient when the game was still played more below the rim than above it. Just as often, Cousy shredded defenses with his dribbling, outsmarting taller players for layups. Cousy soon emerged as the Celtics' marquee name.

A few years earlier, one Celtic was a 6-foot-7 forward named Chuck Connors. He was on the roster for parts of two seasons before starting a more successful career in Hollywood as an actor. Connors starred in the 1950s TV series *The Rifleman*, in which, regrettably, he was a more accurate shooter than he had been with Boston. Connors stayed in touch with the Celtics and on West Coast trips sometimes gave Auerbach and players tours of Hollywood sets.

Besides Sailors, some of Cousy's more prominent Celtic teammates during his rookie campaign were guards Sonny Hertzberg and Ed Leede and, above all, "Easy" Ed Macauley. Macauley was one of the league's most prolific scorers, a 6-foot-8 soft-touch shooter whose main drawback was that he weighed just 190 pounds and couldn't really bang underneath. He averaged 20.4 ppg for the Celtics that season and became the pivotal Boston offering in the multi-player, franchise-altering trade that brought Bill Russell to Boston. Cousy and Macauley were the headliners.

One thing Hertzberg, Leede, Macauley, and Cousy had in common was their skin pigmentation. They were all Caucasian. From its inception in 1946 through the end of the 1949–50 season, the NBA was a lily-white league. In contrast to minority opportunities presented decades later, professional basketball was a white-man's private club.

However, one additional historical figure made his Celtics debut during that 1950–51 season. Never a star, with a career of limited duration, Chuck Cooper's name does not resonate so vividly with Celtics fans as Auerbach's, Cousy's, and Macauley's. But he stands out from others because of the social significance of his draft selection. With all of the hullabaloo surrounding the No. 1 pick and Cousy, the Celtics' No. 2 pick did not receive quite as much attention as might be expected.

What set Chuck Cooper apart from those associated with the team that season was his skin color. Cooper was the first black player drafted by an NBA team.

4

THE NBA'S FIRST BLACK PLAYER

On April 25, 1950, Walter Brown and Charles Cooper II wrote a chapter of history together. When the Celtics second-round turn came in the NBA draft at the Bismarck Hotel in Chicago, Brown simply said, "Boston takes Charles Cooper of Duquesne."

No bells, whistles, or flashing lights. No announced master plan for integration. Just a name mentioned, as if the player was the same as any other player. And that was the point. Auerbach told Brown that Cooper was the player he wanted, the best fit for the Celtics frontcourt, so Brown drafted him.

Cooper was not a superstar, but he was a known quantity with promise, a collegiate All-American at the Pittsburgh-based university. The owners of the other NBA teams in the room also knew Cooper was black. They were silent, surprised by Brown's choice, but for the most part willing to let the moment pass. Then one anonymous owner (Brown never said who), blurted out, "Don't you know he's a colored boy?"

To Brown, skin color was not an issue. He vehemently defended his selection in broad, but powerful words. "I don't care if he's striped, or plaid, or polka dot!" Brown might have been describing Auerbach's wardrobe, but this was a far more substantial matter. By selecting Cooper, Brown picked the first black player ever chosen in the NBA draft. He also set the tone for future Celtics lineups. The Celtics were the first team to liberally stock their roster with black players, the first to have a black All-Star, and later became the first team to start five black players.

At a time when blacks were still being lynched in the South, when water fountain usage was divided by skin color, when registering to vote took courage, and when a black man might be beaten or killed merely for conversing with a white woman, the Celtics were in the forefront of social change. The Celtics did not undertake this acquisition of Cooper, or other black players, as a sociology project, but because Red Auerbach wanted the best available talent. If Auerbach saw any color, it was the silver that glistened on championship cups, or the gold that glittered on first-place awards.

Merely drafting one black player was significant. But there was no true outcry against the move for the simple reason that in a general way the NBA was ready to break the color barrier. Several picks later in the same draft, the Washington Capitols took West Virginia State's Earl Lloyd, who actually became the first black player to participate in an NBA game. And that same season the New York Knicks signed Nat "Sweetwater" Clifton as a free agent. Clifton had played with the Harlem Globetrotters.

Later, Cooper, who was thrilled to be drafted by the Celtics both from a personal and barrier-breaking standpoint, said none of the other teams would have acted if Brown hadn't picked him.

"Walter Brown was the man who put his neck on the line," Cooper said.

Although Lloyd played in a game one day before Cooper did, Lloyd later acknowledged that he considered Cooper to be the first black player in the league. Lloyd said he did not think he would have been drafted by Washington if the Celtics had not taken Cooper.

The move was a twofold risk for Brown. Cooper was not a major star who would turn the franchise around, just the best player available in the mind of the coach. Who knew how fans would react to the selection of a black player? Beyond that, Harlem Globetrotters owner Abe Saperstein, who founded the world-famous, all-black touring basketball comedy team in 1927 or 1928 (depending on who you talk to), was angered by the NBA invading what he considered to be his territory.

Saperstein was after Cooper as a full-time player, and although Cooper played several off-seasons with the Globetrotters to boost his income, Saperstein realized he now had competition to sign the best black hoopsters. The Globetrotters used the Harlem appendage, but were not really based in that section of New York (their main office was in Chicago). Harlem itself represented the pinnacle of black culture and society and was more of a geographic symbol in the title than a geographic location for the team.

Besides visiting just about every country on the planet that could be reached by any means short of overland safari, the Globetrotters also played an important role in conjunction with the NBA. The Globetrotters played exhibition games around the league before the home team met a foe in a doubleheader. Frequently the Globetrotters, with their snazzy uniforms and the clowning routines that appealed to kids of all ages, were a bigger draw than the visiting pro team. Abe Saperstein dreamed in dollar signs, and with the world at his command he was a valuable business partner.

To alienate Saperstein was a chancy business. He had more options than NBA owners. He could yank his product and make just as much money on the same date elsewhere. An NBA owner would find it difficult to rebound so easily. When Brown drafted Cooper, there were ominous rumblings that Saperstein was furious and might threaten to boycott the Boston Garden. Word reached Brown, and before the issue even surfaced his famous temper kicked in. He declared that the Globetrotters were no longer welcome in his home, aka the Garden.

This meant the simple act of drafting Cooper became not merely a basketball decision, but was magnified as both a social statement and a financial one. Other than his legendary remark at the draft about not caring about a player's color, Brown never matched Branch Rickey's social justice oratory when Rickey tried to ease Jackie Robinson's way through the minefield of his early Dodgers years. Brown, whose Celtics were not drawing particularly well, put his pocketbook where his mouth was.

Just as it was in most walks of American life, the acceptance of blacks in the NBA was overdue. The NBA, of course, was a much younger league than that of other major professional sports. Its 1946 start-up following the merger of two fledgling leagues, the National Basketball League and the Basketball Association of America, made it a baby on the national scene.

That was the same year Jackie Robinson signed with the Brooklyn Dodgers organization and by design played a season for the less racially-oriented Dodger minor league team in Montreal to crack organized baseball's color line. Robinson's rookie year in 1947 was a milestone in American racial advancement. Baseball, in the form of the National League, dated back to 1876. The National Football League, which to date had suited up only a few black players, was founded in 1920. The National Hockey League, formed in 1917, did not have a black player until later in the 1950s. By these standards—a glacial pace of improved opportunities for blacks—the NBA was running the 100-yard dash.

Blacks were denied the limelight stemming from participation in the nation's top basketball league for a shorter period of time, but they had shown an ability to play the sport at a high level for years. Although the Globetrotters became the most famous basketball team in the world, the African-American New York Renaissance, or Rens, might have been the most famous basketball team in the United States before the creation of the NBA.

The Rens were an all-black professional team founded in 1922. Like the Globetrotters, their roots were traced to Harlem, in their case to a club called the Harlem Renaissance Casino. Over a twenty-seven-year period, ending when the NBA was just three years old, the Rens compiled a won-loss record of 2,588-539, and they played all comers. During the 1932–33 season, the Rens won 88 straight games and in 1939, they won the World Basketball Tournament in Chicago by besting the Oshkosh All-Stars. On the way to the title, they defeated the Globetrotters.

Unlike the Globetrotters, the Rens actually did play some of their games in Harlem, as part of the thriving entertainment scene of the 1920s, '30s, and '40s. They also competed in an epic series of games with the Original Celtics, widely considered to be the best team of the era. Those Celtics were led by Nat Holman, Dutch Dehnert, and Joe Lapchick, who always insisted the Rens were the equal of his team and lobbied unsuccessfully to have the Rens accepted as a group into one of the pro leagues.

Chuck "Tarzan" Cooper (no relation to the other Chuck Cooper), Harold "Fat" Jenkins, Leon Monde, and Willis Smith were among the Rens' stars. In 1949, when the Rens' clout was fading, Saperstein bought out owner Bob Douglas and turned the Rens into a Globetrotter subsidiary.

During the height of their fame and abilities, the Rens faced many of the same challenges and difficulties that barnstorming black baseball teams encountered. They were denied service in restaurants, were turned away from hotels, and had racial epithets shouted at them. More than once, when they played the all-white Original Celtics, race riots broke out.

Baseball, with Robinson, Larry Doby, Roy Campanella, Don Newcombe, and others, set the foundation for the integration of basketball. Baseball, widely identified as the national pastime, laid the groundwork. It had become clear by the end of World War II that consigning black players with the skills of Satchel Paige, Josh Gibson, Cool Papa Bell, and Buck Leonard to the shadows of the Negro Leagues was a national disgrace. Black men had enlisted in the armed services in droves to fight German and Japanese imperialism and racism overseas. After putting their lives on the line to save America, they were not going to accept the same second-class citizenry standards imposed on them before the war.

A revolution had begun. And if baseball rosters were going to feature black players, how could a fighting-for-respect basketball league do any less? By comparison to the taunts and humiliations heaped upon Robinson in particular, and his co-workers in general, the battles waged by Cooper, Lloyd, and Clifton were skirmishes. But they didn't win their war without firing a shot.

During his brief stay with the Celtics, Kenny Sailors roomed on the road for a while with Chuck Cooper. "In some places, the hotels would not let the black man stay with the team," Sailors said, "and Cooper slept in the homes of local black families.

"It took people a while to get used to it [a black player]," Sailors said. "It was completely different. I asked him, 'How can you put up with it?' He said he wasn't bitter. He said, 'Nah, I don't mind. I get my meal money and I stay for nothing.'"

Perhaps Cooper was putting on a good front, careful not to rock the boat and jeopardize his opportunity. On the team, Auerbach made it clear that no bigotry would be tolerated, that if you were a member of the Celtics you were a member of the team on and off the court.

Bob Cousy was a New Yorker like Auerbach, raised in a basically prejudice-free environment. Much like owner Brown, Cousy didn't care about a man's color. If you could play, you had his respect. Cousy considered himself a liberal on social issues even as a young man. He made no secret of his convictions and he thinks that's one reason why Auerbach asked him to room with Cooper for part of that 1950–51 rookie season for both players after Sailors left for another team.

"We were so focused on winning—Arnold had a lot to do with it—and that's why we assimilated black players so easily," Cousy said. "Arnold knew my feelings about civil rights and so he put us together and we became lifelong friends. I never saw Chuck as a black basketball player. I saw him as a basketball player who was 6-foot-7, whose skin happened to be different. But he was a bright, sensitive, articulate guy. We shared some interests in music and other things so we developed a relationship very quickly and hung out together."

Cooper was actually 6-foot 5-inches and weighed 220 pounds. He was twenty-four his rookie year and he averaged 9.3 ppg in 66 Celtics contests that season. In his professional debut, November 1, 1950, Cooper scored 9 points in a loss to Fort Wayne. He spent four years with the Celtics before continuing his career elsewhere in the NBA, but never averaged more than 8.2 ppg again.

When the 1950–51 training camp opened, Cooper was not the only black player seeking a roster spot with the Celtics. Hank DeZonie, formerly of the Rens, was one of three others. However, when the final cuts were made, Cooper was the only one left. Auerbach frowned on DeZonie's flamboyant personal style and the brazenness of bringing his girlfriend to camp. Isaac Walthour was one of the other hopefuls, but he was a point guard and could not beat out Cousy. He later played briefly with the Milwaukee Hawks.

Auerbach said that while there was racial discrimination displayed toward Cooper from outside the team, there was never a problem with the players. Cooper was from Pittsburgh, earned a degree in business management, and loved jazz. He was as educated and sophisticated as the next player in a sport where most players attended college.

During his second season with the Celtics, Cooper was on the floor for a contest against the Milwaukee Hawks at the neutral site of Moline, Illinois, when he was involved in a bench-clearing fight. Cooper said an opposing player called him a "black bastard" and he wasn't going to put up with the slur. Cooper asked, "What did you say?" and the player repeated it, so Cooper pushed him in the face. Another opponent started swinging and Celtics enforcer Bob Brannum entered the fray. Auerbach, who had the moxie of a boxer, faced off with Milwaukee coach Doxie Moore.

Cooper was suspended and fined, but he said when Commissioner Maurice Podoloff heard what started the incident, he cancelled the financial penalty. Years later, Cooper, who died in 1984 at the age of fifty-seven from liver cancer, said he never had racial problems with his teammates and that they were all supportive. Much later he suggested in a newspaper article that his scoring opportunities might have been limited because he was black. But Cooper was not as much of an offensive threat as Cousy, Ed Macauley, or some others.

Regarded as a friendly man who was living out his dream as a professional basketball pioneer, Cooper was also not as much of a threat to the so-called American way of life as racists must have imagined. During Cooper's tenure with the Celtics, the team often played preseason exhibition games in cities that did not have professional teams. Some of those cities were below the Mason-Dixon line.

When the Celtics showed up for a game in Raleigh, North Carolina, they were informed that Cooper could not play. When Auerbach said he was going to call the game off, local officials relented; however, Cooper was forbidden to stay in the team hotel. Instead of searching for an alternative bed, he decided to take the train back to Boston immediately. Cousy joined him.

Waiting at the train station for their escape, Cousy couldn't help but stare at the white-only and black-only drinking fountains. Aggravated, embarrassed, angry, and saddened, Cousy did not know what to say to make Cooper feel better. For years afterward he felt guilty that he did not say something soothing. Cousy believed he should have had it in him to be a better friend, ignoring that he had already demonstrated the depth of that friendship by fleeing the hostile community with Cooper.

By the time Cooper retired from the NBA, the Boston Celtics were poised to initiate their great dynasty. At the heart of it were such great black players as Bill Russell, Sam Jones, K. C. Jones, and Tom Sanders.

After playing one season with the Harlem Magicians, a team begun by players who broke away from the Globetrotters, Cooper earned a master's degree in social work at the University of Minnesota. He returned to Pittsburgh, where he became director of the city's parks and recreation department, was a member of the Board of Education, and served as a bank official.

Cooper never received the level of fame or prestige of Jackie Robinson—his circumstances differed—but he was always proud of the part he played in integrating the NBA.

5

BUILDING A TEAM

Sometimes it seemed farther from second place to first than from last to second. Sometimes it seemed the building of the Celtics took longer than construction of the nation's Interstate system during the 1950s. Piece by piece, Red Auerbach's construction project took form, but just like the renovation of the country's highways, it took years to make progress.

Auerbach came to Boston to win, but he couldn't turn the roster over in one year, or even two or three years. The addition of Bob Cousy and Ed Macauley was critical for the 1950–51 season, and they brought the Celtics their first winning record.

It wasn't a fluke, but rather the beginning of a habit. The next year the Celtics finished 39-27, a year later they were 46-25, and the year after that the Celts ended up 42-30. The line on the graph pointed upward, but it did not yet lead to a championship. The Celtics were solid, but not deep enough or dominant enough to make a run through the playoffs.

But Auerbach's eye for talent was true. In the draft and through trades, through shrewd maneuvers and superior coaching, he singled out the men he wanted and he made them Celtics.

Bill Sharman was the prize addition for the 1951–52 season. The 6-foot-1 dead-eye shooter from the University of Southern California was the perfect complement to Cousy in the backcourt. Auerbach drafted Frank Ramsey out of Kentucky in 1953, even though he knew he had a military service obligation that would delay his arrival. And he picked up agile 6-foot-8 Gene Conley with a 10th-round throwaway pick in 1952, even though he knew Conley's first commitment was to baseball. In 1955, the Celtics first-rounder was Jim Loscutoff, the power forward from the University of Oregon who became the team's enforcer with his strength. They were all building blocks, guys you could win with, guys who strengthened the roster for the long haul.

Sharman was born in Texas in 1926, but grew up in Southern California as an extraordinary all-around athlete with golden-boy good looks. His wavy hair appeared as if a little dab of Brylcreem would do him and he looked able to step into television's *Route 66*. Sharman was superb at tennis, broke into the NBA with Washington in 1950, and came within an eyelash of playing for the Brooklyn Dodgers after receiving a $10,000 signing bonus.

"I was right out of college, and I didn't have $1,000 in the bank," Sharman said of the impressive baseball offer.

By 1951, Sharman was playing for the Dodgers' Fort Worth affiliate, and when rosters expanded in September he got a call up for a look-see. The Dodgers were cruising to the National League pennant and manager Charlie Dressen said he would get Sharman into a handful of games when they clinched. Those who know their baseball history realize that event never happened. It was the autumn of the miraculous New York Giants comeback and Bobby Thomson's stunning, pennant-winning home run off Ralph Branca. Sharman had a terrific seat to witness the closing act of the pennant race—except for one day.

Sharman may be the only player in Major League Baseball history to be ejected from a game without ever playing in one. In a late-season Dodgers game against the Boston Braves, there was a close play at the plate and the umpire ruled the Brooklyn runner out. A yelling Dressen ran on the field to protest. There was also a lot of noise from the bench.

"I don't think I said one word," Sharman recalled more than fifty years later.

The umpire thought he did, however, and tossed the whole bench from the game, including Sharman, who never did get his on-field Major League chance.

"It was kind of funny," he said. "Or unique."

The professional seasons were shorter during that era, though there was still some baseball-basketball overlap. Sharman spent his winters scoring in double figures for the Celtics and his summers in the Dodgers minor league system, trying to work his way back up to the parent club. In a game in Memphis during his fifth year, Sharman fractured his right hand sliding into home plate. He retired from baseball after that and stuck with basketball.

Sharman played nine seasons with the Celtics, always scoring between 16 and 21 points a game, before becoming a coach. Sharman led teams to championships in the old American Basketball League, the American Basketball Association, and the NBA, the only coach to do so, and was elected to the Basketball Hall of Fame as a player and a coach, one of three people, along with John Wooden and Lenny Wilkens, to accomplish that feat.

Sharman and Cousy were a perfect backcourt match. Cousy was the playmaker who could shake up defenses with his scoring prowess, particularly driving. Sharman was the shooter making phenomenal outside jumpers and a very high percentage of his free throws.

"He complemented me very well," Sharman said. "When I played college ball, I played forward. I was a pretty good shooter. But I never did handle the ball. I'd be on the baseline and pop out. Cousy is maybe the greatest ball handler of all time. I could run around and get free. It was just wonderful the relationship we had on and off the floor. We spent almost ten years as roommates—nobody on our team had a room alone—and we never had a fight or got mad at each other."

Gene Conley had one of the most remarkable careers of any professional athlete. Deion Sanders and Bo Jackson both starred in football and baseball. Dave DeBusschere played baseball and basketball. But Conley, the lanky fastballing pitcher, is the only one to win championship rings in basketball, with the Celtics, and in baseball, with the Milwaukee Braves.

"I had such a unique and unusual career," Conley said. "Those two sports, it's a tough one now. I went without spring training for years. They tried to keep me from doing it in those days. Just about the time they wanted me to stop, I'd have a halfway decent year—the timing was perfect—and I'd say, 'See? It really helped me.'"

The comings and goings were even wackier than they seemed on the surface. Conley, who attended Washington State, where he played just one year of basketball, played 39 games for the Celtics during the 1952–53 season, concentrated on baseball for a while, and rejoined the Celtics for the 1958–59 season. Auerbach was tolerant because he needed what Conley brought to the team. Conley was a genial fellow, with a sense of humor, and a limited enough basketball ego that he didn't expect to play long minutes. Some years, Conley said, the Braves actually paid him not to play basketball and he agreed. It was like a farmer being paid by the federal government not to grow certain crops.

With the Celtics, Conley eventually became known as "Bill Russell's backup." But he always felt that label was inaccurate.

"Nobody backed up Russell," Conley said. "I played with Russell. Russell never came out. I said, 'Red, give me a minute or two.' I had some fundamentals that he liked. I could always block out and I was a hustler like a son-of-a-gun."

Conley was a so-called locker-room guy, a player who could get along with anybody and help keep the atmosphere light during tense times. When he tired of silly civilian questions about his height like, "How's the air up there?" Conley said he was "5 feet, 20 inches tall."

At one time, Conley, who also conveniently pitched a bit for the Boston Red Sox, appeared on television game shows *What's My Line?* and *To Tell The Truth*. In the modern era of widespread sports coverage, it would be impossible for a Conley to go unrecognized on *What's My Line?*

In an exploit during the 1962 baseball season that lives on in Red Sox lore, Conley and infielder Pumpsie Green left a team bus stalled in traffic in New York and melted into the pedestrian crowd. It was after a frustrating loss, in a vehicle with faltering air-conditioning on a hot summer day. Conley wanted to hit a corner bar for a break while the bus was held hostage in gridlock. When the duo emerged from their refreshments, the bus was gone.

Since the next day was an off day before a series in Washington, Conley suggested he and Green do the town in New York before hooking up with the club. Green became worried and said he was going to find his own way to D.C. Conley told him to go right ahead, but that he was going to jump on a plane to Israel. Israel?

After considerably more imbibing, Conley headed to the airport, ticket to Jerusalem in hand, only to be stymied in his quest for overseas adventure by the lack of a passport. By then, with Green back in the fold, the Red Sox were treating the Conley situation as an AWOL missing-person case. After sobering up, Conley rejoined the Red Sox and was penalized with a stiff fine.

Red Sox officials might have been angry enough to have steam coming out of their ears like cartoon characters, but fans more or less laughed off the quirky misadventure. For many years after that, however, a small radio station in the area that did not broadcast twenty-four hours a day, signed off with the signature phrase, "Good night, Pumpsie Green, wherever you are." Illustrative of his own sense of humor, some years later Conley ended a speech at a baseball dinner by uttering the same line.

It would be simplistic thinking, though, to write off Conley as merely a good-time guy. Auerbach called him "one of the greatest athletes of our generation." And in an admiring story in a Philadelphia newspaper, sports columnist Sandy Grady wrote, "Donald Gene Conley is the most versatile invention since the safety pin. Given enough time, Mr. Conley could play for the Eagles, race at Indianapolis, score respectably in the U.S. Open, and shoot a snappy game of nine-ball on the side."

Frank Ramsey, the 6-foot-3 forward drafted No. 1 by the Celtics in 1953, said Conley had the talent to be the best player on the team if he wanted to. That may have been an exaggeration, but it was obvious Conley wasn't merely taking up space on the bench.

It was Ramsey, it turned out, who occupied a special spot on the bench emblematic of Auerbach's cleverness. The NBA now annually presents a Sixth Man Award. Auerbach, using Ramsey, invented the role. A player good enough to be a starter instead came off the bench some minutes into the game to ignite his team. It was a cute strategy. Always it was understood that teams started their best five and that there was a drop-off in ability when a coach turned to his bench. Not with Ramsey. He was a starter in a sub's body, and he had the ability to come into a game cold, like a baseball pinch-hitter, and make something happen.

Ramsey grew up in small-town Madisonville, Kentucky, and he still lives there. As a youth, his identification with a basketball dynasty was the Kentucky Wildcats and his idea of a dictatorial coach was Adolph Rupp. True enough on both counts and strange enough that he moved from one dynasty to another and from one famous coach to another.

Coaches and teams look for quick fixes in the draft. Their No. 1 picks are more valuable than diamonds. It is expected that the top choice will not only make the team, but contribute and perhaps even start. But in a move that foreshadowed Auerbach's later patience waiting for Larry Bird, the Celtics mentor drafted Ramsey knowing full well he would not have his services for a year or more.

In Ramsey's case, although taken No. 1 in 1953, he did not play his first game for the Celtics until the 1954–55 season. Ramsey was in the Army, but through creative scheduling of a 60-day leave and a series of three-day passes, he was able to periodically swap uniforms. It was a different kind of vacation than other grunts had.

"I wasn't released [from the Army] until two days after we won the first championship in the 1956–57 season," Ramsey said.

Ramsey, a redhead whose hard-nosed style resulted in his legs seemingly being taped up as thoroughly as a mummy, first met Auerbach well before graduating from Kentucky. During the summer of 1950, Ramsey, as did many of the top players of the day, competed on one of the basketball teams at Kutsher's Country Club in the Catskill Mountains. The resorts of the "Borscht Belt" sponsored teams as part of the entertainment for their clientele. High school and college players picked up spending money working summer jobs during the day, and they played ball at night. In fact, in 1953, Auerbach spotted a very tall, slender center in the Catskills who at first glance convinced him he would be a great player in the future. That was the first time Auerbach watched Wilt Chamberlain play.

Another future NBA star who played in the Catskills with Ramsey on a team coached by Auerbach was Cliff Hagan. Auerbach drafted Ramsey, Hagan—key bait in the most important trade of Auerbach's career—and forward Lou Tsi-oropoulos from the same Kentucky team, and all had NBA careers.

"Red was our coach [in the Catskills] and from there I would see him every now and then when we played in New York," Ramsey said.

Ramsey's Kentucky years more or less coincided with the Korean War, so if someone contacted you announcing you had been drafted, you were more likely to think it was the Army than the NBA. In Ramsey's case, it was both. He had also been in ROTC, so he knew he was going to do military time. The funniest situation for Ramsey was that he ended up with a drill sergeant in each place.

Cousy, among others, said Auerbach treated all of the Celtic players the same way—badly. Ramsey laughed at the comment, but said, "He would come up to you and if he knocked ashes off his cigar on you, that meant he liked you."

Using that as the standard, Auerbach must have loved Jim Loscutoff, dubbed "Jungle Jim" by Celtics broadcaster Johnny Most for his less than subtle ways of protecting teammates who were smaller and not as powerfully built. At 6-feet-5 and 230 pounds, Loscutoff played bigger. He was every-one's bodyguard. "Loscy" was never shy about taking or dishing out hits under the basket where the traffic was thickest. In an era before weight lifting was popular, Loscutoff had the broad shoulders, thick thighs, and wide butt of a body builder. Neither his body nor his shooting touch was soft.

It was a fallacy to think that Auerbach treated all of his players the same. He treated each man according to the way he thought it would best motivate him. If Cousy's reciprocal yelling showed that he was not going to accept Auerbach raising his voice to him, Loscutoff's water-off-the-back reaction to Auerbach's high-decibel verbal assaults made him a whipping boy to be used as an example for messages to the entire team. Just as he did on the court when taller, heavier players banged him, Loscutoff could take it.

Loscutoff, who ran a summer basketball camp for high school and col-lege players for decades in the Boston suburb of North Andover, wore a blonde crew cut and had the most memorable nickname in the league. Jungle Jim—even the words sounded fearsome.

"It was fashionable at the time," Loscutoff said, laughing many years later. "Everybody recognized the nickname Jungle Jim, so I was very recognizable. I didn't mind it at all. I don't know how to associate Jungle Jim with myself now. It was just me at the time."

Loscutoff averaged in double figures (10.6 ppg) only once during his career that spanned 1955 to 1964 and in lifetime totals scored just 2 points for every foul he committed. During the 1958–59 season, he fouled out of 15 of the 66 games he played, six fouls at a time, a phenomenal rate. On a team densely populated with terrific shooters, Loscutoff was counted on to rebound, play defense, and when necessary throw his weight around.

"Red never told me to go in and kick the crap out of our opponents," Loscutoff said. "I just did that on my own. Some particular players had to know they couldn't take advantage of us."

Auerbach, who was a survivor of the streets of New York, understood that all the players had to be scrappy, but that it took the sum of all parts to make a team. Every player brought a different skill set to the table. The blend of shooter and passer, rebounder and defender, short man and tall man, may have looked like goulash on paper, but it was a fine cuisine recipe when mixed together on the court.

By the mid-1950s, the Celtics were becoming the Celtics.

6

WILD DAYS
IN THE EARLY NBA

Dr. James Naismith invented basketball in Springfield, Massachusetts in 1891, but Danny Biasone saved it in Syracuse in 1954. The NBA's biggest problem in its early days trying to woo fans already enraptured by college basketball and other sports was that it was boring them into a coma.

Owners seeking to convince the public that professional basketball was an exciting game were thwarted by their own product. Nothing illustrated the stagnation like a 1950 game when the Fort Wayne Pistons beat the Minneapolis Lakers 19–18. That wouldn't even be a satisfying quarter today. The Pistons would not have survived to move to Detroit and the Lakers would not have lived to move to Los Angeles if the rules had not changed.

Much of the beauty of NBA basketball can be attributed to the speed of the game, the balletlike moves made by great athletes on the fly. However, until the 1954–55 season, running was not always the most successful strategy. Games bogged down because teams were not forced to shoot. A 5-point lead could be insurmountable if the team ahead chose to hang onto the ball, dribble around, pass it in circles, and refuse to shoot. Nothing in the rules made them get rid of the ball; instead, they were rewarded for holding on to it.

Games like the 19–18 beaut left the owners groaning. Only newspaper-men fighting a tight evening deadline could remotely be expected to cheer a result like that.

"Boy, it was dull," said Biasone, who owned the Syracuse Nationals.

Biasone cooked up a remedy. After studying the pace of the average game, he suggested that the league adopt a rule requiring teams to shoot within 24 seconds of gaining possession of the ball. The method worked so spectacularly, increasing scoring and making for more pleasing play, that the 24-second clock remains in effect today.

The first game played with the shot clock was on October 30, 1954, and the Celtics were in it. They also lost, 98–95, to the Rochester Royals. The pace of NBA play, however, had changed forever.

The impact of the shot clock was dramatic. In the clock's first year of use, NBA teams averaged 13 points per game more than they did in the prior season. The Celtics became the first team to average 100 points for a 48-minute game. Celtics coach Red Auerbach called the innovation "the single most important" rules change in half a century.

This is one time Auerbach recognized the common good since he actu-ally possessed the single most effective freeze-the-ball weapon in Bob Cousy. Cousy had the talent to dribble the other team crazy and keep the ball out of the reach of lunging defenders. When they got desperate, they fouled him and Cousy hit the free throws. Nothing seemed to drive hostile fans of opposing teams madder than the sight of Cousy manipulating the clock, all the while making their heroes look foolish.

The NBA of the mid-1950s was almost an alien solar system com-pared to the NBA of the early 2000s. Arenas were old. Except for Madi-son Square Garden in New York, none possessed much charisma. Locker room decor was plainer than the interior of mobile homes. The audience was less knowledgeable and often vicious toward visiting players. A shake-down of money-losing teams winnowed the number of clubs to eight by the 1954–55 season. The Eastern Division consisted of the Boston Celtics, the New York Knicks, the Syracuse Nationals, and the Philadelphia Warriors. The Western Division lineup was the Fort Wayne Pistons, the Minneapolis Lakers, the Rochester Royals, and the Milwaukee Hawks.

Since there were only eight teams, intramural division rivalries were particularly intense. The teams played each other so often that fans in respective cities knew everything from the place a guy liked best to shoot to how he parted his hair to what time he woke up in the morning. And yes, familiarity did breed contempt.

In an era when it was manly to settle problems with fists rather than lawyers, on-court scuffles were more savage and in-the-stands confrontations and player-taunting more direct. For the Celtics, the worst environment was Syracuse, with Philadelphia running second. In Syracuse's case, it was probably a small-town inferiority complex. In Philadelphia's case, well, that's the city where Santa Claus and injured home players were later booed at sporting events. There's no reason to believe the populace was more enlightened in the 1950s.

"I hated Syracuse," Cousy said more than 50 years later.

Boy, did Syracuse make a negative impression on Cousy. As a senior citizen, he spends part of each year in Florida, where he often golfs with snowbirds and transplants from Rochester, Buffalo, and Syracuse.

"I constantly needle them," Cousy said. "I say it snows in Syracuse in August and all this stuff. It was a blue-collar town. They would have to pay me more money than exists to live in that town. It wasn't my favorite place to visit, and the fans were obnoxious. Oh, they were rabid. The smaller markets in those days, you took your life in your hands."

Fans screamed louder at the Celtics in Syracuse than anywhere else. Much like the pro wrestling stereotype, little old ladies really did poke players with umbrellas. Fans spit on players, threw coins at them, and even ran on the floor to try to take a swing every now and then. When the buzzer sounded to end a game, win or lose, the sprint to the visitors locker room was such a green-and-white stampede it looked like the start of the New York Marathon. The atmosphere was more like the hockey minor leagues in the movie *Slap Shot* than basketball.

"I recall literally being frightened because when you've got fans on the floor, and there we were, semi-nude, with fans running up, and all over the place, they can do almost anything and probably get away with it," Cousy said.

It was not as if the men in blue did much to protect the Celtics either. Police presence was minimal at arenas. Owners did not want to pay for heavy security. Cousy became so paranoid about Syracuse that he didn't even want to spend the night at a hotel after a game. He discovered there was a sleeper train heading to Boston 300 miles east that passed through Syracuse about 12:30 a.m.

Cousy pleaded with Auerbach to let him go, saying, "Arnold, I want to get out of here." Cousy grabbed his stuff from the hotel, took a cab to the station and rode the train to Worcester, where he disembarked and his wife, Missie, picked him up.

On-court play was hard-nosed, and despite their long-term record of excellence the Celtics found it difficult to beat Syracuse on the road. The Nationals, who won their only league title at the end of the 1954–55 season, always had top-flight talent. With Al Cervi, Paul Seymour, and Alex Hannum on the bench over the years, they were also led by coaches who burned to win and didn't mind distributing a few bruises along the way.

"Our coaches were tough guys," said Mr. Syracuse Dolph Schayes. "Hate is a tough word, though. They never had a liking for Red Auerbach. They would have loved to push the cigar into his face. We were scrappers."

The 6-foot-8, 220-pound, wavy-haired Schayes, who was born in 1928, played from 1948 to 1964, averaging 18.2 points a game, and was later inducted into the Basketball Hall of Fame. He settled in Syracuse and his son Danny not only played for Syracuse University, but also had a lengthy NBA career.

Schayes has his own insight into why Syracuse displayed the personality traits it did at the time. "Yes, it was a blue-collar town. But the 1950s was a golden era of sorts," Schayes said, "a time of full employment when a General Electric provided 20,000 jobs.

"It was a town with a lot of factory workers," he said. "It was a great town for wrestling."

Wrestling? Gorgeous George–flavored wrestling. It was a great town for the Nationals too, because they were the only professional game in town, competing with the New Yorks and Bostons.

"We had very vociferous fans who considered themselves the under-dogs," Schayes said. "We're David. They're Goliath. We were the Green Bay of the NBA. The fans got into it."

They got into it at the Onondaga War Memorial Coliseum, which held 6,000 or so fans for basketball.

"We could have gotten double the number," Schayes said.

The basketball palaces of today that seat 20,000 fans and are routinely filled were unimaginable at the time.

"You didn't have the big-facility arenas," said Bob Petit, the Hall of Fame Hawks forward.

Crowds were smaller and that meant paydays were too. Petit said he made $11,000 early in his career in the 1950s and topped out at $60,000 before he retired in 1965—and as an eleven-time all-star he was one of the biggest names in the NBA.

"There were no no-cut contracts," Petit said. "I didn't know of those."

The Celtic who was more of a lightning rod for trouble than most of the players was broadcaster Johnny Most. Most was a one-of-a-kind announcer, who really did bleed green and white, or at least tested the thesis often. His away-game broadcasts, where he was often overheard by the crowd, made him as much of a target as the players.

Not to worry. The gravel-voiced Most, who seemed to live on coffee, Danish pastries, and cigarettes, and who coped with insomnia, was a New Yorker who played college football at Brooklyn College and during World War II won a Purple Heart, seven battle stars, two presidential citations, and a flying cross. He had done some boxing and was not scared to use his fists if provoked. Most even got into a fight while on the air. Naturally, the incident occurred in Syracuse. His radio setup was courtside in the War Memorial in 1958, and he observed a fan coming out of the stands, taking a run into the Celtics huddle during a timeout where he was punched by Auerbach. Another fan threw a punch at Cousy. It missed the player, but Most was hit in the shoulder. That contact transformed Most from bystander to participant.

"Excuse the interruption," Most said into his microphone, "but I have to restrain an unruly, overweight, sloppy, pathetic drunk." Most rose and shoved the guy back into the stands. Then the broadcast resumed.

Either the action found Most, or Most found the action. During one Boston Garden game in 1959, Most's zeal in describing a play resulted in him spitting out his false teeth. The home broadcast booth was located in the balcony, and luckily Most plucked the flying teeth out of the air before they landed in the mezzanine.

The announcer worked himself into a one-sided frenzy broadcasting games. At home, his signature opening line was, "High above courtside at the Boston Garden . . . ." Generations of Celtics fans grew up comforted by that phrase every time they switched on a broadcast.

Don Chaney, a prominent Boston guard of the 1960s, once was hospitalized during the season and was watching his team play on TV. A nurse chastised him for not listening to Most's commentary while he stared at the tube. Chaney turned down the sound on the TV and turned up Most on the radio. That's when Chaney realized Most might as well have been calling a different game.

No doubt Most could be inflammatory. He considered guard Al Bianchi one of the dirtiest players in the league, someone always trying to take advantage of Celtics Frank Ramsey and Sam Jones. Most accused Bianchi of faking contact and falling on the court to attract a foul call. In Syracuse (of course), Most waited until Bianchi was nearby on the court and shouted into his mike, "Bianchi is a poor excuse for a human being. He gets humiliated out there because he couldn't defend a one-armed midget. He thinks he's a hard-nosed player, but he's nothing more than a coward." And people wondered why Most, a mere broadcaster, got into fights.

Most was a great find for Walter Brown. He had broadcast Knicks games and Brown worried that a Boston audience would not accept a New Yorker. But Auerbach reminded his boss that he was a New Yorker and was doing fine. Most adapted well to his Boston constituency. His enthusiasm rubbed off on listeners. Every game Most called was thrilling. Every Celtics shot was a big one. Most sold seats at the Garden by making the action sound irresistibly exciting.

"He was the best ticket salesman the team had," Cousy said.

Most began his stint in 1953 and despite late-life diabetes and emphysema leading to his death in 1993, the announcer essentially held on to the

microphone for the next thirty-seven years. Most suggested that the opposing players were evil incarnate and the Celtics were angels. In Most's mind,
the Celtics were brutalized by foes like Bianchi, who were all out-of-control
hatchet men. Celtics fans ate it up. Most taunted refs on the air, loudly
claiming that they were going blind. Sometimes they overheard him and
shot him dirty looks during games. Celtics players loved Most. They knew
he was on their side and very much part of their family.

The fourth black player in the NBA was another Celtic. Don Barksdale,
a 6-foot-6 forward out of UCLA, was a member of the 1948 United States
Olympic basketball team (the first black man to perform that duty) and
played two seasons with the Celtics, averaging 7.3 and 10.5 ppg, respec-
tively. Barksdale was also the first black player to compete in the NBA All-
Star Game, in 1953. Most was one of the most color-blind guys around—he
joined the NAACP in the 1940s—and he and Barksdale became close
friends, often spending nights out on the town. When late hours were kept,
Most made sure Barksdale woke up early enough to make it to practice on
time. Barksdale said Most saved his career.

The mid-1950s marked the transition between the set shot and the jump
shot, too. When Schayes turned pro out of New York University, he was in
the vast majority who shot two-handed set shots when attempting to make a
long-range basket. Schayes was aware of Kenny Sailors' new-fangled jumper
and over time adapted, shifting to a one-handed set shot. By the time Schayes
ceased coaching in the NBA in 1972, nobody shot any kind of set shot.

"The set shot has gone the way of the dodo bird," Schayes said. "Kenny
Sailors was the darling of the sportswriters. He was a wonderful player from
the prehistoric NBA days. I used the two-hand set shot because everybody
used it. I became very adept at this shot. I used it to set up my driving. It
wasn't a quick shot to get off. The kids would laugh at you today. But in the
early days, if you shot a jumper, coaches went so far as to put you on the
bench. They didn't think it was accurate."

But gradually there became a need to release shots more quickly to
counter more agile defenders.

Jack Twyman, a 6-foot-6 forward who was another great scorer of the
time as a decade-long mainstay of the Rochester and Cincinnati Royals, said,

"I think the evolution of the jump shot came with the 24-second clock. I was a set shooter and I had to change from a set shot to a jump shot, probably in 1955 or 1956. I came in as a quasi set shooter–jump shooter. But I probably took my last set shot in 1956. The set shot was a thing of the past."

Johnny "Red" Kerr, who played nine of his twelve NBA seasons in Syracuse as the reliable double-figure scoring center lined up next to Schayes, said the league was definitely rougher in the 1950s and that Schayes was the subject of other teams' elbowing and banging.

"We had a lot of guys who wanted to beat up on Schayes," said Kerr, who is a longtime broadcaster for the Chicago Bulls. "He was our star and I guess if anybody was a protector or a bodyguard Mr. T for him, it was Earl [Lloyd]."

Not that Kerr, at 6-foot-9 and 230 pounds, couldn't do some damage in close-quarters infighting.

"There were no suspensions," Kerr said of the way the NBA was administered at the time. "There was no fine. You may have got kicked out of the game for fighting, but the next game you were playing and all was forgotten. I was in the same division as Wilt Chamberlain and Bill Russell. We had to play eight or nine times a year. I had to go eight or nine times a season against the two best centers of all time. I thought it was rougher in those days. We only had one rule and that was if a fight started, or if you were going to start a fight, start it in front of your team's bench."

The Nationals won their one title, but they could never get past Boston in the playoffs again. They were hungry, but were always denied. The Celtics had just a little bit more talent, and the continuous big-game losses grated on the Nationals, Kerr said. Not to mention the Auerbach victory cigar.

"We all hated the Celtics," Kerr said. "It was a natural rivalry. I think if you ask any of the old Chicago Bears players what their feeling is about the Green Bay Packers, you'd hear the same thing. When we were playing, I had fights with Tommy Heinsohn, the Celtics forward. I didn't like him at all. But when it's all over, you step back and I think you respect them more for what they did."

A half century after the under-the-basket confrontations, when the Celtics and Bulls play, Heinsohn, also a broadcaster, and Kerr, get together for pre-game meals and talk about the old days.

One NBA fight the likes of which is unlikely to ever be duplicated is the on-the-floor war in the 1956–57 season between Auerbach and Hawks owner Ben Kerner, who by then had moved his club to St. Louis. A pre-game argument broke out before a playoff game at Kiel Auditorium over the height of one of the baskets. Bob Cousy, Bill Sharman, and Bill Russell argued the hoop was not set at precisely 10 feet.

Auerbach started to intervene and raise the issue with officials. Kerner, seeing his old employee trying to monkey with the home team's equipment, intercepted him at midcourt. The men began yelling, Kerner swore at Auerbach, and Auerbach punched him with a right cross to the face. Down went Kerner. The duo wrestled around on the floor until they were separated. Kerner suffered a bloody lip. Auerbach was proven wrong when officials measured the basket and found it to be regulation height. Play ball. Auerbach didn't even get a technical foul for instigating the battle. In the present-day NBA climate, he might have been suspended for a year.

Earl Strom, who spent thirty-two years refereeing NBA ball, starting in 1957, had a unique perspective on fighting in the league's early days. He believed that the owners who came from hockey backgrounds— where skaters routinely ended up toothless from contact—thought fans responded to hard hitting in any form and didn't want to crack down on miscreants.

"There were some damn good fights, the heavyweight haymakers coming from left and right," Strom said. "A lot of times you didn't get it stopped until one guy went down."

Strom recalled ejecting Cousy from a game in Boston after he swore at him. Strom said it was like throwing the Pope out of Rome and the fans' cascading boos seemed to agree. A year later, Strom said, fans in St. Louis began throwing eggs at the Celtics during a playoff game that was televised back to Boston. Sure enough, the next day, when the series resumed in Massachusetts, fans who watched the first game came armed with eggs and began pelting the Hawks. Strom noted that unsurprisingly no eggs were landing near Cousy, so he stood next to him under a basket. Then Cousy moved to the Celtics bench and Strom went with him. When Cousy went to get a drink of water and Strom followed him there, he asked Strom what the heck he was doing. Strom said he felt that sticking with Boston's biggest hero was the safest place to be.

Strom selected an all–tough guy team featuring seven players from the 1950s. The fame of most did not transcend the decade, but Al Attles, who later coached the Warriors to a title, and 7-foot center Walter Dukes still carry some name recognition. Oh yes, and one Celtic was among them—Jungle Jim Loscutoff.

Once, Strom clobbered a fan seated near the court who twice had maligned him with the F-word. Strom blew his cool and belted the guy in the face. The fan's friends jumped him and Celtics players bailed out Strom. Tommy Heinsohn got Strom in a bear hug and pulled him out of the pile, and Bill Russell lifted the main protagonist out of the way. In another incident, Strom was walking off the court through a tunnel in Syracuse when a fan lunged over a barrier at him, Strom didn't even see him coming. Walking behind Strom was 6-foot-8 Gene Conley, who apparently reached up and belted the interloper and kept right on strolling off the court. Strom said he heard a smack and saw the guy upstairs slowly sink into his seat.

It may not have seemed like it when the whistle blew to start play and calls were questioned, but the players and the referees of the 1950s were generally on the same side.

At the time, the NBA was more compact. Not only were there only eight teams compared to the current thirty, but teams were also more geographically bunched. The Midwest was the West in terms of league outposts. It usually took more time to reach other cities for road trips than it does now. These days teams jump on charter flights immediately after night games and players are frequently in their own beds by 3 a.m. Although DC-3s gained in popularity in the 1950s, much of the travel was by train.

"We would get on a sleeper after a game, ride into Chicago, change trains, and go about six hours, or whatever it took, to Minneapolis," Kerr recalled. "Sometimes they [opposing players] were on the court warming up when we were just checking into our hotel."

Nearly every aspect of the NBA is more player-friendly now. Modern players are pampered compared to their predecessors, and not just with expanded legroom on their airplanes. Prudently, teams invest in well-educated trainers and provide them with assistants in order to give players top-notch care if something happens during games, or to help them with rehab from injuries. With multimillion-dollar investments in players, their well-being is paramount. In the 1950s, sports medicine was a bit more haphazard. Teams had part-time trainers for home games (never mind practice), and trainers did not travel to road games. The attitude toward an injured player seemed more casual. No blood, no foul might have been the rule on the court, and no bone protruding through the skin meant you were capable of playing.

Petit, who was born in 1932 and starred for Louisiana State University before making his mark in the NBA, is still very much a sports fan. Back living in Louisiana, he roots for his alma mater and attends nearby sporting events like the Sugar Bowl. When he compares the treatment of athletes from his playing era with the players of today, he laughs.

"I taped my own ankles for eleven years," Petit said.

And it hardly mattered if he was falling apart. If he could stand by game time he pulled on his Hawks jersey. Petit broke his arm during a game in St. Louis and played two nights later in Minneapolis. Another time, Petit said he sprained his ankle in a game against Fort Wayne. He was 215 pounds of dead weight, but when the Hawks checked out of their hotel the next morning, his teammates carried him. And he played the next night. Petit also took seventeen stitches in his eyelid at halftime at a game in St. Louis. The doctor admitted it was a rush job so that Petit could go back in, and that he would have to restitch after the game. Petit said that if you could will your body to do so, you played.

Twyman's Royals were a team on the rise during the 1955–56 season, a team led by the rookie sharpshooter out of the University of Cincinnati and an even more precocious rookie, the unstoppable Maurice Stokes. Stokes was 6-feet-7, weighed 240 pounds, rebounded like a center, and passed like a guard. He averaged 16.8 points and 16.3 rebounds a game as a rookie and hit a high of 16.9 points and 18.1 rebounds per game as a third-year man, as well as breaking into the list of top assist men.

Stokes's story is one of the most heartbreaking in NBA history, though the role Twyman played is one of the most heartwarming. On March 12, 1958, near the end of a game at Minneapolis, Stokes fell to the floor and banged his head on the hardwood. He felt funny, then ill, then panicked, as his body seemed to go haywire on the ensuing flight out of town. He said aloud that he thought he might die.

It was not initially clear what was wrong, but Stokes had suffered a traumatic brain injury from the blow to his head and fell into a six-week coma. When he awoke he was completely paralyzed and could not speak, and with only minor improvements he lived that way until 1970 when he died of a heart attack at thirty-six. In the meantime, teammate Twyman, in a stunning act of generosity, became Stokes's legal guardian, supervised his care, and for years organized benefit basketball games as fund-raisers to pay Stokes's bills. This was considered even more noteworthy since Twyman was white and Stokes was black, and the 1950s was not the leading decade in the history of American brotherhood.

Even after the Royals acquired Oscar Robertson in 1960, perhaps the greatest all-around player of all-time, they could never overcome the Celtics' control of the Eastern Division. Twyman, now past seventy, believes that with a healthy Stokes, a lineup featuring Robertson, Stokes, himself, and center Wayne Embry, the Royals might have disrupted the Boston dynasty.

"If he [Stokes] had stayed healthy," Twyman said, "they wouldn't be talking about the Celtics the way they are, because he was some ballplayer. We had a lot of good ballplayers. We had the ingredients. Once we took the Celtics to triple overtime in a deciding playoff game. But we didn't do it [win the big series]."

"Red Auerbach had a mystique, an aura." Twyman continued. "Casey Stengel had it with the Yankees. I guess maybe Vince Lombardi had it with the Green Bay Packers. They refused to lose and that's a very unique and wonderful talent to have. He passed it along to the players. They bought into it. I'm not sure any team ever, in any sport, dominated their sport like the Celtics did from 1957 to 1969."

7

A BIG MAN WILL PROVIDE

Howie McHugh, the publicity director of the Celtics, was the designated driver assigned to pick up Bill Russell at Boston's Logan Airport in December of 1956. There was no game that day, so he asked his good friend Bill Sharman to accompany him.

At Logan, a banner read WELCOME BILL RUSSELL TO THE BOSTON CELTICS. Did that ever turn out to be the truth. Slender, athletically muscled, and standing 6-feet-9, Russell had the right build. Sharman looked over his new teammate and thought, "He looks like a basketball player." And did that ever turn out to be the truth too.

No one truly knew what to expect from Russell, direct from the United States' gold medal victory in the 1956 Summer Olympics in Melbourne, Australia, a victory that followed his leadership of the University of San Francisco to two straight NCAA championships. Word was that Russell was pretty good. But there were no scouting services or clearinghouses to inform basketball fans about the best pro prospects. There was no wall-to-wall TV programming of college basketball games giving fans a sneak preview of the best players to come. All most people around Boston knew was that coach Red Auerbach said this guy he drafted could rebound and that the school headmaster seemed willing to mortgage the franchise to hire him.

In private conversations with players like veteran guards Bob Cousy and Sharman, team leaders who along with Auerbach suffered through near misses in the playoffs, the coach said Russell was going to be the championship difference maker.

The nightmare days of the Celtics' last-place finishes were history. Auerbach was building winners. At the end of the 1954–55 season, Boston beat the Knicks two games out of three in an opening playoff series, but lost the next round to Syracuse. After the 1955–56 season, the Celtics lost in the first round to Syracuse.

These were not upsets. The Celtics's lost because they were not the better team. Cousy and Auerbach spent six seasons on the outside looking in, waiting their turn. They were not happy with the results, but Cousy reflected many years later that those Celtics' clubs lived up to their potential.

"I think we all could sit back after the season without regrets or recriminations," Cousy said. "I think Arnold was always able to extract the most out of the players and he proved that later on. But even in those years, when Ed Macauley was our center and weighed about 185 pounds soaking wet, and we had Bob Brannum and Bob Harris as forwards, not Hall of Fame candidates, at the end of the day we could say we basically did as well as we could. I suppose that's what it's all about in the final analysis in sports. You can look in the mirror and say, 'Well, Goddamnit we lost, but at least we played as well as we could.'"

Neither Cousy nor Auerbach were men content to be associated with teams that were just okay. They wanted more, and things changed forever after the 1955–56 season when Auerbach's acumen produced the greatest draft class of all time. In order, he selected Bill Russell, Tommy Heinsohn, and K. C. Jones, three future Hall of Famers. Heinsohn, who starred at Holy Cross 35 miles away, was a territorial pick. This means the Celtics had first dibs on him because his college was located within the club's home territory. Jones was Russell's teammate and co-conspirator in leading San Francisco to a then-record 56-game winning streak and those two NCAA crowns.

Tipped off by his West Coast sources, Auerbach knew Russell was something special. But the big man's greatness could not be hidden, and even if other teams didn't quite recognize Russell's unique capabilities as clearly as

Auerbach did, Russell was still on draft radar screens. Boston's acquisition of Russell was not without intrigue and wheeling and dealing.

The St. Louis Hawks and Rochester Royals were ahead of the Celtics on the draft list that year. The Hawks seemed likely to take Russell. Instead, Auerbach bargained with Ben Kerner. Auerbach dangled Macauley, a proven All-Star scorer with roots and an off-season home in St. Louis, and Cliff Hagan—under duress, since Auerbach had been waiting two years for the former Kentucky star to emerge from the service.

Although Macauley was happy in Boston, his one-year-old son Pat was ill with spinal meningitis that had caused brain damage and he needed special care. Six seasons into his career with the Celtics, Macauley wasn't even sure he could continue to play in Boston, so that made him amenable to a trade. He viewed the exchange with St. Louis as a favor from Walter Brown, who was very fond of him. Also, "Easy Ed" grew up in St. Louis and attended St. Louis University.

Macauley was a seven-time All-Star. Hagan became a longtime star for the Hawks. As phenomenal as the trade turned out to be for Boston, it was not a slam dunk when it occurred. Macauley and Hagan were players of value. No one figured Russell would be a franchise maker and go down in lore as the greatest winner in team-sports history.

"Where were the Celtics before Russell got there?" asked K. C. Jones. "They couldn't get that far. Bill joined the Celtics in mid-December, coming straight back from the Olympics, and he takes them to the championship."

The trade was the hard part. The Celtics still had to persuade Rochester not to choose Russell. The financially ailing franchise worried about the big money Russell might command. Walter Brown also had a trump card. He controlled the bookings of the family-friendly figure skating show, the Ice Capades, a surefire winter moneymaker for anyone looking to fill otherwise empty arenas. Brown promised that the Ice Capades would play Rochester if Rochester steered clear of Russell. That was the story anyway, and if there has been some tentative revisionist commentary hinting otherwise, it is now impossible to prove since all of the principals are dead. Except Russell, and he likely never knew the details about his availability to Boston. At least no one made him skate with the Ice Capades in Rochester.

William Fenton Russell was born February 12, 1934, in Monroe, Louisiana, but attended high school in Oakland. His height was listed at 6-feet-9 and his weight at 220 pounds. He was a track-and-field high jumper and high hurdler whose long fingers reached to the top of the backboard for rebounds. He possessed a left-handed jump shot that looked awkward, and a high, arching free throw that was no prettier. He was not an overwhelmingly high scorer, but made shots in the clutch, and he virtually invented defense.

Russell was a vacuum cleaner on the backboards and brilliant at throwing a two-handed outlet pass to jump-start fast breaks. Before Russell, the NBA's tallest players swatted shorter players' shots away and out of play, sometimes gleefully watching them bounce into the fifth row of the stands. But with impeccable timing, Russell jumped, blocked the shot, then caught the ball on its way down. He swooped down from outside shooters' peripheral vision and plagued their thoughts and shots. He intimidated with his agility and a deep glower. Opponents grew paranoid that Russell would appear like some wide-winged bird to ruin their shots, their psyches shattered from hearing real or imaginary footsteps, so the battle was half-won. It made him almost a ghostly presence, abruptly materializing. Cousy said he couldn't begin to count the number of times he heard someone say, "Russell came out of nowhere!" He was just quicker than anyone else.

Russell was also the cog that made the Celtics machine complete. He was the missing piece in Auerbach's scheme. Despite the coach's fast-break philosophy, the early Celtics teams couldn't live up to the plan because they did not have the weapons. Adding Russell to the mix linked everyone's skills. Now the Celtics of Auerbach's dreams could become the Celtics on the floor.

"We had a very competitive team," Cousy said. "The fast break was our basic offense, but we didn't control our backboard. Obviously, there's a need to do that. Arnold told me the year before [the draft] he had a guy hidden away, a guy on the West Coast, and if he could get him he would solve our rebounding problems. He never said a word about defensive abilities. Russ ended up revolutionizing the game defensively."

Russell's early childhood was spent in meager circumstances in a racially charged Monroe, Louisiana. His father Charles, known as "Mister Charlie," worked in a paper-bag factory, but one day he courted serious trouble by seeking to preserve his dignity with a tire iron in his hand. That prompted the move to California.

Russell's mother died soon after when she was thirty-two, and his father raised him and his brother alone. Mister Charlie instilled a sense of pride and independence in his sons. Russell absorbed the lessons well and determined he would never let himself be bullied by a white man's world. Snubs stemming from the color of a man's skin were not difficult to collide with, but Russell carried himself with an erect carriage and a regal bearing. If some people thought he was aloof, tough. Russell was always going to be his own man, always going to do what he wanted and not be pressured into doing things to merely get along. The longer he played and the more he achieved, the more that success gave Russell the power to act the way he wished. Over time there seemed to be a dichotomy between a reserved, public Bill Russell and a friendlier, inside-the-team Bill Russell.

In 1956, when Russell stepped off the plane at Logan with his wife, Rose, and shook hands with owner Walter Brown, he knew little about Boston and Boston knew little about him. Russell's skills had been sufficiently touted so that the sportswriters expected someone who could step in and make a contribution, but they had no inkling that a savior had zipped in on a jet plane.

Heinsohn, the 6-foot-7 forward who soon enough would be christened "Tommy Gun" for his propensity to shoot often and without conscience and blow opponents away with daring hook shots, had a better idea than most Celtics what Russell was bringing.

One of the best college players in the East his senior year, Heinsohn was the leader of an accomplished Holy Cross team entered in the Holiday Festival at Madison Square Garden. The San Francisco Dons, on their way to a second NCAA title, were also competing. Heinsohn said eastern basketball people knew little about the Dons other than that they had a "mysterious big black guy in the middle."

In hindsight, Heinsohn is sure Russell was psyched to the rafters because public relations hyping the tournament implied it was a showdown between the two big men. They banged in butt-to-butt, hip-to-hip contact during the first half. In the second half, Russell dominated, blocking Heinsohn's shot at will. Heinsohn thought he had better moves than Fred Astaire, but Russell never fell for his fakes. San Francisco won, 67–51. Heinsohn said "Thank God" the next time he saw Russell they were playing on the same team.

Listening to Heinsohn speak, his intonations sound like a *Goodfellas* "dese" and "dose" guy. That's on the surface, but he is nothing like that in real life. It's just his Jersey City accent talking. Heinsohn is an accomplished painter, coach, and broadcaster who was also a successful insurance salesman. The artist who most fascinates him is Van Gogh, and Heinsohn and the Celtics painted their own share of masterpieces over the years.

Heinsohn's family was the only one of German heritage in his neighborhood. That didn't matter much until World War II started, when the boy was seven. Then local toughs taunted Heinsohn, calling him "Nazi!" and ganging up on him to make him fight his way home from elementary school. It was a lonely and frightening time for the boy who said he did not outgrow that trauma completely for decades. In a sense, Heinsohn was confined to his own internment camp during the war, stuck in his house for self-preservation. A move to Union City, New Jersey, three years later represented a fresh start and the start of his life in basketball.

One neighbor who regularly took advantage of the outdoor basketball courts at Gilmore School playground was a Villanova player named Paul Arizin, who matured into a star pro and a Hall of Famer. Heinsohn offered to rebound Arizin's missed shots, and Arizin taught him to shoot. Neither could imagine they would one day face each another in the NBA, Arizin with the Philadelphia Warriors. In fact, Heinsohn's rookie year, when the Celtics charged to their first title, Arizin led the league in scoring with a 25.6 points per game average.

Although the hook shot (before it was basically forgotten in recent years) was an unstoppable shot for centers, Heinsohn recognized a proficiency when he was still young and much smaller. He made uncountable numbers of the sweeping, arcing shots at the playground and later electrified fans at the Boston Garden with his accuracy from surprising distances. Nobody in basketball history, except perhaps Kareem Abdul-Jabbar, the NBA's all-time leading scorer, took or takes hook shots from a distance greater than 12 feet. Heinsohn's hooks were sometimes tried from the corner and his makes boggled observers. It was no accident that Heinsohn entitled his autobiography, *Give 'Em the Hook*. He was that identified with the weapon.

Heinsohn became so good at the game so fast that private Catholic high schools began recruiting him. Deemed to be a somewhat unsavory practice in the 2000s when it has accelerated, such recruiting was almost unheard of in the 1950s. When he graduated, Heinsohn had about one hundred pen pals writing flattering notes to him from colleges located around the nation. He chose Holy Cross, Cousy's old school, because he thought he wanted to become a doctor and because he knew two players from Jersey on the Crusaders roster.

Heinsohn was a smash at Holy Cross, becoming an All-American and leading the Crusaders to the NIT championship in his sophomore year. One of the teams Holy Cross vanquished was Louisiana State, led by a player named Bob Petit. Heinsohn and Petit saw each other over and over in championship situations over the years.

As good as he was, all Heinsohn needed to stay humble was to keep up with the exploits of the ex-Crusader Cousy, who was dazzling fans in downtown Boston. Cousy earned the nickname "Houdini of the Hardwood" because of the way he made the ball do tricks. Heinsohn said Cousy also earned the nickname Mister Basketball because his flash and style "made the sport." If a player tried to emulate Cousy (and especially if a pass went awry), Heinsohn said other players and fans derisively said, "Who do you think you are, the Cooz?"

Heinsohn said he suspected all along that Auerbach would choose him with a territorial draft choice, and his rookie year he signed with the Celtics for $9,000. The once-fragile kid from New Jersey was one of eighty professional players in the NBA.

Bob Cousy and Bill Sharman finished seventh and eighth in the league in scoring. Heinsohn tied for eleventh. Jim Loscutoff recorded his only double-figure season. Frank Ramsey had one foot out of the Army and the other in the Celtics' camp. The Celtics got off to a good start, even without Russell. One secret of the Dynasty was the way Auerbach drove his players to get into superb early-season shape. His training camps were as rigorous as the Army's. Auerbach knew that some teams eased into shape and could be plucked in the early going. Why not pile up wins fast and build a lead in the division race?

"It was an arduous training camp," Heinsohn said. "Longer than the current ones. We tried to get off to a great start."

Compared to off-season workout schedules maintained by most NBA players today, players of the 1950s were too busy to run, lift, and shoot daily because they worked seasonal jobs. They needed the money to support families and pay mortgages. If anything, Heinsohn's conditioning was worse than many others' because he was a heavy smoker during his career. Cousy urged him to give up the habit, but he kept on puffing. Frank Ramsey said his playing time benefited because Heinsohn's stamina was harmed from smoking. Heinsohn did not stop smoking until years after he retired.

The season Russell came to Boston, the Celtics did get off to a good start. Russell did not have to lift his new team from the basement. They were already moving into the penthouse.

"Heinsohn and Loscutoff provided a lot of immediate help rebounding and now Russ joins us," Cousy said. "We were a first-place team before Russ got there. I think maybe we might have got to the finals, but we probably wouldn't have beaten St. Louis without him."

Maybe, maybe not. But with Russell in the lineup for forty-eight regular-season games, the Celtics showed they were the class of the tougher Eastern Division. They posted the best regular-season record in the sport at 44-28. The Western Division was the have-not division with St. Louis, Minneapolis, and Fort Wayne tying for first with dismal 34-38 records. St. Louis emerged as the first seed after tiebreaker playoffs and won its way into the league finals too.

The Celtics were waiting. When it came to the playoffs, they still had something to prove.

8

A TITLE FOR BOSTON

The last shot bounced off the rim, once, twice, and rolled away as the buzzer sounded. Time ran out on the St. Louis Hawks and the Celtics were victors, 125–123 in double overtime. It was the moment the Dynasty began, April 13, 1957, the moment that Red Auerbach, Walter Brown, and Bob Cousy in particular had been building toward. From the seventh game to seventh heaven.

Cousy ran, skipped, hopped, jumped, heck, triple-jumped from the defensive end of the Boston Garden court to mid-court. In delirious joy, he repeatedly threw his arms up in the air as if exhorting the already applauding and cheering fans. Bill Russell met Cousy at center court and jumped up and down, as if consecutive center jumps were required, or he was imitating a Masai warrior. It was a wild and memorable scene, years in the making. The Boston Celtics were the champions of the world!

You have to win a first title to start a Dynasty, and if the ball had dropped in that basket the Celtics would have been runners-up, not champs, bemoaning a close call, not extolling a triumphant performance. They did it, but nearly couldn't. They did it, but it was a wring-you-dry, excruciating struggle with the Hawks. Double overtime by two in the seventh game. Wow!

"As you grow up you always want to be the best at something," Bill Sharman said. "That's something you always wanted to do sometime in your life. And we were the best that year."

Bill Russell made the Celtics whole. He made his regular-season debut in December in a nationally televised game. Auerbach didn't even start him, but that circumstance was remedied quickly after Russell grabbed 16 rebounds in 21 minutes of playing time.

Cousy remembers walking off the court that day after Russell played less than half a game and thinking, "You know, we may be getting a little more than we bargained for here. It was obvious seeing this guy's rebounding presence and it also was obvious very early on that he was going to be a defensive presence as well. He completely complemented the skills we already had in place. And the rest, as they say, is history."

Literally.

Very quickly, the Celtics adapted to Russell's rhythms. When Russell signed his contract and met with Auerbach, the coach promptly made it clear what he expected. He told Russell to concentrate on playing his defensive and rebounding game and not to worry about points. He told the player he would never judge him on statistics. In a league where scoring average counted heavily in the minds of the public and owners who signed checks, that was innovative thinking.

Although Russell did take his share of short hooks and medium-range jumpers, it was understood that he didn't have to score to earn his pay, so he obliged and mostly passed off to better-shooting teammates.

"There was no pressure," Russell said.

In his thirteen seasons with the Celtics, Russell never led the team in scoring, although he did compile a lifetime average of 15.1 points per game. But he led the league in rebounding five times and his career rebounding average was 22.5 per game. Sometimes it seems entire teams don't gather that many in a game these days.

It was soon apparent that Russell had extraordinary mannerisms off the court as well. Russell arrived in Boston wearing a goatee (his careerlong personal trademark) when no one else in the league wore facial hair. When he laughed it was a reverberating cackle, the sound of ice cubes shaken in an empty glass, only more high-pitched. Pregame, Russell would sit around the locker room, joking, playing cards—making Auerbach a little bit edgy with his nonchalance—and then suddenly he would bolt for the bathroom to throw up. Russell was not game-ready unless he puked his guts out at least once before the contest and sometimes more than once.

Heinsohn called Russell "a lion of a competitor" and said that if it was getting too close to tip-off and Russell hadn't yet thrown up, Auerbach actually walked up to him to tell him to get into the men's room and barf. "That's how much he gave of himself."

A review of Russell's background suggested that wherever he went, championships followed. University of San Francisco went undefeated for nearly two straight seasons and the U.S. won the Olympic gold medal with Russell in the middle. He brought the same attitude to the pros, though if the Celtics didn't go undefeated (and no one ever would in the NBA), it wasn't his fault.

"I had dedicated myself to trying to win every game," Russell said.

Frank Ramsey was like that too when he joined the Celtics. After playing on an undefeated Kentucky team in college, he wasn't used to losing and when he suffered his first defeat with the Celtics he started crying. Ed Macauley told Ramsey to cut it out, that in the pros the season was too long to think of winning every game. Ramsey seemed so youthful, gap-toothed, looking like the farm boy he was. They all looked so young, faces free of wrinkles, smiles full of expectation.

In his two-thirds of a rookie season, Russell averaged a league-leading 19.6 rebounds per game. With him controlling the backboards, the Celtics matured into a polished unit. They won six more games than any other team that season and averaged a league-high 105.5 points per game.

"We were blowing those suckers out of there," Cousy said after Russell began controlling the rebounding.

"Heinsohn" would be the surprising answer to a trivia question: Given the splashiness of Russell's debut and his spectacular statistical start, most fans would assume he was chosen rookie of the year. Probably because he did not play the entire season, he was not. It was Heinsohn, who averaged 16.2 points per game, who was voted top rookie.

Heinsohn was tall and slender in those days, with a crew cut that in no way resembled the mod hair he displayed in his 1970s fashion-plate days, and minus the filled-out shoulders too. Heinsohn elevated well on his jump shot, was creative near the basket, and froze defenders in place with the hook. He was a born scorer and a shooter by nature. Cousy kidded Heinsohn all the time about his proclivity to shoot, but Heinsohn comprehended right from the start that's what Auerbach wanted from him.

"My job on the Celtics was not to pass the ball," Heinsohn said. "My job was to get free and get open so Cousy could deliver the ball. He was the assists man. I gave it back to him, saying, 'Well, if it wasn't for me, you wouldn't have gotten all of those assists.'"

The Celtics won the NBA title every year but one during Heinsohn's career, the year he retired at thirty.

"You know, the first title was the best," he said.

It was the best for all of them.

On paper, just going by the teams' regular-season records, the 1957 finals should have been a Celtics gimme. They were ten games better than the Hawks. But winning four more from St. Louis was a tougher task than predicted. The Hawks were late bloomers that season. The roster was dotted with notable players, but they didn't jell until late.

The undisputed leader of the Hawks was Bob Petit. He was second in the league in points scored with a 24.7 average and is still regarded as one of the greatest jump-shooting forwards and rebounders of all time. Macauley was still playing at an All-Star level in the pivot, though he was not nearly as strong or as great a jumper as Russell. Charlie Share, the 6-foot-10 player whom Auerbach drafted instead of Cousy in 1950, had found a home with the Hawks.

Playmaker Slater Martin, once the floor leader of the NBA's first dynasty, George Mikan's Minneapolis Lakers, came to the Hawks in a trade. Cliff Hagan, part of the deal that allowed Boston to draft Russell, was also a Hawk. So were future coaches Jack McMahon and Alex Hannum, as was underrated double-figure scorer Jack Coleman. The Hawks bumbled through the regular season somewhat, but made a run at crunch time.

"We had a very, very good team," Petit said. "Cliff and I were the scorers. Jack McMahon, Charlie Share, and Slater Martin were willing to do a lot of the dirty work. We were very confident that we would be able to play with Boston."

Why shouldn't they be? The Celtics hadn't accomplished anything yet. There was no reason to fear them as anything other than the team that happened to emerge from the Eastern Division playoffs that year. And Petit was a formidable scorer, in the middle of a years-long stretch during which he led the league twice and never fell out of the top five in points-per-game average.

"Who's better?" demanded Hawks owner Ben Kerner.

Petit averaged nearly 30 points a game in the playoffs, and Heinsohn later complimented him lavishly.

"Petit was probably as strong as any man I've played," Heinsohn said.

Boston had home-court advantage for the best-of-seven series because of its superior regular-season record, but St. Louis negated that immediately with a 125–123 double-overtime opening-game victory (which nearly mirrored the seventh game) in Boston on March 30, 1957.

The Celtics woke up and captured the second game at home, 119–99. The teams split the next two games in St. Louis and the Celtics took a three-games-to-two lead after a single-game return to Boston. The Celtics could have clinched in St. Louis in Game 6, but lost 96–94.

That set up the epic seventh game in Boston two days later that frayed everyone's nerves with thirty-eight lead changes. In what became typical of Celtics championships, a fresh hero stepped up to quell the Hawks' hopes. In later years, one of the team's running jokes was Frank Ramsey's annual postseason speech in the locker room. He announced that now that the playoffs had begun, the team was playing with his money, so they had better take care of it.

"Yeah, I did that," Ramsey said years later. "We all needed the playoff money. The most I ever got in playoff money was $3,200, but that got us through the summer."

Heinsohn scored 37 points and collected 23 rebounds in the championship decider, and Russell scored 19 points and gathered 32 rebounds. But Ramsey was the man in the clutch. In the first overtime, Ramsey scored 6 of Boston's 10 points. In the second overtime, with the game tied, 121–121, he hit a free throw and on Boston's next possession sank a 25-foot one-hander. The title belonged to the Celtics.

"I knew there was no one around to rebound and maybe I shouldn't have taken it," Ramsey said of his long shot, "but it went in, so that's all that counts, I guess."

Heinsohn, however, led the team in scoring during the playoffs, surpassing Cousy and Sharman, who usually were the high men. In the seventh game, neither shot particularly well.

"I didn't really have a good game," Sharman said. "The seventh game was one of the worst I had all year."

In 1953 Cousy had carried the Celtics to a remarkable playoff win over Syracuse by making 30 out of 32 free throws in a four-overtime game. He scored 50 points in that game, as cool as Arctic snow in the clutch and at the free-throw line when eyes were all on him. Near the end of the St. Louis game, with the championship truly in reach for the first time, Cousy made just 1 of 2 free throws and said he was the most nervous he had been in a game since high school.

Like Sharman, Cousy did not play well in the seventh game, his shooting erratic. Boston survived because the Hawks' last shot was a half-inch off. Boston survived because the team had Bill Russell.

The Celtics were giddy in celebration, champagne soaking the locker room. They were very much in the moment, with no crystal balls to consult to read the future. They completed the quest for a title, and they would come back the next season and try to do it again. What these grateful, happy, momentarily satisfied players could not know after they deposited title No. 1 in the bank is that in the coming years they would make the impossible reality.

Riding the shoulders of a racehorse named Bill Russell, the Boston Celtics would stamp themselves as the greatest basketball team of all time.

9

DYNASTY DETOURED

On November 1, 1957, before the opening of the 1957–58 season at the Boston Garden, the Celtics were rewarded with a perk for becoming world champions. Mark Furcolo, son of then-governor Foster Furcolo, presented the players with Massachusetts vanity license plates with their uniform numbers on them.

Bill Russell, No. 6, Bob Cousy, No. 14, Jim Loscutoff, No. 18, and the others might not have been able to take the gifts to the bank, but it was a nice gesture.

Then the Celtics won the first game, 107–83, over the Syracuse Nationals. Cousy and Loscutoff sat out with the flu, but Frank Ramsey scored 27 points and Russell grabbed 27 rebounds. One of the things that had to make Walter Brown the happiest was the crowd of 12,681. It was the largest turnout to date for a Celtics opener.

With essentially the same roster—plus the addition of a new guard named Sam Jones—and confidence from capturing last season's championship, the Celtics got off to a swift start. Two weeks into the season, Russell set a league record by gathering 49 rebounds in a 111–89 victory over Philadelphia.

Compared to when the team began and Boston newspapers did not even cover every Celtics game with a staff writer, the explosion of interest in daily print was remarkable. It was around this time that the word *amazing* became a regular descriptor in Celtics game reports.

During the first month of the new season, Commissioner Maurice Podoloff predicted that the geographically compact NBA would soon place teams in the West Coast cities of Los Angeles, San Francisco, and Portland, Oregon. He was right on all counts, though it took considerably longer for the Trailblazers to find their way to Oregon as an expansion team than it did for the Lakers to move from Minneapolis to L.A. and for the Warriors to move from Philadelphia to San Francisco.

One subplot to the first half of the 1957–58 season was the extraordinary foul shooting of Bill Sharman and Dolph Schayes. Game after game, head-to-head, the two marksmen made every free throw. Sharman was well into his streak that would hit 55 straight on Christmas Day, when, of all people, Russell had a hot game from the line. After making 12 in a row, Russell joked with the press.

"Tell Sharman I'm going after his foul-shooting record," the big man said.

Russell was an erratic foul shooter throughout his career, though he often made clutch shots with the game on the line, but Schayes was a forreal threat to catch Sharman. On January 3, however, Schayes's streak ended with a miss at 50 in a row.

Sharman, who scored 44 points in the Christmas Day game, was a career 88.3 percent free-throw shooter. He made those mid-game tosses look easy from 15 feet. What is little remembered, however, is that Sharman actually improved his seasonal averages the longer he played.

Playing word association with the names of his old teammates, the first words guard K. C. Jones (who at one time served as an assistant coach to Sharman with the Lakers) thought of when it came to Sharman were: "Great shooter."

Sharman hit 88.9 percent of his free throws as a rookie with Washington, but he never stopped practicing. Sharman is credited with the invention of the game-day shootaround that every college and professional team now uses. Halfway through his ten-year NBA career, Sharman said he simply grew weary of killing time on the road in uninspiring hotel rooms. You could say that boredom contributed to Sharman's accuracy.

"Game days seemed two or three times longer," Sharman said.

Sharman challenged himself to find a better way to use the time he felt was being wasted. He went for a walk and came across a high school with an empty gym, picked up a ball, and began shooting. He had a good game that night and decided that the extra shooting made him feel crisper. So it became a habit. Wherever the team was, Sharman sought out a private practice place. At first the shooting was casual. Then he developed a routine. His jump shots were followed by free-throw shooting.

"I decided, 'I'm not gonna go back home till I hit ten in a row,'" Sharman said. "Then it was fifteen in a row. Each time I missed I had to start over. I made it so there was some kind of pressure on me. I shot 86 percent for my first five years and I shot 91 percent for my last five. I knew it helped me."

Indeed, in the last five years of Sharman's NBA career he had individual season foul-shooting marks that included 90.5 percent, 93.2 percent, and 92.1 percent. When Sharman later coached Cal State-Los Angeles, Cleveland in the ABL, San Francisco in the NBA, Los Angeles and Utah in the ABA, and the Lakers in the NBA, his teams followed the procedure. But it wasn't until Sharman coached the Lakers to the NBA title in the 1971–72 season, and his team won a record 33 games in a row, that other teams emulated him.

"And then everyone used it," Sharman said.

Sharman said he wonders how well he would shoot today with less to overcome compared to the inconsistent arena conditions of the 1950s.

"Today they have breakaway rims," he said. "When we played in the fifties, the rims were rigid. We played where the lighting was bad. In some places the rims were a little bit tilted down on one side. It makes a big difference. In Syracuse, one day the roof was leaky. In the hockey arenas, sometimes the floor would be slippery. The conditions in the 1950s were not the same."

The one key roster addition for the 1957–58 season was Sam Jones. This was one instance when Red Auerbach really did outsmart the known world. Jones, a solid 6-foot-4 and 205 pounds, was born in Wilmington, North Carolina, played high school ball at the Laurinburg Institute and college ball at underpublicized North Carolina Central. Not even Auerbach would have known about Jones without the telephone assistance of his old buddy Bones McKinney, who was then coaching at Wake Forest. McKinney knew what kind of players Auerbach sought and he assured him Jones was his type. Good matchmaking.

Sam Jones came close to accepting a different job offer, however. When he finished college, he planned to stay in North Carolina and become a teacher. He was offered a teaching position that paid $5,500 a year. When he asked for $6,000 and school officials said no, Jones signed with the Celtics. It was one of those fork-in-the-road decisions that alter the rest of a person's life.

The designated successor to Sharman, Jones was a terrific shooter. No one in NBA history shot more accurately, banking his jumpers into the hoop off the glass. Not only was Jones unheralded because he was from a tiny college, but after his first three seasons he left school to enter the Army for two years. Then he returned and played his senior year. Jones, who ultimately would be named among the NBA's 50 greatest players of all-time in 1996, was probably not on any other team's draft list. Yet Auerbach drafted Jones No. 1, his fourth future Hall of Fame draft pick in two years.

Jones was so serious on the court that his perpetual frown seemed to give him major forehead lines even as a young man. The new man only appeared in 56 games his rookie season, with limited playing time, and he averaged just 4.6 points a game. But Jones never averaged less than double figures again and his lifetime scoring average was about 18 points a game.

"I was totally amazed with his ability to shoot balls," said K. C. Jones, who in their early backcourt partnership was often mistaken for Sam's brother by virtue of both being black and having the same last name, although they looked nothing alike. "I recall one time he was about 6 feet from the basket and he's saying to the guy going up to block his shot, 'Oh, baby, you can't get this.' He was talking at the same time he was dribbling with one hand and going in the other direction. He had a way of coming down the sideline with the ball when he was running, but it looked like he was just taking his time. Then he'd fly by you at 80 miles per hour."

What initially surprised—and pleased—Auerbach about Sam Jones was his ability to defend. Jones was no garden-variety shooter, but it was easier to find a scorer than a top-level player who could guard. Early in the season Auerbach said that Jones was the Celtics' quickest defender and "he can guard just about anyone except the other team's center."

Jones got off to a slow shooting start, however, and became hesitant to take shots when he was open.

"I'm way off the mark, and I'm killing the team," Jones said at one point.

Russell confronted Jones and comforted him. He told him to take the shots that were in his range and whether he missed or not to keep on shooting. The encouragement helped Jones's confidence and he got past the bad patch.

Jones was soft-spoken, but he didn't lack confidence in many areas. He was multitalented, able to outrun teammates in sprints, and outplay them in cards, pool, and dominoes. And yes, he was able to outshoot them when his slump was over and his stroke was on. Announcer Johnny Most nicknamed Jones "Slippery Sam" for his ability to elude defenders.

The 1957–58 opening-day attendance was not always matched at the Garden. Owner Walter Brown worried, and at a late January sports luncheon he said, "I can't believe that Boston won't support a winner. I hope we don't go broke winning a world championship."

A couple of days later the Celtics drew 8,093 fans to a game when Bob Cousy pumped in 39 points in a win over the rival St. Louis Hawks, a marquee visiting attraction. Cousy received a standing ovation, but there were nearly 6,000 empty seats.

The Celtics clinched the Eastern Division title on February 25 by beating the Pistons, who had moved to Detroit. Auerbach grinned as he said to reporters about his players, "I asked them not to throw me in the showers. I don't have fresh clothes. We'll save that for when we win the playoffs."

When? Oh yes, that was the cocky Auerbach. His self-assuredness was ahead of the curve of team achievements. The Celtics were defending champions, but they had not yet established in the minds of their fans that winning the NBA title was their birthright and opposing teams had not yet become fatalistic. Although the team was more confident than ever. The Celtics won eight more regular-season games than any other club in either division. The veterans were a year better. And they still had Russell, the dominant player in the league. Put the foot on the gas pedal, rev it up to 60, and put it on cruise control, baby. What could go wrong?

The Celtics marched through the eastern playoffs while the Hawks battled through the Western Division. The previous year's championship series couldn't have been tighter, so the Hawks merely felt this was their turn.

The Hawks, who returned all of their major weapons (typical of the general league roster stability of the time), won the opening game by 2 points in Boston. The Celtics won the second game and that moved the series to St. Louis. The Hawks won the fateful third game, 111–107, not alone a shocking result. But there was a stunning byproduct. Russell had collapsed to the Kiel Auditorium floor writhing in pain with a sprained left ankle. He could barely walk, never mind run and jump. The Celtics were shaken. Russell did not play another minute in the series and St. Louis won the championship in six games.

Cliff Hagan, at 6-foot-4 undersized for a forward, averaged more than 27 points per game in the series. Bob Petit scored 50 points in the deciding game. The Hawks had their title. The Celtics and Hawks met twice more in the finals in the next three years, but with a healthy Russell each time Boston was victorious. The Hawks cobbled together a nice little mini-run, but it was an also-ran run.

"That was our championship," Petit said of the 1957–58 season. "We could never do it again. There is no question in my mind the Celtics were the greatest dynasty assembled in any sport."

Frank Ramsey, whose Kentucky team was in the same Southeastern Conference as Petit's LSU team, said Petit improved incredibly in a five-year period.

"He's killing the league with [his jump shot]," Ramsey said. "But I still believe it is something he added when he came into pro ball. I have no recollection of him using a jump shot [in college]."

For the Celtics, it was Dynasty interruptus. The wounds suffered by losing healed at approximately the same pace as Russell's ankle. Maybe there was a worthy lesson in losing. Maybe that blotch on the record kept the Celtics a bit more humble, a bit more focused and hungry to win again. Though Frank Ramsey later said one reason the team succeeded for so long was collective amnesia. "Each year we set out to win and you really didn't think about what you did the year before," he said. "That group was together year after year, and we set out to win and we did."

Auerbach chose his men wisely. And besides, one thing he would not accept was complacency.

10

NEW FACES ADOPT THE CELTICS WAY

After two years in dry dock, marching with a rifle on his shoulder, and serving his country in a way quite different than he had during the 1956 Olympics, K. C. Jones officially became a Celtic.

Jones played in the shadow of Bill Russell in the Olympics and at the University of San Francisco, but if you were going to hitch your wagon to a star you could do worse. Just like Russell, wherever Jones traveled, championships followed.

And the Celtics were very much in pursuit of a championship during the 1958–59 season. They didn't doubt for a moment they would have been champions the previous year but for Russell's bum ankle. So they had to prove all over again that they were the best team in pro basketball.

If Auerbach and others thought Sam Jones was a clever defender, they were about to meet a guard who at 6-feet-1 was shorter, but more tenacious, someone who had the body strength and quickness to cover any other guard in the world. It just may be that K. C. Jones is the greatest defensive guard ever.

One of the things that gave K. C. an advantage when he matched up against NBA guards was his football background. Jones, who weighed 205 pounds, tried out for the Los Angeles Rams of the National Football League as a defensive back. The same type of coverage skills, tackling aside, were applicable as an NBA defender.

When he was in the Army, Jones was stationed at Fort Leonard Wood in Missouri. For amusement, he played wide receiver on a football team where a teammate was John Morrow, a center for the Rams. Morrow was impressed by Jones's skills and told him he should try the NFL upon discharge. Morrow telephoned the Rams' then-general manager Pete Rozelle, the future NFL commissioner, and put in a good word.

The Rams gave Jones a tryout as a pass catcher. He played poorly at first, and coach Sid Gilman moved Jones to the defensive backfield. Three exhibitions into the preseason, he was very comfortable in that role, and he enjoyed himself until he injured a thigh muscle. The trainers told him to sit out, but when Jones went to practice without pads and had his desire questioned by some assistant coaches, it offended him. He spent the night weighing the pros and cons of football versus basketball, and the next day telephoned Red Auerbach and asked if the Celtics still wanted him. They did. Jones packed and walked out of Rams camp without telling anyone, never again flirting with football except on television.

"Had the injury not occurred, I'd have been there [with the Rams]," Jones said years later.

Jones has always said that going into the Army toughened him up for pro sports, and that coming to the Celtics a couple of years after being drafted benefited him. It also didn't hurt that he was friends with Russell. In college they were a veritable Mutt and Jeff of the hardwood, 6-1 and 6-9. Russell had good things to say about Jones. K. C. made the team, but he knew he was not going to start over Bob Cousy, Bill Sharman, or Sam Jones.

K. C. Jones was never a big-time scorer. If Sharman's jump shot was smooth as silk, Jones's was as rough as wool. He never averaged in double figures, but his defense hounded foes to distraction and he passed like a quarterback. Even as a rookie, when Jones was feeling his way, Auerbach trusted him in important situations. When Jones played, good things happened. The other team was disrupted. The Celtics scored.

Another addition to the Celtics that season was Gene Conley. It seemed Auerbach was stocking his bench with everyone who had ties to the club. Conley hadn't played for the Celtics in six years, busying himself as a pitcher for the Milwaukee Braves in-between basketball stints. As a member of the starting rotation for the World Series champions, Conley's idea of resuming his basketball career did not play well with Braves team officials.

"These sports don't mix," Braves general manager John Quinn said.

Contrary Conley signed with the Celts anyway. He thought the two jobs mixed just fine. Other Braves may have sold cars or insurance in the off-season. Conley played hoops.

"I feel very positive about this," Conley said, adding he thought his legs would be strengthened by basketball for baseball. Quinn steamed. And he became grumpier still when spring training opened and Conley opted to stay in Boston to complete the basketball season.

"I feel I have an obligation to owner Walter Brown to stick with the Celtics, and help if I can, until the playoffs are over," Conley said.

Conley was 9-9 in the Braves' starting rotation during the 1957 regular season when they also bested the New York Yankees in the Series, but 0-6 in 1958. Not good ammunition to plead his case before a jury. His insubordination, coupled with his bad year, prompted the Braves to trade Conley to the Philadelphia Phillies for the 1959 season. In between, Conley averaged 4.2 points per game for the Celtics. The trade worked out well for Conley, who rebounded (in a different way) to go 12-7 and make the National League All-Star team for the Phils.

Around the time Conley was blowing off spring training for the Braves, the Celtics engaged in one of the most noteworthy regular-season games in NBA history. On February 27, 1959, the Celtics defeated the Lakers, 173–139, in the highest scoring game in league history. It would take ingestion of mass quantities of LSD to imagine a game like that being played in the pre-24-second-clock era. The game at the Boston Garden broke or tied 21 records. And an injured Bill Russell didn't even play that day.

One of the records was set by Bob Cousy, whose wizardry reached its apex with 28 assists. The mark lasted until 1990 when then–Orlando

Magic guard and future Chicago Bulls coach Scott Skiles passed off for 30 assists. Tommy Heinsohn led the Boston scoring with 43 points and Cousy sank 31.

"He is the greatest man ever," said Laker guard "Hot" Rod Hundley of Cousy. "He's just too much, that man. Fantastic."

Around that time, Conley's Braves manager, Fred Haney, exhibited irritation with his favorite dual-sport athlete. "What is he, a baseball pitcher or a basketball player?" Haney asked. Both. But a lot of people had difficulty getting used to the idea.

About ten days after the 173-point game, Walter Brown tried something new to boost the box office. To attend what became a 141–131 win over Cincinnati, the Celtics offered discount tickets to kids under sixteen. The demand was so high that more than 3,000 fans were turned away from the Boston Garden. That season the Celtics won a league-record 52 games and Cousy led the league in assists for the eighth year in a row.

A month after the children's charge on the Garden, April 9, on the same day famed architect Frank Lloyd Wright died, the Celtics were crowned champions for the second time. In an NBA first, they swept the Minneapolis Lakers four straight games in the finals, making it twenty-two consecutive wins over a team that was soon to become their biggest rival, replacing the Hawks. The series scores were 118–115, 128–108, 123–120 and 118–113. Russell totaled 30 rebounds in the finale.

"What a bunch!" said a gleeful Auerbach, who had been carried off the floor at the Minneapolis Armory by his players. Cigars were lit.

Minneapolis featured the new big star in the league that year. Elgin Baylor, a 6-foot-5 forward who rebounded way beyond his size, and who glided untouchable through traffic, came out of Seattle University to average 24.9 points per game as a rookie. He was the prototype of the future (though players of his talent remain exceptionally rare), the NBA athlete who moved the game above the rim. Baylor got his 25 points per game in the finals, but it only helped keep the games close.

"We tried everything we could think of," Baylor told Johnny Most in a postgame interview. "We had no one to match up with Russell and no one to stop Cousy on the break."

Who did?

With two NBA titles and three finals appearances in a row, people were beginning to probe what made Boston so good. A half-century later the questions are still valid. One of the most difficult things in professional sports is to repeat as a champion. Players age and retire. Players get injured at inopportune moments. Players grow envious of one another. Players want their own turn in the spotlight and seek trades. Coaches leave.

Yet the Celtics maintained continuity. They retained the core of the squad without letting the petty distractions that afflicted other teams affect their drive and cohesiveness. Auerbach was a puzzle master, piecing together selected parts to make a beautiful whole. Auerbach drafted white and black players from the South. He fitted in New Yorkers like himself. He found players on the West Coast and in the heartland. As Brown famously said when selecting Chuck Cooper in the draft, he didn't care what color your skin was, he cared only that you could play basketball.

The Celtics could play basketball. That was the simple truth. They were men from different backgrounds with a common goal, smart enough to know that they needed one another to achieve that goal. Auerbach set a special tone, letting each individual player know that he brought a uniqueness to the team.

Ramsey knew he was never going to beat out either Bob Cousy or Bill Sharman for a starting guard spot. Nor was he going to be the No. 1 scoring option ahead of Tommy Heinsohn in the frontcourt. But he knew his time would come. He knew his job as relief man gave him an advantage over tiring opponents and he would get his chances. For years—several years—K. C. and Sam Jones were backup guards and then they were stars. Tom Sanders, drafted out of New York University in 1960 where he was a high scorer, had to sublimate his offense in the Celtics' scheme. His value came from being the NBA's most stifling defensive forward.

These were all men with egos, who had been leaders in high school and college. Auerbach asked them to be backups, or to specialize in different things. To his credit, Auerbach told them they didn't have to be among the league's top point-getters in order to stick with the team and to be well paid. To their credit, they listened and believed. During the Dynasty years, you didn't hear a Celtics player clamoring to be traded so he could take a star turn on another team. What would that say about a player's selfishness? If professional athletes can be believed, winning is the paramount thing. With the Celtics, when the season tipped off between 1957 and 1969, you knew you had the best chance of any team to win the NBA title.

"We had a unique group of people," Frank Ramsey said, "and Red drafted almost all of them. He picked people that he knew would fit in. There was no jealousy on the team. If something went wrong, Red would say, 'You'd look good in Minneapolis.' But I don't think he ever traded anyone but Ed Macauley, and he wanted to be traded to St. Louis. There was no jealousy."

It is a constant refrain from the Celtics of that era. No jealousy. One of the seven deadly sins, a sin that could bring a team down, was avoided. Everyone will also say without Russell there would have been no Dynasty, the literal proof of which being the length of Russell's career matching the Dynasty years. The sidebar to that story is that Wilt Chamberlain, as great as he was, as dominant as he was, could almost never beat the Celtics out of championships with his supporting cast. So the other Celtics men were something special too. They couldn't have done it without Russell and he couldn't have done it without them. And none of them could have done it if they hadn't liked and respected one another.

"There was harmony," K. C. Jones said. "There was never a negative word on or off the court about a teammate."

11

THE BEST SIXTH MAN
IN BASKETBALL

The Kentucky that Frank Ramsey knew as a youth in the 1930s and early 1940s was farm country and coal country. Unless you owned a Thoroughbred horse-racing operation, it seemed that farming and mining was how you made a living.

He was like so many of the Celtics of the Dynasty years. Ramsey did not come from comfort or wealth. Like Red Auerbach, Bob Cousy, Bill Russell, K. C. Jones, and others, whether city kids or country kids, one of the hallmarks of the Celtics' roster in the championship years, one of the areas of common ground, was certainly a shortage of silver spoons. They were men who from childhood on had to earn what they got and work for what they earned. It was true in real life as well as basketball life.

They were tall and taller. They were black and white. They were from cities and farms. But always their similarities rose to the surface and their differences were forgotten or repressed. To Auerbach, it did not matter where you came from, what type of background you came from, or if you were black or white. You had to play his way and follow his rules and want to win so much that you were willing to sublimate your ego and maybe some of your skills to the team. He wanted his players to be hungry to win whether or not they had once been hungry otherwise.

"I give Arnold the credit," Cousy said of Auerbach. "Because he treated everybody the same—badly. I think if you were a minority, and working within a group or organization, what you would want—and I'm anticipating this since I obviously don't say it from someone with a black skin—but my thought would be if I was in this situation, I would want to be treated like everyone else. I wouldn't want my hand to be held. And hey, if you're going to treat everyone badly, fine with me."

When Cousy says badly, he means being the object of sarcasm for making a mistake. Auerbach was an equal-opportunity yeller at heart, though he made modifications occasionally based on his belief that yelling at the wrong guy could hurt the team. He didn't pal around with his players. He had his quirks, like banning the consumption of pancakes, a rule that applied to everyone.

Ramsey was born—and still lives—in Madisonville, a town one hundred miles north of Nashville in western Kentucky. The current population of the community is listed at about 19,000, though Ramsey remembers it being much smaller when he was a kid. Madisonville celebrated its Bicentennial in 2007 with the theme "the Best Town on Earth."

Ramsey said the seat of Hopkins County had two high schools when he was younger and has fourteen now. The country kid felt a bit overwhelmed when he moved to Boston. Driving a car in Boston has always been a serious adventure. The streets are not laid out in a grid and motorists seem to drive with one foot on the gas pedal, one hand on the horn, and like many of those Thoroughbreds, with blinders on. Ramsey and Jeanne, his first-year wife, seemed most perplexed by nearby Harvard Square, near the famed university.

"Harvard Square is a circle!" Ramsey said. "You certainly can get lost because everything they say is a square is like a traffic circle."

There were no such complications in small-town Madisonville.

Ramsey's family owned a dry-goods store in town and a farm on the outskirts. Instead of attending basketball camp or competing on summer AAU teams as so many basketball hopefuls do these days, Frank held a summer job. When he was ten, eleven or so years old, he did farm chores. He plowed and planted corn and put up hay. Ramsey drove a team of mules.

"Everybody had their own team and you worked from six in the morning till six at night," he said.

Churning butter was another assigned task. The butter was churned, and because there was no refrigeration on the farm, it was placed in a butter mold and dropped in a well "to cool it off," Ramsey said.

Ramsey was born in 1931 and grew up during the Depression and spent his early teens hanging on information reported from the European and Pacific fronts during World War II. The Ramseys were not rich, and no one really mentioned the words middle class around them either.

"The farm didn't even have electricity and it had no refrigerator," Ramsey recalled. "They probably didn't get electricity down on the farm until about 1949. At the farm we didn't have indoor toilets. We had what they called two-holers, one for adults, one for children. It was a pretty rural place at that time."

There was some irony that the nickname ascribed to Ramsey in the pros was "The Kentucky Colonel." Even though living circumstances were a bit fancier in the Madisonville home, with indoor plumbing and lights, Ramsey didn't have the type of patrician background that awarded real or mythical officer's rank. Primarily, he brought his southern accent with him to big-city Boston.

Auerbach's father ran a dry-cleaning establishment, and Auerbach worked hard for every dollar he earned. Cousy came from modest circumstances and he too rustled up odd jobs on the streets of New York. Ramsey never uses the word poverty to describe his family's station in life, but he doesn't pretend he hung out at mansions sipping mint juleps on the porch either.

It was a novel idea when Auerbach employed Ramsey as a sixth man coming into games late in the first quarter to shake things up. He had a look of a choirboy about him that belied fierceness, and longtime opponent Jack Twyman of the Cincinnati Royals said it worked to Ramsey's advantage.

"Ramsey comes off the bench and turns it on," Twyman said. "He looks like an angel with that sweet face, but he's knocking people around and throws them off their game. And the officials think he's so innocent."

It was years after the Celtics Dynasty was assembled that little boys grew up dreaming of becoming professional basketball players. "NBA star" was not on the list of career options discussed in the 1950s and 1960s. Oh, college stars knew it was possible to make a living from playing professional sports, but the attitude was more of "If I get drafted, I'll give it a try" than of training, working out, practicing with single-minded devotion to the game for years to the exclusion of many other of life's pleasures.

K. C. Jones could as easily have become a football player for the Rams as a guard for the Celtics. And he just as easily could have missed out on professional sports altogether. Jones spent two years in the Army, and if he hadn't starred with the San Francisco Dons alongside Russell he might not have been noticed.

"I was lucky to get into college," Jones said. "I had no intention of going to college. What did I know with the neighborhood I grew up in? My history teacher, and I didn't know this until later, she made contact with the coach. Had that not happened, I'd have been working in the post office in San Francisco."

Jones was born in 1932 and said his family of seven, led by dad K. C. and mom Eula, spent much of the Depression seeking odd jobs and opportunities in Texas. He says in a 1986 autobiography, "I grew up in the Jim Crow South." With vague knowledge of his family heritage, Jones said he had grandparents and great-grandparents who were Cherokee and Cheyenne Indians and even German-Jewish. Yet his skin was black, and he said it was a hard world for African-Americans trying to make ends meet.

The man who grew up to not only play on many world championship basketball teams, but also coach a later generation of Celtics to world titles, said he saw discrimination everywhere as a youngster. He said he'd hated the white world that contrived to deprive blacks of basic rights, set up colored and white water fountains, and treat blacks as second-class citizens.

The K. C. Jones that the sports world got to know was somewhat shy but friendly and became a leader on the court as a player and off of it as a coach. Yet there is some bitterness in his memories. He recalls in sixth grade being accused of cheating by a teacher because he figured out the right answer in front of the class on a long division problem. And he will never forget his parents separating between his ninth and tenth grade years, with his mother taking him and his four younger siblings to San Francisco.

San Francisco, however, was a more liberal city. People of color—many colors, from Asian and Indian to black and white—shared buses and classrooms. Jones found out that not everyone who was white was mean and thought ill of black people. He developed an interest in sports, and heavyweight champion Joe Louis, sprinter Jesse Owens, and baseball player Jackie Robinson became his idols.

It was a white woman, incredibly enough to Jones, who jump-started his future. His history teacher Mildred Smith cold-called San Francisco basketball coach Phil Woolpert and convinced him that not only was Jones a worthy high school player, but he also deserved a scholarship. The Jones family, with his mother working as a part-time maid, had no money to send K. C. to college. But a teacher who saw beyond Jones' mediocre grades to his potential, won him the college opportunity.

She didn't do it all by herself. Jones had basketball credentials as a local all-star, but was being recruited by absolutely no one. As luck would have it, a sportswriter wrote fictionally that Jones was being sought by many other California schools. This cajoled Woolpert into closing the deal. Jones has no doubt that without the intervention of those allies he would have become a mailman because that career also interested him and the post office offered long-term job security. Jones considers it fortunate that he ended up on the right professional basketball team too. The Celtics were a team of no prejudices or jealousies. They lived the motto of The Three Musketeers: one for all and all for one.

"On the court there was no, 'He's getting more shots than me,'" Jones said of the Dynasty Celtics. "There was none of that. It was total togetherness. Russell was a leader in that department, along with Cousy. You got that right down the whole team."

The hardscrabble backgrounds of many contributed to the tenacity that made the Celtics winners, Jones said. Those who lifted themselves from difficult backgrounds were not about to squander an opportunity.

"Some of us came from poor sections," Jones said. "Football players playing tackle football without pads at the public playground and getting hurt and all that stuff, but not going to the hospital. You might walk up a hill, a mountain, about two or three miles, to play three-on-three basketball and you had to walk all the way back home. In school being in sports was bigger than other things."

Celtics players knew they had something special going when they kept winning and winning, but they also recognized they had a special bond that aided them. Yes, it was the talent. They had Russell, but they had the complementary parts. They didn't all worry about making contributions in high-profile ways. Auerbach was always up front. He told the players what their roles would be and they accepted them. He didn't sugarcoat the facts, or lie to them. And he rewarded them appropriately. You could be a defensive specialist on the Celtics, or a sixth man, and earn as much as other teams' higher-scoring starters did. And you got that bonus playoff money, the chance to play for a championship every year and to play on a team where the players got along well.

"It was the togetherness on and off the court," Jones said of one thing that set the Celtics apart. "We'd go out with different guys."

There were no Celtics cliques. There was no division on the team by race. Both Jones and Ramsey owned homes in Framingham, about 25 miles west of the Boston Garden. They lived about fifteen minutes apart, so when the team was going on a road trip, they rode to the airport together.

"And we would come back together," Jones said.

If someone decided to throw a party, everyone was invited, not just black guys going to black guys' parties, or white guys going to white guys' parties. The more normal schisms of other teams didn't apply to the Celtics.

"We'd all show up," Jones said. "It was really such a positive atmosphere. We didn't take jealousies onto the court. We had none of that. That was really fantastic."

Just as Jones and Ramsey lived near one another, Cousy and Tommy Heinsohn, who both attended Holy Cross, made their homes in Worcester, the home of the college. They commuted to the Garden and airport together for years. For all the talking they did over thousands of miles of driving, basketball was a small fraction of the subject matter. They took their minds off the games during the trips.

"We talked about everything in the world," Heinsohn said. "We talked basketball, but to borrow the expression, we left the basketball on the court and immediately afterwards in the locker room, or sometimes at breakfast when you were on the road. Other than that, you went and lived your life. So we talked about life."

John Havlicek, a late addition to the Dynasty roster who enjoyed a career that long outlasted his championship teammates, could probably do a stand-up comedy routine just on Celtics' driving habits. When you spend so much time with a group of guys you can't help but learn things.

During Havlicek's rookie year and his earliest seasons on the club, the Celtics played preseason exhibitions all over New England. These were in medium-size towns and it was easier for the Celtics to drive their own cars in small groups than to fly in. Havlicek quickly learned what being low man on the rookie totem pole meant—he had to ride with Tom Sanders.

Sanders grew up in New York City, and unlike the typical suburban kid who covets a license at the first possible moment coming of age, he never bothered to get one. He went to college, at NYU in Manhattan, one of the most unnecessary places in the universe to possess a license. But when he moved to Boston, Sanders did need a driver's license. The story went that he sideswiped more than one car immediately after he obtained the license and that he ran into a policeman in slow motion, tipping the officer over onto the hood of his car. Nobody wanted to ride with Sanders. But nobody wanted to ride with Russell either, because he drove so fast, so the center usually drove to the New England games alone. And nobody wanted to ride with Auerbach, Havlicek said, because he sometimes fell asleep at the wheel. There was a lot of jockeying to get into cars piloted by Heinsohn and Ramsey, as they were supposedly the best drivers. For all this worry, there was never a major accident.

Auerbach was a somewhat imperial leader. He was always conscious of his role and job as the boss, the coach who was on a different level than the players. He was responsible for their playing time, negotiating their contracts, and setting their pay scale. He knew he couldn't be too buddy-buddy, be one of the boys. For the most part that made for a lonely existence for the team leader. He roomed alone in the hotels, lived alone in Boston, and kept his fraternization to a minimum. Players went out to restaurants and bars together. Auerbach hung out alone, except in later years when trainer Buddy LeRoux traveled with the team.

The players followed the rules, but sometimes they reached out and risked playing practical jokes on Auerbach. It was a gesture of affection, of inclusion, but at the same time was meant to bring him down to size a little bit in the only safe way the players knew how.

At the end of his last season as a player, Cousy revealed some tales of team-and-Auerbach interaction where the coach was on the fuming side of the punch line. During a preseason trip to Maine, Auerbach bought a red fedora and was gaga over the purchase. He even warned the players not to touch the hat. Ed Macauley sneaked over to the same store, bought a duplicate, and stashed it.

After the game, as Auerbach strode into the locker room, he saw a player toss "his" red hat to Cousy standing in the shower. Cousy put it on and let the water pour down. Auerbach's reaction abruptly shifted from disbelief to fury. He erupted in a full-fledged tirade, and then Macauley walked into the shower, plucked the hat from Cousy's hat, and sliced it into pieces, almost as if he was making cardboard cutouts for a nursery-school class. When Auerbach walked out in a rage and reached his car, he saw the other red fedora on the seat—intact—and realized he'd been had.

Every team must have locker room leaders besides the coach, and Bill Russell and Bob Cousy assumed that function. They were the leaders on the court, perennial All-Stars, so that gave them credibility. But they were forceful personalities as well, and their teammates knew how much they burned to win. They were agog that Russell threw up in the locker room before every game. And they were intimidated that Cousy not only was not ripe for a joke after a loss, but was so bothered by defeat he didn't always seem capable of rational conversation.

Heinsohn said all of the players growing up in the Depression era, or during World War II, shared a commonality of personal and American hard times that may have shaped them as dedicated individuals. But more occurred behind the scenes that revealed the soul of the Celtics.

"There were two guys on that team, Russell and Cousy, their whole reason for existence was basketball," Heinsohn said. "Psychologically, they had to win—the other guys just rolled along—and they [the center-playmaker duo] were responsible for making it a team. They did the things that made the team. One was Mister Defense, blocking shots, rebounding the ball, playing defense. One was Mister Offense, getting the ball to players in the right spot. When things weren't going well and we had a little slump going on, one of those guys would stand up in a little private team meeting and say, 'What do you think I can do to turn this around?' They opened themselves to criticism. I think that was the secret of the camaraderie on the team. If the top guys were inviting criticism, certainly you could listen too."

When the Celtics of the 1950s and 1960s traveled, they did not receive the special treatment of the clubs of today, with charter flights winging them between cities as soon as a game ended. The old Celtics spent extra nights at hotels, and just like regular passengers they spent time waiting around airports. They killed that time playing cards together and talking, learning about each other's spouses and children.

"I guess that's why we were close and we still are," Ramsey said. "Red drafted by personalities. They had to have basketball talent, but he wanted you to be a winner, to come from a winning program. And he always said, 'You're not paid on the points you score. You're paid on whether we win or lose and your contribution to the team.'"

Ramsey did not grow up in a wealthy family and basketball didn't make him rich in the bank account sense the way things are measured today, either. But that's not why he played.

"The most I ever made was $20,000 in a year," Ramsey said. "And I felt like I was overpaid because I was doing something I loved."

12

NO BLACK OR WHITE ON CELTICS

The greatest shame of America is slavery. The great sorrow of American history is that a hundred years after the Civil War ended, cities of the South were still fighting it and discriminating against the blacks who lived in their midst and the black people who visited their towns.

The Boston Celtics organization may have acted colorblind, but the places the team traveled were not. In November 1958, the Celtics went to Charlotte, North Carolina, for a neutral-site game. When they reached their accommodations, black players Bill Russell, K. C. Jones, and No. 1 draft pick Ben Swain, who spent just one year with the team, were told they must stay at a "Negro hotel." Sam Jones, who was from the area, boarded with a family he knew. Celtics owner Walter Brown was furious.

"I don't care if we ever go back there," Brown said. "I know one thing. I'll never do anything to embarrass my players."

Russell was quoted in the *Charlotte News* as saying he did not believe in segregation. "It's against my principles," Russell said. "I came down here with my team and had to eat and sleep apart from them."

The Minneapolis Lakers' Elgin Baylor stayed in a black-only hotel and said he would never play basketball in Charlotte again.

In January 1959, a couple of months later, Baylor and two black Lakers teammates were shuttled to an all-black hotel in Charlestown, West Virginia when there for a game. When the situation was reported to Mayor John Coppenhaver, he refused to apologize.

"The incident was something over which our city has no control," Coppenhaver said, citing local laws.

A questionable response, and symbolic of race relations in the South at the time. Nearly two years later, the Celtics once again encountered unexpected discrimination while on tour for a game. In October 1961, as a thank you for the years of their dedicated play (and no doubt considered a good business move), the Celtics and Hawks hatched a plan to honor Frank Ramsey and Cliff Hagan at their old arena, Memorial Coliseum in Lexington, Kentucky. It was a homecoming exhibition for University of Kentucky basketball players made good.

Only somebody forgot to tell The Phoenix Hotel. Celtics black players Russell, Sam and K. C. Jones, Tom Sanders, and Al Butler, as well as black Hawks players Woody Sauldsberry and Cleo Hill, were refused service in the hotel coffee shop. Shocked for the second time, and once again enraged, Walter Brown said, "I will never be embarrassed into a situation such as this again."

Instead of playing in the game to honor their teammate, the frustrated players left town with Ramsey's blessing. Ramsey, the honoree, said he was "100 percent behind Bill Russell and the other boys. No thinking person in Kentucky is a segregationist. I can't tell you how sorry I am as a human being, a friend of the players involved, and as a resident of Kentucky for the embarrassment of the incident."

Cousy said he thought the black members of the team made the right choice and he bristled when he heard an NBA referee in town to work the game say he thought those players who left were selfish and had not taken into consideration the league. "It's so easy to sit back and take that reasoned, objective view when it's somebody else's dignity being affronted," Cousy said.

Not that Boston was so innocent of racial guilt. Boston calls itself "the hub of the universe." In many ways it could fairly be described as one of the most liberal cities in the United States. But unbeknownst even to many of the solid citizens of the time was an undercurrent of bigotry that manifested itself more openly in several ways over the ensuing years. Brown sometimes wondered if fans failed to support his winning clubs in the numbers they might have if the Celtics hadn't featured as many black players. At the same time the Celtics were winning world championships, the all-white Boston Bruins of the National Hockey League were finishing in last place, but outdrawing the basketball team in the Boston Garden.

When the Celtics won the 1956–57 NBA championship, their first, Bill Russell was the only black man in the team picture. The Boston Red Sox, the heartthrobs of New England, were the last team to integrate in the Major Leagues in 1959. Russell was something new on the local sports scene, being a proud black man with strong opinions, a tremendous sense of self who was the driving force on the best team in town. He said what he thought and sometimes what he thought made white people—even those who rooted for him—cringe. Some felt he was aloof. Russell was determined to live life on his own terms, not spend effort coping with artificial barriers erected by a wrong-headed, insensitive society.

Hall of Fame football star Jim Brown, a man perceived by the public much as Russell was because he too refused to be bullied or slighted by white society, said, "Bill Russell is a person of great integrity. And if you can't stand the brutal truth, don't talk to Bill Russell."

Russell once bluntly told Boston sportswriter George Sullivan that Boston was the most racist city in the country. Sullivan asked if he really meant for him to print that and Russell retorted that he bet Sullivan's editors wouldn't let him put it in the paper. Russell was correct.

The harshness of the world—with black men being pulled over by police merely for being black and driving a nice car—taught Russell lessons that he reflected back at society at large. He wanted no special privileges accorded to him because he was a basketball star. He wanted to be welcomed places because he was a man.

"I'm acceptable most places as somebody's guest because I'm Bill Russell, pro basketball player," he said. "But in many of those same places I wouldn't be acceptable as Bill Russell, U.S. citizen, so why should I fool myself?"

Celtics fans were happy for the team's success and admired Russell's skills. Yet there were hecklers, nasty ones, who did attend games at the Boston Garden, sometimes yelling insults such as "Chocolate boy!" and "Nigger!" at Russell. He heard them because he later repeated the slurs to others, but he never acknowledged his antagonists while running up and down the parquet court. Such racist commentary was limited, and it was possible to sit in the stands and never be aware that Russell was being verbally assaulted. The bigots were a definite minority and unless a ticket buyer was unlucky enough to be seated nearby, an entire 48-minute contest could pass without overhearing.

When Russell joined the Celtics, he and his wife, Rose, who later went to work for the Boston chapter of the National Association for the Advancement of Colored People, had a son. They wanted to live in a suburban community where the school system was richer and the educational opportunities better than in Boston. Trouble followed the Russell's housing search: They were not welcome in all-white areas. Finally, Russell bought a house in the town of Reading, a dozen miles north of Boston. The Russells were the only black family in the neighborhood among mostly Irish-Catholic residents. Twice the home was broken into, and once an invader defecated in Russell's bed. It was a disgusting and distressing signal that the break-in wasn't all about theft.

For the longest time, Celtics fans who did not know of these incidents, or count them as racist, wondered why Russell was cool to Boston in his public pronouncements. Indeed, Russell almost never reacted to the wild cheers he received when he rebounded so expertly, blocked shots, or made key plays for the Celtics. He seemed to treat praise and insults with the same indifference. He was not playing for the fans, but for himself and his teammates, Russell said.

Even Cousy, who enjoyed playing golf with Russell elsewhere, said he never invited him to play at the Worcester country club where Cousy held membership because he was certain Russell would be turned away and all would be embarrassed. Decades after they were teammates, Cousy was being filmed for a Celtics documentary and when discussing the prejudice inflicted on Russell, he broke down and cried, saying he wished he could have done more to help the big man.

Cousy, who has participated in book projects and written articles that speak out against racism, said he admired the strength Russell exhibited. Russell, he said, never compromised his views, never went along for the sake of going along at an event or advertising promotion if he felt the circumstances were demeaning, whether financially or in content. Russell displayed respect for Cousy at all times. Onetime Celtic, Don Barksdale, who in 1953 became the first black player to compete in the NBA All-Star game, called Cousy "A real down-to-earth cat."

Cousy said he believes racism is rooted in insecurity, but that the racism the Celtics encountered and Russell faced came from outside the organization, not from within. In the locker room, the "great, bearded one," as teammates came to call Russell, was a different person, joking around, sharing stories, boosting the spirits of players in a slump and cackling loudly. Outside the locker room, Russell wore an impenetrable mask.

Bill Sharman, star guard of the 1950s, said Russell's public and private selves differed. Russell might have told newspaper reporters that he didn't like white people, a response to slights, but he seemed to like his white teammates just fine.

"I was at his house a few times," said Sharman, who is white. "I played golf with him. We were very good friends. I can't think of anybody who didn't like him who played with him. When you're winning, it's so much easier. Everyone has a smile."

During the late 1950s, the role of black players in the NBA was still scrutinized. Sportswriters speculated in print that owners had quietly established a quota system. Four blacks was probably the most any team would ever carry, writers said. Russell was angered by the reportage and he confronted Walter Brown. He demanded to know if this was true. Brown again uttered a variation of his draft-day speech when he chose Chuck Cooper, saying he didn't care about any player's skin color. Russell didn't know whether to believe him or not.

Following seasons proved Russell's suspicions unfounded. Boston was not only the first team to draft a black player, but the Celtics became the first NBA team to put five black starters on the floor. That was in 1965, when Red Auerbach began a game with Russell at center, Sam and K. C. Jones in the backcourt, and Tom Sanders and Willie Naulls as the forwards.

"Five black men," K. C. Jones said. "We are all proud of that."

In 1966, when Auerbach stepped down as coach to focus on front office duties, he named Russell as new coach of the Celtics, making him the first black head coach in any major professional sport in the United States. Baseball did not have its first black manager until Frank Robinson took over the Cleveland Indians nine years later.

The Celtics essentially formed a club, a group aligned against distractions of any kind, a brotherhood that shared feelings as well as the basketball and disdained any negative influences that might impinge on their lives and goals. White players and black players circled their wagons against attack. The Celtics were a haven for black players and the white players didn't care what other whites outside the family said.

"Jocks live in their own little, isolated world anyway, I think," Cousy said. "But in those days, current events were the furthest things from our minds. We were so honed in and so competitive. This was a credit to Arnold. We had complete dedication to the job at hand. Most of us came charging out of those ghettos and shared this animalistic, sustained, intense desire to accomplish the competitive goal. We came self-motivated for the most part. But to have him [Auerbach], who fought his way out of that Brooklyn ghetto in the same manner, we just blocked everything out. It is a testimony to his leadership."

Washington Post sports columnist Tony Kornheiser said Auerbach was considered the best basketball coach of all time, but his impact on sport and society transcended the court.

"He had a profound effect on the culture," Kornheiser wrote, comparing Auerbach to baseball's Branch Rickey, who signed Jackie Robinson. "Basketball was at the forefront of racial progress and Auerbach was at the forefront of that."

Players who lived in the Celtics locker room during the Dynasty were never known to say an unkind word about each other that touched on race, with the exception of Russell's generalizations about society.

One day on his way to a game, Ramsey stopped at the North Station newsstand beneath the Boston Garden and picked up a copy of *Sports Illustrated*. In the locker room his attention was arrested by an article headlined, I HATE ALL WHITE MEN. So said Bill Russell.

Russell came into the locker room and Ramsey said, "Russ, hell, I'm reading this. You hate all white men? Do you hate me?" Russell seemed taken aback and said, "Frank, I was misquoted."

Nobody made any more of an issue about the magazine and Ramsey knew at heart that Russell didn't hate him. "We all respected each other as an individual and there was not anything because of the color of skin," Ramsey said.

Clif Keane, the longtime Boston sportswriter said, Auerbach "was great with the black guys" because he never allowed cliques to form. Whenever Auerbach had the power to assign seats or to arrange gatherings, he made sure that black and white Celtics mingled. When it was pointed out to him, Auerbach denied any conscious effort to do so, but few believed him. He simply compared the team mix to when he was growing up and Jewish, Catholic, Irish, and Polish guys were all members of the same teams he played on.

Still, some took notice. The Boston chapter of the NAACP gave Auerbach a special recognition award. And at a Boston brotherhood luncheon, Dick O'Connell, the Red Sox general manager, somewhat ironically noted (speaking as a representative of a team that had not practiced what O'Connell was preaching) that the best living, breathing example of integration in the community "can be found right down the street. The best illustration of all is right in front of our eyes. Just look at the Celtics."

Perhaps the rest of the nation should have looked at the Celtics. The Celtics were a testimony to the fruits of integration at a time when the United States was being ripped asunder by racial conflict. The Dynasty run coincided with the most turbulent years of the Civil Rights movement, as blacks agitated to attain rights that had been abrogated. Outside the doors of the Boston Garden a revolution was going on.

On December 1, 1955, Rosa Parks, a Montgomery, Alabama, tailor's assistant at a local department store, was tired and not feeling well when she caught a bus to take her home. She took a seat, and as the bus filled, she refused to give her seat to a white man. Parks, forty-two, was arrested for violating Montgomery's bus segregation law.

Three-quarters of the Montgomery public-bus system riders were black and local activists had long searched for an appropriate test case to challenge a law that said Parks was wrong. Parks was a willing subject. A few days later, in a five-minute trial, Parks was found guilty and fined $10. But with the religious community backing her, and Ralph Abernathy and Dr. Martin Luther King Jr. organizing, protests had just begun. King was only twenty-six and the event catapulted him onto the national stage. The drawn-out boycott of local buses started, with residents carpooling and walking miles to work rather than submitting to the clearly racist rules any longer. It took 382 days to resolve the issue, allowing blacks the right to first-come, first-served service, decreed by the U.S. Supreme Court.

Religion and civil rights melded to form the foundation of the Southern Christian Leadership Conference. American blacks' war on the system that had repressed them, deprived them, lynched them, and haunted them had begun in earnest. And Martin Luther King Jr. became the most important African-American figure of the 20th century, a passionate, but pressured leader who espoused the nonviolent principles of India's Mohandas "Mahatma" Gandhi and who met with presidents in hopes of guiding them into the path of righteousness.

As early as 1957, a determined, but frequently depressed and exhausted King exposed his feelings about the risk his work brought upon himself and his family.

"My cause, my race, is worth dying for," he said.

His home in Montgomery was bombed when King was not present, but neither his wife, Coretta, nor his children, were harmed. The message was clear. The descendants of those who fought the Civil War were not surrendering without another round of battles. The presidents with whom King parlayed, Dwight Eisenhower, John F. Kennedy, and Lyndon Baines

Johnson, were held back by political expediency, willing to take only steps limited in scope to rectify woeful treatment of blacks.

More and more the fight for equal rights, to be able to register to vote in peace, to drink water from any fountain, to be served in any restaurant, to lay one's head on any pillow in any hotel, was taken to the streets, with marches, sit-ins, and speeches.

The dramatic sit-in at a Woolworth's lunch counter in Greensboro, North Carolina, begun by students from nearby North Carolina A&T, gained nationwide attention. The vicious response to marchers when Sheriff Eugene "Bull" Connor of Birmingham, Alabama, unleashed attack dogs and fire hoses on children gained worldwide condemnation. Worse, when racists bombed a church in Birmingham, killing four little girls attending Sunday school, anger inflamed the Civil Rights movement. Many thought King's nonviolent approach had overstayed its usefulness. Firebrands wanted to meet violence with violence. There were schisms where there needed to be unity. There was skepticism where there needed to be belief. Lobbying for honor in civil rights victories, King prayed for the guilt of good people in power to overwhelm the evil of bad people like a Ku Klux Klansman who performed dastardly deeds at night under the anonymity of white sheets.

Blacks were downtrodden, abused for centuries, second-class citizens in the land of opportunity. It was no wonder than anyone who preached patience was scoffed at, no wonder that rebellion seethed in souls. The song "We Shall Overcome" became an anthem widely sung. In Montgomery, where the bus boycott stretched beyond a year, an elderly woman so eloquently commented, "My feets is weary, but my soul is rested." My soul is rested. It was another battle cry for the movement.

At a time when the law was unjust and law-enforcement officers broke the law, it took federal troops on the doorstep of state capitols to help justice prevail. And it took the powerful words of courageous local newspaper editors and national media exposure, in words, pictures and film, to bring the plight of the discrimination against blacks to the forefront of a nation's conscience. Upon seeing photos of the attacks on demonstrators in Birmingham, President Kennedy remarked that they made him sick to his stomach.

The Civil Rights movement spread and continued. Violent, ugly, broad-based racism was confronted at Little Rock Central High School in Arkansas and at the doors to the University of Mississippi. Innocent school girls were taunted in Little Rock, James Meredith was challenged in Mississippi, all simply for seeking an education. Governors, from George Wallace in Alabama to Orval Faubus in Arkansas and Ross Barnett in Mississippi, shunned all opportunities to be statesmen and at every chance pandered to the lowest common denominator IQ of their people. Proof arose almost daily that the Confederacy was not dead in a South stuck in 1864. Rather, it was displayed in the form of flags tattooed in the windows of pickup trucks.

At various times, Martin Luther King Jr. nearly despaired over the apparent deafness of the white world. Where is the decency, he railed in private meetings with the men who formed the backbone of the Civil Rights movement. Always, he gathered himself, rejuvenated himself, and returned to the pulpit of the Baptist churches he led, in Montgomery, then Atlanta, and to the podiums at demonstrations, seeking to spread a message of hope to the masses who so desperately wanted to believe that the world was changing for the better.

Federal troops forced George Wallace to allow the registration of the first black students at the University of Alabama. In June 1963, John F. Kennedy delivered a nationally televised speech that touted freedom for all Americans and outlined a Civil Rights bill he intended to send to Congress within days. Just one day later, June 12, Medgar Evers, the head of the Mississippi NAACP, was murdered in front of his home. Events seemed to unfold at the sprint pace of a 100-yard dash.

The Boston Celtics were not immune to the mood of the land. Bill Russell saw Charles Evers not long after his younger brother Medgar Evers was killed and offered to help him in any way possible. So Charles asked Russell to come to Mississippi to give basketball clinics in Jackson. Russell said the state was pretty much on the verge of racial warfare at the time, and he fretted for his safety while second-guessing the rashness of his volunteerism. Teammates teased Russell mercilessly before he went, urging him to stay inconspicuous and try to travel incognito. One thing the 6-foot-9 Bill

Russell could never do was blend. In Mississippi, there were no major incidents. Nobody shot at him.

Wayne Embry, nicknamed The Wall by announcer Johnny Most because of the candy machine–like width of his 6-foot-8 frame, was a star with the Cincinnati Royals. But he also played on the Dynasty Celtics near the end of his career before becoming the first black general manager in the NBA with the Milwaukee Bucks in 1972.

Embry was the only black player in his high school in Springfield, Ohio, and survived that experience reasonably well. As a rookie with the Royals in 1958, however, segregation in Cincinnati meant he had to reside in a black-operated hotel before finding more permanent living quarters. His onetime hero, pitching star Don Newcombe, recently traded from the Dodgers to the Reds, lived downstairs in the same building. In the NBA he entered, Embry said there was usually only one black player per team, the exception being the Celtics.

When he joined the Celtics for the last two seasons of his playing career, Embry said Russell invited the black players to his Reading home for pregame meals. Steak, baked potato, greens, and dessert were usually part of the menu provided by Rose. Russell, who knew he was just going to throw up when he reached the locker room, didn't eat much.

In contrast to the Celtics, Embry said there was not so much harmony in the Royals locker room during the Civil Rights era. Embry said black players talked about what was going on in the streets of America constantly, but team officials cautioned them not to get involved. Owners didn't want to alienate white ticket buyers. Such a prohibition did not apply to spouses though, and Embry said his wife, Terri, and Oscar Robertson's wife, Yvonne, decided to march in Selma, Alabama, when protests were staged in 1965.

Concerned about her safety, Embry's first reaction to his wife was, "Are you crazy?"

Yvonne Robertson did not even plan to tell her husband she was going until she was on the ground in Alabama. As the Royals traveled to Boston for a game, their wives went to Alabama to march for freedom. Embry feared that his wife would be clubbed or bitten by a German Shepherd. While Terri sang "We Shall Overcome" in the South, the Royals tried to overcome the

Celtics in the Boston Garden. White mobs threatened the Alabama marchers and the players' wives were among those who fled to the airport under cover of blankets in the back of a truck.

"There was a lot going on in society at the time," Embry said years later.

Never was Martin Luther King Jr. more eloquent than on the day he stood before several hundred thousand demonstrators congregated for the March on Washington on August 28, 1963. Estimates of the crowd that day range from 200,000 to 500,000, but at the beginning of an era of protest, it was then the largest such gathering on American soil.

On that hot summer afternoon, standing on the steps of the Lincoln Memorial, King spoke from the heart to an audience that had just been singing gospel songs, an audience that ached to believe justice was imminent after a century denied. In part, he said, ". . . I still have a dream. It is a dream rooted in the American dream. I have a dream that one day this nation will rise up and live out the true meaning of its creed—we hold these truths to be self-evident that all men are created equal.

"I have a dream that on the red hills of Georgia, the sons of former slaves and the sons of former slave owners will be able to sit down together at the table of brotherhood.

"I have a dream that my four little children will one day live in a nation where they will not be judged by the color of their skin, but by the content of their character. I have a dream today!"

The next year, 1964, the thirty-five-year-old Doctor of Divinity Martin Luther King Jr. was awarded the Nobel Peace Prize, the youngest person so recognized. Fearful of assassination with every step, worried about fractionalization within the movement, worn down from lack of rest and unceasing pressure, King was at first more thoughtful than joyful at the news.

Admittedly honored beyond words, King believed the award was a validation of the Civil Rights movement. His worry never ceased, but he viewed the awarding of the Nobel Prize as encouragement to fight on.

Against the backdrop of such turmoil, basketball seemed of minimal importance. But in their small way, the Boston Celtics were living Martin Luther King Jr.'s dream. They were a team of blacks and whites, cooperating, sharing, an integrated unit that was not on the frontlines of a revolution, but in its own way a visible, cohesive example of brotherhood at its best. How did they do it when the world around them was going to hell?

"They [the Celtics and Auerbach] kept the same players, didn't they?" Gene Conley noted. "The core was the same. They didn't break up. Race was not an issue. We were too busy going to the Y and working out and playing the next game. Black or white, the players didn't know the difference."

The Celtics got to know one another well, and learned to understand and appreciate personalities and moods of teammates. They became so used to their shared experiences and moments of glory that to some extent they forgot that as a group they were not at all like society at large.

Once, Russell brought his father, Mister Charlie, and his grandfather, whom he called the Old Man, into the locker room after a Celtics game. Russell's grandfather was transfixed and suddenly began to cry. When Mister Charlie asked his father what was wrong, he replied that he never thought he would live to see what was happening in front of him. John Havlicek, a white man, and Sam Jones, a black man, stood in the shower soaping up and chatting at the same time. The sight of that natural act, that simple sign of integration, stunned and impressed him more than any teamwork he saw on the court.

It was a touching moment for Bill Russell. One that stuck with him and helped him realize in one more small way that the Boston Celtics were different. He said that his grandfather told the story to anyone who would listen back in Louisiana. Imagine, water running off a white man onto a black man, water running off a black man onto a white man. And the white man and the black man looked as if they liked one another, too.

13

RIVALS RISING

The Celtics whipped the Minneapolis Lakers in four straight to win the 1958–59 title, but Boston was introduced to the Lakers' newest and best weapon, the rookie Elgin Baylor.

Later, when Michael Jordan was proclaimed the greatest basketball player on earth and touted as the greatest player who ever lived, it was as if the world had developed collective amnesia. For a while, fans acted as if Jordan was the first player who ever dunked, the first player who ever elevated, the first player whoever showed hang time. Maybe Jordan is the best basketball player of them all, but he is not a super vertical leap above the rest. There are others in the best-ever photo, and during a remarkable wealth-of-talent period of time, they poured into the NBA and undertook the mission to dethrone the Boston Celtics.

In a society with the attention span of a televised news cycle at best, players like Wilt Chamberlain, Oscar Robertson, Jerry West, and Elgin Baylor of forty-five and fifty years ago are only dimly remembered. With a tic that provided a built-in head fake and jumping ability that provided him with the rebounding ability of a center, the 6-foot-5 Baylor was the first to emerge.

Baylor averaged 24.9 points per game as a rookie during the Lakers' unexpected charge to the finals in 1959 and he was even better his second season, averaging 29.6 points a game.

Early that next season in Minneapolis, Baylor's sublime talents foreshadowed the budding of a new rival for the Celtics. In a 136–115 defeat of Boston that ended the Celtics' 22-game winning streak over the Lakers, Baylor scored 64 points.

Only a handful of years earlier, before the invention of the 24-second shooting clock, entire teams did not score that many points in a game. Almost exactly a year later, in November 1960, Baylor set an NBA scoring record with 71 points in a game. He also had 25 rebounds that day.

"We were determined he'd get the record," Lakers guard "Hot" Rod Hundley said. "He's a wonderful guy and the greatest player ever."

Lakers coach Fred Schaus said that when Baylor reached 59 points, he instructed the other players to keep setting him up. "I told the team to feed Baylor," Schaus said, a not unexpected choice given that the man was unstoppable that night.

In a follow-up newspaper story a few days later, Baylor spoke for himself and the fresh blood arriving in the league with skills better than fans had ever seen before. "With the kind of shooters there are around today," he said, "a man could score 100 points."

Less than two years later, Wilt Chamberlain did. But by then the 7-foot-1 former Philadelphia schoolboy great and Kansas University All-American had already surpassed Baylor. On Pearl Harbor Day, 1961, the NBA witnessed one of its splashiest shootouts. The Lakers, by then in Los Angeles, bested the Warriors, 151–147 in triple overtime. Chamberlain scored a record 78 points. Baylor had 63 points in the same game. What a show. The game lasted past midnight with only 4,022 spectators in Philadelphia's old Convention Hall.

During the 1960–61 season, Baylor averaged 34.8 points a game and he was joined by a rookie whose jump shot was so sweet that his silhouette became the logo symbol for the NBA. Jerry West grew up in West Virginia, in a little-known place called Cabin Creek. He was a basketball prodigy, a miraculous scorer in high school and for the Mountaineers in college, and he acquired the nickname "Zeke From Cabin Creek," mainly because it rhymed.

As a rookie, West averaged 17.6 points per game. But in his second season, he averaged 30.8 points per game. Baylor missed thirty-two of the team's eighty games because he was borrowed by the U.S. Army, but averaged 38.2 ppg in the forty-eight he played. West was a big guard for the time at 6-feet-3, and although he weighed less than 200 pounds he had more strength than defenders expected.

The Lakers' time was coming, but for a few more seasons, after the Minneapolis Lakers' last hurrah in the finals, the St. Louis Hawks remained the chief threat to Celtics domination. St. Louis reached the finals at the end of the 1960–61 season. Man-for-man, the Hawks were a better team than the one that won one title and nearly captured a second a couple of years earlier.

Bob Petit was still The Man in the Hawks' offense. Cliff Hagan had matured and improved. But the Hawks also added heady 6-foot-1 guard Lenny Wilkens out of Providence College, who became a Hall of Fame player and coach. And big, bruising, all-elbows-and-power Clyde Lovellette joined Petit and Hagan as a trio of 20-point scorers. Lovellette possessed neither the hops nor the timing of Bill Russell, but he used his 6-foot-9, 240-pound body to pound on the Celtics center. No one ever used the words *dainty* and *Lovellette* in the same sentence.

It took the full seven games of the championship series for the Celtics to take out the Hawks in 1960. Boston won 122–103 in the deciding game at the Garden. By then, Russell's special talents were universally admired across the NBA, but at the beginning of the season, St. Louis owner Ben Kerner said he had no regrets about the trade that brought him Hagan and Ed Macauley.

"Yes, I'd make it again," Kerner said. "When I traded away Russell, I wasn't established in St. Louis the way I am now."

Call it a vote of confidence in his own players, stubbornness in refusing to admit he had been outsmarted by the Celtics, or Kerner still feeling the effects of Auerbach's long-ago punch to his head, but there is little doubt he would have presided over a better ball club if he'd kept Russell. Maybe

Kerner, the new sportsman in town, wasn't secure enough to hitch his franchise's future in the new market to an outspoken black man. The racial climate in St. Louis, the farthest-South club in the league at the time, was as hot as the city's summer weather.

There was as much stability on the Celtics roster between the start of the championship run in 1956 and 1961 as could ever be expected on a professional team. But things were changing. At the end of the 1960–61 season, with ten years in the league, guard Bill Sharman retired to begin a coaching career. Carefree Gene Conley, content with his multisport championship rings, signed off at the end of that season too.

Professional sports leagues are structured to reward the best teams with trophies and the worst teams with high draft picks, so in theory they will not remain the worst teams. The Celtics kept winning and the Celtics kept picking last. For all his genius as a judge of talent, Red Auerbach made mistakes. The 1958 No. 1 choice, Ben Swain, spent just one year with the team. Ditto for 1959 No. 1 choice John Richter. The No. 2 1959 selection, Gene Guarilia, a rugged 6-foot-5 forward out of George Washington University, Auerbach's alma mater, stuck around for four seasons, but never played major minutes.

In 1960, however, the Auerbach magic returned. The team's top pick was 6-foot-6 forward Tom "Satch" Sanders. Sanders wore glasses thicker than Buddy Holly's and white elbow- and kneepads that combined to give him a dorky look. The pads were the equivalent of an office worker's pocket protector. In the world of professional sports, they just weren't cool. Auerbach ordered Sanders to get rid of the pads and he got himself contacts too. If the accessories seemed overdone, Sanders's new look reinforced his capability as a marvelous defender. With his long arms and long legs and quickness, Sanders now seemed like a ferocious big cat poised to pounce. The league's high-scoring forwards hated dates with Boston because they understood they had to battle twice as hard to get open for passes.

The other player still on the board when Auerbach was debating which forward to take was Dave Budd, who went to the New York Knicks, but never had the accomplished career of Sanders. Auerbach had seen Sanders play three times before the draft and he felt good vibes from him.

"I'd say, first of all, his defensive ability struck me," Auerbach said. "And he is a hungry ballplayer, one who wants to make good, who wants to win. He has long arms and can clear the boards. Mainly, he has the desire, the right attitude."

Sanders was a scorer at New York University, but Auerbach made it clear to him that his main responsibility would be shutting down the other guys. Sanders didn't let the job description bother him too much.

"I looked at it as an opportunity to play with the Boston Celtics and worry about the other things once you get in the door," Sanders said. "The Celtics were already winners. They'd won three titles. Good things will prevail. You will find a way."

What Sanders's role boiled down to once you shifted through the general description was being hired to turn off the Bob Petit and Elgin Baylor point spigots. They were the best frontcourt scorers on the teams that could challenge the Celtics. If Sanders made life a little bit more difficult for them, the Hawks and Lakers had to find other sources for their points. Given the depth of scoring talent those clubs had, they could, but Auerbach acquiring Sanders was like adding another chess piece to the board.

Baylor's abilities spoke loud because of his slashing ability to the hoop and his flashy moves with the ball. The only thing that could really slow Baylor was injuries. Going one-on-one, Sanders just did the best he could and that was better than almost anyone else.

Baylor, vice president of basketball operations for the Los Angeles Clippers, said he always thinks of Sanders first when evaluating the Celtics defense of the time.

"Satch [Sanders] was the toughest defender I ever went against," Baylor said. "Very aggressive, but never dirty."

Even though he was a guard, Oscar Robertson was the same height as Baylor. The Big O, as Robertson was nicknamed, thought of Baylor as an offensive dynamo. "Animal, vegetable, or glowing, green radioactive minerals couldn't stop him," Robertson said.

If Baylor was a sorcerer, Bob Petit's consistency was his strength. He had an uncanny jump shot, but his contributions to the average watcher were more subtle than Baylor's. It was only later, when box scores were examined, that someone might realize how much damage he had done.

"Bob Petit was a player who got the most out of his talent, which was an awful lot," Sanders said. "But he knew what he wasn't so great at: He wasn't going to bring the ball upcourt and he didn't go behind the back with his dribble. He focused on what he could do well and that's why he did it so well. He was 6-foot-9 and when he decided to take that little, short-range jump shot at a distance when guys focus on driving, he didn't miss."

Sanders was nicknamed "Satch" after legendary baseball pitcher Satchel Paige. He had a great appreciation for jazz music, sometimes wore a beret (a far more dapper look than the elbow- and kneepad swaddling) and submitted his bid for the greatest, or at least one of the more brazen comments, for *Bartlett's Quotations* when the Celtics visited the White House and President John F. Kennedy in 1963 after that year's championship victory. Kennedy, being from Boston, was a Celtics fan, not simply going through the politically correct motions of meeting with the sports champion of the moment.

Although there was a group shot of the occasion, it was not merely a grip-and-grin moment with the leader of the free world. Celtics players sat around a conference table pretending they were cabinet officers and joked with the president. When Kennedy and the basketball champions parted, Sanders uttered his famous comment, "Take it easy, baby," to Kennedy.

Sanders's defensive mind-set apparently went beyond the court. Wayne Embry roomed with Sanders on the road and said he was paranoid about hotel break-in possibilities. Sanders locked the door religiously and often moved a desk in front of it. If he could not move furniture to employ as a barrier, Embry said, Sanders tied a rope across the entryway to trip a potential robber. Embry said this was all fascinating to watch unfold, and he only hoped he remembered all of the obstacles if he got up in the middle of the night to go to the bathroom.

John Havlicek also roomed with Sanders for a time and echoed Embry's recollection. He said Sanders rigged up creative alarm systems, such as balancing an ashtray on the edge of an empty waste basket at the door, so if it fell it would alert him to an intruder. The main problem with all of these systems, Havlicek said, was that he came in late and had to wake up Sanders every time just to be let into the room.

Ultimately, Sanders did need knee braces again, but he was a comparatively unheralded winner on eight title teams. Sanders never made the NBA All-Star game, but the Celtics retired his No. 16 jersey. Later, Sanders coached the Celtics and also at Harvard University, and became a vice president of the NBA. Sanders, along with K. C. Jones, was regarded as the quietest Celtic of the Dynasty period. Yet Jones says Sanders kept him laughing all the time, often with scary exploits from behind the wheel. Seemingly, his later-in-life driver's ed lessons didn't take immediately.

If Sanders disrupted the opposition's best offensive forward with his stare-at-the-belly-button defensive focus, then the 6-foot-1 K. C. Jones led a parallel existence in the backcourt. Much like Sanders, Jones earned his paycheck by checking offensive stars, not for putting the ball in the hoop. In both circumstances, the confrontations were supposed to be the immovable object stopping the irresistible force. But as basketball observers know, the offensive man always has the advantage. He has the ball in his hands and he knows where he is going. The defender is expected to ignore the ball handler's fakes, anticipate his destination, and get there first. Even then, the truly talented offensive player may score on an off-balance shot, or make the defender commit a foul.

K. C. was expected to cover Jerry West when the Celtics played the Lakers and 6-foot-5 Oscar Robertson when the Celtics played the Cincinnati Royals. It probably doesn't matter who is asked from that era, the answer is probably the same, but Jones bluntly stated the toughest guards he covered were Robertson and West.

"They kept me in the league," Jones said.

Not because he stole their lunch, but because the challenge of facing them was so great that Jones invested all his pride in trying to stop them.

"Most guys experienced a little fear regarding Oscar and Jerry West," Jones said. "Their ego made them the best. For me to match the ego of Jerry West and Oscar I had to master the fundamentals of defense and be as creative potentially on defense as they could be on offense. I had to find things that would work."

Jones recalled one playoff game against the Lakers in the Boston Garden when he held West to only 16 points. In the locker room his teammates were patting him on the back and praising him and asked what the secret was to stalling West.

"I said something about he likes to throw the ball down to the right as a fake and then take his first step," Jones said. "So the next game we played them he got 45 points. Guys are gonna have those nights, but then sometimes they're not. You've got to learn from when he had a bad night. That's competition. You worked as best as you could in those situations without a sense of fear."

Jones was such an adept theft, swatting the ball away from dribblers for turnovers that announcer Johnny Most said of K. C., "He steals the ball so often that he is actually on defense an offensive weapon."

With West and Robertson, not even Auerbach could ask for much more than containment. It is doubtful Oscar Robertson would admit that Michael Jordan was a better player than the Big O was in his prime. And old-timers who saw Robertson play might well back him up.

At 6-feet-5 and 220 pounds, Robertson was really the NBA's first big guard with superstar talent. He was a handful, not only because he was such a great shooter and scorer but also because he could outmuscle other guards. The famous photograph of Robertson that adorns his autobiography is a summation of his athleticism. Robertson has just caught a rebound and he's holding the ball below his waist. The picture captures him with legs thrust wide in a split that only the most agile and flexible athletes can dream of performing, but Robertson hasn't landed in the split, he is still in mid-air, his heavily muscled arms taut and legs virtually parallel to the ground. Can guys do that?

Robertson was a star at Crispus Attucks High School in Indianapolis and an even bigger star at the University of Cincinnati, where he averaged 33.8 points and 15.2 rebounds a game. As a guard! Robertson was such a Bearcats hero that a bronze statue of him now stands outside of the basketball team's campus home arena, as the sentinel of the program.

Robertson was an instant sensation in pro basketball. Jerry West called him "a man for the ages," who in terms of maturity was never a rookie. "He was the measuring stick for how players should play."

NBA statisticians keep meticulous count of players' triple-doubles—an accumulation of double figures in points, rebounds, and assists in a game.

Such record-keeping focus was unknown in 1960 when Oscar entered the league and the numbers were not tracked closely until years later.

When it became fashionable to take note of triple-doubles, essentially in the 1980s when 6-foot-9 Magic Johnson emerged as the world's tallest point guard, someone with a sense of history dredged up Robertson's record. In his second year as a pro with the Royals, Robertson averaged 30.8 points, 12.5 rebounds, and 11.4 assists per game—for the season. A triple-double every day.

Fans now are aware of that feat. What has been given less attention is the fact that Robertson actually came within a whisker of averaging a triple-double for his entire first five seasons. Between 1960 and 1965, Robertson's statistics in the categories of points, rebounds, and assists read as follows: 30.5, 10.1, 9.7; 30.8, 12.5, 11.4; 28.3, 10.4, 9.5; 31.4, 9.9, 11.0; 30.4, 9.0, 11.5. There is no comparable performance by another player.

Nonchalantly, perhaps jokingly, Robertson once said that maybe if he had known people would care he might have done even better. Heck, there was no three-point line in Robertson's day and he said he surely would have worked on that shot if the rule was in effect. Robertson says he sometimes hears of his single-season triple-double average mentioned in the same breath as Ted Williams's .406 batting average of 1941 when he was the last baseball player to bat .400.

"The truth is, I didn't know what I achieved," Robertson said, since he didn't study stat sheets and no one made a big deal of it at the time.

Actually, the odds are likely better that a baseball player will hit .400 again before anyone else in the NBA averages a triple-double on the season. The modern player with the best chance is probably the Cleveland Cavaliers' LeBron James. His style is appropriate for the feat, but in an era when shooting percentages have improved, there aren't enough rebounds to go around.

As Oscar's numbers suggest, he came to the NBA readymade. But pure athleticism was not the only reason he did so well immediately: Going to college in the same town where he played professionally also helped immensely. In his undergraduate free time, Robertson attended Royals games, and future teammate Jack Twyman said Oscar took notes all of the time.

"He probably had as much of a book on the doings of the NBA as the seasoned veterans," Twyman said early in Robertson's career. "Oscar will make it his business to become one of the all-time greats in pro ball because he's such a thorough student of the game along with being endowed with tremendous natural ability. He's been priming himself for his career in this league for some time."

Bob Cousy, the first great point guard, was just 6-foot-1, much smaller than Robertson, and he recognized what a force Oscar was. Covering Robertson, he said, "is no worse than taking on a windmill with your bare hands."

The first time they met on the court, Robertson thought of Cousy as the ultimate point guard and Cousy said of Robertson that he adapted to the NBA so quickly it seemed he had been in the league a long time. Cousy added later that teams couldn't double-team Oscar because he always found the open man with a pass. Yet later still, when Cousy became coach of the Royals, Robertson chafed at the boss's style. Robertson was traded to the Milwaukee Bucks, where he won a world championship ring.

Robertson's background made him very sensitive to racial issues. Despite their status as enemy combatants on the court, Oscar was friendly enough with Bill Russell to invite him into his home for meals before Celtics-Royals games. Cincinnati in the early 1960s was not a hospitable place for blacks to go searching for restaurant dinners.

Robertson says race has played a big part in his life and there are many examples why. He had a great-grandfather raised as a slave in Tennessee. His grandfather was a sharecropper and Robertson was born in a farmhouse in 1938 before the family moved to Indiana. In high school, he received a phone call death threat before a big game. Indiana was a hotbed of Ku Klux Klan activity at the time. Robertson said he was sometimes called nigger, but was used to it from being born in the South. He never forgot those slurs though.

Robertson could do anything on a basketball court. Anything, that is, except beat the Celtics. The first big showdown came during the playoffs after the 1962–63 season. The Royals took the Celtics to seven games in the Eastern Division finals before losing in the final game, 142–131. The next year Boston beat Cincinnati in the division finals in five games.

"It was horrible to have played my career during that time—we always managed to finish second to the Celtics in the division," Twyman said. "One year we took them to a triple-overtime game and we were beaten. So we almost beat them. You know, if you're any kind of an athlete, it's wait till next year. We'll get them next year. It was frustrating, but they always figured out a way to win. We always thought we had a pretty good team."

They did, but the Celtics—as Robertson said—had a great team.

14

NBA GROWING PAINS

Sam Jones was on the run. Bobbing and weaving on the fly, he darted off the end of the court in the Boston Garden, leaned over, and scooped up a photographer's stool. Then he turned to face a rampaging Wilt Chamberlain. The lion tamer was looking for an equalizer to ward off the bigger, stronger beast stalking him during the April 1, 1962, game between the Celtics and the Philadelphia Warriors.

The 6-foot-4, 205-pound Jones needed to put some kind of barrier between himself and Wilt, the 7-foot-1, 300-pound center who everyone agreed was the strongest man in the NBA. It was quite a sight, memorable for all those present, and an incident talked and written about for decades afterward. It was a boxing match that never would have been sanctioned by the World Boxing Association because of the weight inequity. It was a matchup that Jones could only lose after making the mistake of tugging on Superman's cape. In under-the-basket infighting, Jones either stepped on Chamberlain's toes, annoyed him with hacks on his arms, or ticked him off with a stray elbow. The two yelled choice words at one another.

Chamberlain showed grimaces of aggravation when things did not go his way on the basketball court, but he rarely flashed a temper that might lead to fisticuffs. Sometimes he simply flexed his powerful biceps and sent a persistent opponent to the floor. That usually ended the physical confrontation. For once, Chamberlain was enraged and Jones wanted no part of a one-on-one. Where was Jim Loscutoff when you needed him?

"I did not want to fight him," Jones said at a sports memorabilia convention near Chicago a few years ago.

Jones settled for a footrace and armed himself with the nearest available protective device. Others, from Bill Russell to police officers, intervened and Chamberlain never got a chance to belt Jones. The game resumed without combat. Jones's postgame account for the newspapers explained the prospect of using the stool as a fighting utensil.

"He wanted to break my arm," Jones said. "If I'm going to fight him, I'm not going to fight fair. So I grabbed the stool. Naturally, I wasn't going to tangle with a guy that size, so I made sure I had some protection."

There were boxing cards at the Boston Garden that did not include as much action as the basketball game that day. Warriors guard Guy Rodgers, taking a cue from Jones, picked up a stool too. Celtics guard Carl Braun and Rodgers faced off and Rodgers punched Braun in the mouth. Fans and police officers went after Rodgers while referee Norm Drucker put a headlock on Braun. Maybe these were really boxer's stools used in corners between rounds and not stools used for photographers' comfort while shooting the game. In the end, five players, three Celtics and two Warriors, were fined $50 each by NBA commissioner Maurice Podoloff. Chamberlain was not among them.

Although Sam Jones explained his reasons for shying away from the big man pretty clearly at the time—after all Chamberlain was talking about challenging Muhammad Ali for the heavyweight title—K. C. Jones had a different take on the situation years later.

"I think it was a sense of theater grabbing the stool," K. C. said. "Wilt was walking toward him with his right arm out like he was going to shake Sam's hand. Sam didn't recognize that."

Actually, Sam seemed pretty convinced that he was going to get clobbered, didn't he?

"Well, yeah," K. C. said.

Of course, the way Johnny Most saw it, the Warriors were all felons who deserved life sentences at Sing Sing. On another occasion, two years before, Most described the blow-by-blow when Chamberlain tried to deck Tommy Heinsohn with a punch. Heinsohn ducked and Chamberlain's fist smacked his teammate Tom Gola.

"Believe it or not, the Stilt's punches are even less accurate than his free-throw shooting!" Most shouted. "He just decked his own teammate!"

Given that Chamberlain was one of the worst free-throw shooters in NBA history, that was the ultimate insult.

As he did once in a while, after that game Goliath sought sympathy by complaining how he was always a target and never protected by the officials. Most, who must have received a D-minus in diplomacy in school, laid on additional inflammatory commentary.

"Poor Wilt," he said. ". . . he's complaining about all his little bumps and bruises. Please somebody go get him some Gerber's baby food and a pacifier."

If there was such a thing as sports standup insult comedy, Most would have excelled as a Vegas headliner. He could have been the Don Rickles of the athletic world.

One thing sometimes undernoticed during the Dynasty was how, under Auerbach's direction, Boston played beautiful team basketball. The ball movement was exceptional. The players were unselfish. The Celtics were the first great practitioners of the fast break. With Russell inhaling the ball off the backboard and throwing long passes to Cousy, who either shot or fed trailers for easy hoops, the Celtics could demoralize an opponent quickly.

Yet the Celtics were also a team of their time. Syracuse was not the only place where fans incited near riots. And teams that could not compete with the Celtics' finesse game determined to alter the pace into half-court, slow-the-ball-down, grind-it-out affairs. It seemed as if the fans' hostility and the other teams' big bodies worked in concert to create intimidation.

K. C. Jones remembers fans in Philadelphia yelling anything they wanted, with no shame, and no usher or team official suggesting they stop. He recalls one visit that was particularly ugly when Celtics wives made the trip and had to listen to the nasty insults. But even that wasn't as bad as when spectators threw things at the Boston bench.

"They were throwing beer cans down," Jones said. "With beer in them. That was kind of rough."

Auerbach understood what type of team he had assembled. Not that the players were all lovers and couldn't take the abuse. Still, he made sure to keep an enforcer or two on the roster. From 1951 to 1955, the 6-foot-5, 235-pound Bob Brannum was the beat cop. Jim Loscutoff succeeded him, with assistance from Gene Conley. Loscutoff and Conley both were fearless, but both were also smoother on the court than Brannum.

The other Celtics appreciated Loscutoff as a good guy off the court, but liked the security he provided if some bully started shoving them around. Still, even the best guardians must sometimes be reactive. In an April 1962 game against the Lakers, K. C. Jones had his nose broken by a Jim Krebs elbow. Loscutoff worked over the L.A. forward, but Jones obtained some of his own revenge by making full-court drives for baskets, stealing the ball three times from Elgin Baylor, and shadowing Jerry West. A doctor told Jones to sleep that night with one pillow behind his head and pillows on each side of his head so he wouldn't move his head from side to side in his sleep. That would help to stabilize the break. He probably dreamt of Loscutoff taking out the entire Laker lineup.

"He was a bodyguard for Red," K. C. Jones said. "Whenever anybody touched one of our guys out there, Red would say, 'OK, Loscy, get in there.'"

Loscutoff denies being told by Auerbach that he was supposed to retaliate for alleged atrocities. But neither was he a shrinking violet. His presence on the court screamed out that the Celtics were mad as hell and they weren't going to take it any more. Jungle Jim was on the job. Jungle Jim was also a Johnny Weismuller movie character.

"He was in the jungle and he used to take care of animals and stuff like that," Loscutoff said years later, a tone evident in his voice that indicated he was asking you to share the joke with him. The animals Loscutoff tamed were human, but very strong and very fast as well, and they had to be prevented from preying on Celtic teammates. These players needed a good talking-to, didn't they?

"Right," Loscutoff said.

Basketball enemies tried to make out Loscutoff as a thug, and once in a while bad things happened on the court. During a December 7, 1961, Celtics triumph over Syracuse, Loscutoff clocked Nationals forward Dave Gambee one minute into an appearance in the game. Loscutoff was ejected.

"It was physical," Loscutoff said of the 1950s and 1960s NBA. "But the games were never televised, so consequently you got away with a lot more crap than you can now."

Loscutoff was more than a battering ram. When the Celtics won their first title in 1957—Loscy's favorite championship with the club—he made two critical free throws in overtime to help clinch it. He also ran a basketball camp for boys up to college age in Massachusetts, north of Boston, for decades, and his son still runs it. And at one time, Loscutoff coached the Boston State College team.

Loscutoff retired in 1964, after nine seasons of play and as a member of seven world championship teams. The Dynasty was in full bloom, but incomplete, and the true Celtic tradition had not quite been established and certainly not reflected upon. It took some time before evaluations took place, contributions were analyzed, and the organization's enthusiasm to retire player numbers reached its peak. In between, Loscutoff's No. 18 jersey was given to another player who wore it with distinction. Center Dave Cowens, the linchpin of the 1970s rebuilt team, became a star. When Cowens retired, the Celtics did retire No. 18. Upon further review, it was felt more should be done to honor Loscutoff, but what was the proper course with No. 18 already hanging in the rafters?

Thinking out of the box, the Celtics did Loscutoff proud. If they couldn't retire his number in the same manner as other players, they could appropriately recognize him otherwise. Today, Loscutoff, too, has his own tribute hanging on a banner in the Celtics' home arena. But instead of a jersey number, his green-and-white flag reads LOSCY.

"It was a great honor," Loscutoff said.

Not much can touch the big guy so deeply he might bust out crying, but the day his banner was raised was a special one that he will always remember.

Loscutoff was more popular in Boston than he was elsewhere around the league. In fact, with the Celtics winning the championship almost every year it was not difficult to find opposing coaches grousing about their

supposed preferential treatment, or who were at least resentful of Auerbach's game complaints.

Lakers coach Fred Schaus, who had coached Jerry West at West Virginia, was heard screaming at the referees during a 1961 game, saying, "You
got a set of rules for this club, huh? Put the Celtics in a paper bag and
nobody can go near them?"

The Dynasty Celtics won their first crown in 1957, their second in
1959, their third in 1960, and fourth in 1961. By then the Minneapolis Lakers had become the Los Angeles Lakers and had replaced the Hawks as the
new power in the Western Division. Besides Elgin Baylor and Jerry West,
two future Hall of Famers, the Lakers added some extra firepower in forward Rudy LaRusso, out of Dartmouth, a rare Ivy Leaguer in the NBA, and
Frank Selvy. Selvy was a 6-foot-3 guard who had been around the league
for nearly five seasons before joining the Lakers for their wrap-up in Minnesota. In college Selvy played for Furman and remains famous at that institu-
tion for scoring 100 points in a game.

Selvy was a solid double-figure scorer in the NBA, though never in
a class with West or Baylor. But in the seventh game of the 1962 finals,
Lakers and Celtics tied at three games apiece, and game seven tied at
100 points apiece, Selvy had a chance to author some dramatic history.
The Lakers had the ball to inbounds at midcourt with about four seconds remaining in regulation. Selvy passed to "Hot" Rod Hundley, who
considered his options and felt Selvy was more open than Baylor (41
points) or West (35) and fed him about 15 feet from the basket on the
left baseline. Selvy had made the Lakers' last two hoops to force the tie.
He had the hot hand and so was a more logical choice for the last shot
than it initially sounds.

Selvy squared up, shot, and the ball spun through the air. If it's good,
the Lakers are champs for the first time in LA and the Celtics go down. The
ball nicked the rim, Bill Russell (who scored 30 points and gathered 40
rebounds that day) pulled in this one, and the game went into overtime.
The Celtics won 110–107 and were champs again, for the fourth straight
year, and the fifth time in six seasons.

"I thought it was all over when Selvy shot from that corner," Auerbach said in the postgame interviews.

Years later, Hundley, who had ascertained that West and Baylor were covered, was asked what he would have done if Selvy was better defended, too. "I'd probably have shot it," he said.

And, Hundley figured, if it went in he would have been so acclaimed in Los Angeles that he could have been elected mayor.

Baylor was magnificent that day and his slithery moves contributed to Tommy Heinsohn, Tom Sanders, Frank Ramsey, and Jim Loscutoff all fouling out. Auerbach turned to seldom-used backup Gene Guarilia for frontline assistance in overtime. Guarilia was a garbage-time player, meaning just about the only time his name got into the box score was when a game was a blowout. The last men on the bench rarely play in the NBA unless injuries or unforeseen circumstances disrupt a coach's regular substitution rotation. This was one of those unforeseen circumstances. In a few minutes of play, Guarilia scored on a dunk, stole the ball from Baylor, and altered one of Baylor's shots defensively. This time Guarilia sweated for his championship ring.

After the game, Loscutoff said to Guarilia, "You really earned your money, baby." And Guarilia replied, "I think it was about time I did something, don't you, Jim?"

The Celtics persevered, endured, took advantage of others' mistakes, but during the Dynasty years they overcame close calls like that.

Fans love winners, but they get spoiled when their team wins all of the time. It reached a point after several championships in a row that titles were taken for granted, that regular-season divisional championships were assumed. Once in a while, Auerbach felt it necessary to remind the fans that what the Celtics were doing was extraordinary, that victories did not mount by magic, but took heart and will.

"It is not easy winning," Auerbach said during the 1961 season. "It's a lot of hard work and we're winning because we put out so much. Too bad the public can't get a look at the team in the dressing room when it's over. They'd see a lot of thoroughly exhausted men. But you pick up the paper and it says that the Celtics won 'easily' again last night."

Bob Cousy (14), the wizard of the hardwood, was the NBA's first star. The former Holy Cross All-American invented the behind-the-back pass and drove Celtics' foes crazy with his ability to dribble around them. Here he is shown in a 1950s game against the Syracuse Nationals. **Courtesy The Sports Museum**

Frank Ramsey (23) invented the role of basketball's sixth man. A star at the University of Kentucky, Ramsey was used as a fresh shooter off the bench to jump-start the Celtics' offense after the starters wore out the other club's first team. Today the NBA has a Sixth Man Award. **Courtesy The Sports Museum**

Hall of Fame guard Sam Jones (24) unleashes his deadly jump shot from the corner. Jones, who was little publicized in college at a small school in North Carolina, used the backboard glass for support like no other player to hit his bank shot. Here he has the drop on the Cincinnati Royals' great Oscar Robertson (14).

Courtesy The Sports Museum

Bill Russell was the Celtics' top draft pick in 1956 but joined the team late after leading the United States to an Olympic gold medal in Melbourne, Australia. Guard Bill Sharman (left) and owner Walter Brown (right) met Russell's plane and welcomed him to town. **Courtesy The Sports Museum**

Bill Russell (6), the shot blocker supreme, is regarded as the greatest winner in team sports. With Russell as center, the Boston Celtics won eleven championships in thirteen seasons between 1957 and 1969. Russell also became the first black coach of a major American professional sports team. **Courtesy The Sports Museum**

Bailey Howell (18) joined the Celtics near the end of the Dynasty years after a distinguished career with the Detroit Pistons. Howell was a high-scoring forward who was just what Boston needed when Tommy Heinsohn retired.

Courtesy The Sports Museum

Emmette Bryant (7) was a sparkplug player who was a favorite of legendary coach Ray Meyer when the guard played at DePaul University. Bryant played a key role in the Celtics' last title run. **Courtesy The Sports Museum**

John Havlicek (17) did it all for the Celtics, shifting between guard and forward after an All-American career at Ohio State. He succeeded Frank Ramsey as sixth man. Later he became team captain and was the only player who spanned the original Dynasty years and the Celtics championship teams of the 1970s.

Courtesy The Sports Museum

Professional basketball was growing in popularity, but sellouts at the Boston Garden were never automatic. Once in a while an attraction would woo the public and the seats were filled with 13,909 spectators and the rafters were filled with cigarette and cigar smoke that obscured the view of patrons in the higher-than-Most-above-courtside loges. One occasion that caught the fancy of the buying public was a December 26, 1961, doubleheader. Not only were kids on vacation for Christmas break, but the warm-up game before a Boston–L.A. nightcap featured Philadelphia versus Syracuse. Chamberlain scored 51 points. Not a bad appetizer.

The more the Celtics won, the more their trademarks became ingrained in the basketball fan's mind. The parquet floor, the only one of its kind in the league, was famous worldwide. The Celtics wore black sneakers at all times. And jeez, the Celtics won all those championships with only seven basic plays in Auerbach's book. There were more than twenty options off of those plays, but coaches searching for secrets to Celtic success had to concede it was all in the execution. The teams that played the Celts year after year, game after game, knew the plays as if they had been written on the blackboard in their locker room. They just couldn't stop them.

Auerbach was the most famous coach in the league, and Bill Russell and Bob Cousy were the most famous players in the league at the end of the 1950s and shared top billing with the handful of new stars in the early 1960s. And Walter Brown, the rock of the franchise who had once mortgaged his home to keep the team afloat, was the face of the Celtics in Boston and among owners around the league.

The cleverest Celtics learned that the road to a better contract lay on the path to Brown's office instead of Auerbach's. Hard-bargaining Auerbach protected the owner's money as if it was his own; Brown spent it as if he was contributing to charity, something he did with great generosity. Brown was a soft touch for a loyal player who hit him up for a few thousand bucks more than Auerbach was willing to pay.

Brown was old school. He was not a corporate millionaire looking for a plaything when he started the Celtics. It was always his money on the line. He and the original NBA owners believed in pro basketball. Yes, they wanted to make a buck, but they also loved the sport. Yet the NBA was a paternalistic society in the early days. Just as in other major American sports, players had no real rights. They were drafted out of college and had to play for the team that picked them. They signed exclusive contracts with a team and remained the property of that team unless they were traded. Basketball players had no pensions when they retired, stayed in double rooms in hotels, traveled wherever and whenever they were assigned, including all over the map in extended fall exhibition seasons.

Basketball players loved their jobs, loved the glory, played to win titles, but over time they also asked whether or not they should share in the money made by their teams and if they should not have security in retirement, with pensions of some sort rewarding them for years of service.

When the first rumblings of union formation surfaced in the 1950s, most owners were aghast. Many were not making a profit. And like coal-mine operators, auto-plant general managers, and owners in other trades, they did not welcome the idea of their employees forming bargaining units or obtaining outside representation. Talk of starting a union was conducted in whispers at first. It is one thing to have a job protected by a union and quite another to try to start a union in a nonunion environment. Many of the players who were not stars or starters rightly feared for their futures if they signed up for union membership.

That is why Bob Cousy became the driving force behind union startup. Cousy was the league's most visible player when he first thought of a labor organization for NBA players in 1953. The Celtics were not going to cut their biggest star. Red Auerbach was not going to bench the focal point of his offense. Cousy felt the league needed a player's association to add class and stability to the operation. The players wanted a say in decisions that affected their future.

There were only eight teams, with ten players per team in 1954 when Cousy wrote letters to a team leader on each club. He sought out the most important players on each team so they wouldn't face reprisals from ownership and asked them to poll their rosters about union support. Walter Brown even backed the effort.

By 1957 the NBA Players Association was recognized by the league, though it had little power. A key demand was to cut back on the brutal exhibition season. The owners kept all the profits from those games, but players forced into perhaps twenty appearances were worn out before the season began. The players also wanted a say in scheduling, so they didn't have to play a day game after a night game, and they wanted a cap on fines the owners levied for so-called bad behavior.

By 1958 Cousy had his fill of the union presidency and he asked teammate Heinsohn to take over. Heinsohn was an All-Star, but his league stature differed markedly from Cousy's. Heinsohn's image was as more of a fun-loving guy, with a penchant for practical jokes, including fooling Auerbach into lighting up an exploding cigar. Bill Russell said Heinsohn was remarkably patient, waiting three years with that trick for revenge on Auerbach who had pulled a similar stunt on Heinsohn.

All of Heinsohn's patience was required as union president. He repeatedly lobbied owners for concessions to help players. A rookie salary was established, playoff travel adjusted, but he made no headway in getting the owners to hire full-time trainers who would travel with the team, or in setting up a pension fund.

January 14, 1964, became a watershed in the history of the Players Association. The sold-out All-Star game was scheduled for the Boston Garden that night, but on the afternoon of the game, as the owners met at a luncheon, Heinsohn presided over a meeting of the league's best players and urged them to boycott the game unless owners agreed right there that day to create a pension plan.

Feeling bad because his own boss, Walter Brown, would take the most direct hit from a cancelled game, Heinsohn warned him. Brown was furious and wanted to fire Heinsohn and other Celtics on the All-Star team. Auerbach intervened, seeking to change Heinsohn's stance, but Heinsohn said he represented the players and had to follow their wishes. New commissioner Walter Kennedy tried to persuade the players to wait until the next summer's owners meeting for a pension. But the players were tired of waiting. They'd heard excuses for a long time.

A snowstorm delayed the arrival of many players, and so Heinsohn could not convene a meeting for further discussion and a boycott vote until half an hour before the game's scheduled tip-off. With the All-Stars from both divisions meeting in one locker room, the vote emerged 11–9 in favor of a boycott. Oscar Robertson was a strong supporter, and in 1965 became president of the Players Association. He held the position for nine years and often spent his own money on union business. As president, his name appeared as the plaintiff in the 1971 "Robertson versus the NBA" lawsuit that sought to prevent a merger of the NBA and the American Basketball Association. When resolved six years later, the case was instrumental in eliminating the option clause that bound players to teams indefinitely.

During the All-Star game strike deliberations, the owners were frustrated, angry, and felt betrayed by their players. Attempts were made to strong-arm them. When Lakers owner Bob Short tried to storm the locker room door and yelled for Elgin Baylor to come out and talk to him, Baylor sent a brief but blunt message through a security guy, telling Short to go screw himself.

Heinsohn informed Brown of the vote results. Once again, Kennedy attempted to change the players' minds. He feared the loss of television exposure and fan backlash. Ultimately, using the clout of his office, Kennedy returned to the players and announced that he personally guaranteed the owners would institute a pension plan. The players began their warm ups twenty minutes after the game's scheduled starting time.

Walter Brown had supported the idea of the Players Association, but he resented the boycott talks. He held a grudge against Heinsohn for some time afterwards, calling him "the No. 1 heel" in his sports association, though they did reconcile at the end of the season after the Celtics won another championship. It was a good thing that the brief disruption in their otherwise warm relationship was repaired swiftly because later in 1964 Brown died suddenly of a heart attack at his Cape Cod vacation home at the age of fifty-nine. It was a foundation-shaking shock to the organization. Rarely has there been a more admired owner in professional sports.

Stories were told and retold, how the Celtics were so special to Brown, how they once put him $500,000 in debt and how he took out $200,000 in fresh loans while using his house as collateral. In a twenty-first century business world, where not even written contracts are always respected, Brown would have been out of step. He sometimes made handshake deals with Auerbach and his players and at least once handed Russell a pen and asked him to fill in the dollar amount he felt he was worth. No wonder Russell called Brown a man of "nobility." Russell added that the championships that followed Brown's bank-account-warping investment represented "goodness rewarded."

Russell also told stories about how the Celtics sometimes treated Brown as one of the guys, laughing over tales of Brown's commitment to never drive over 35 miles per hour. Some Celtics, Russell said, actually made arrangements with state troopers to pull him over for speeding, just to hear descriptions of the look on Brown's face. Once, Russell added, Red Auerbach borrowed Brown's new Cadillac, and when he returned the keys said with a straight face that the new car seemed to develop a skip in the engine when being driven over 105 miles per hour.

Many years later, John Havlicek recalled his first meeting with Brown after "Hondo" was drafted by the Celtics. He called Brown "a down-to-earth guy" and said his reputation was of a man "who never went back on his word." That is a reputation few men earn and all would be proud to take to the grave.

Cousy said that Celtic tradition and mystique really began with Brown and Auerbach carried it on while referring to Brown as "one of the greatest men who ever lived." After Brown's death, Auerbach was essentially in control of the franchise. It was his decision to retire No. 1 for Brown and hoist the banner to the Garden rafters. Later, the NBA honored Brown by naming the league's championship trophy after him.

Auerbach revered his old boss and partner and missed Brown terribly. During the 1964–65 season Auerbach covertly carried in his pocket Brown's St. Christopher medal. When the Celtics won the title again in the season after Brown's death, Auerbach held up the religious medal and said, "This was Walter Brown's championship."

15

WILT VERSUS RUSSELL

The greatest one-on-one rivalry in American team sports began on November 7, 1959, in a sold-out Boston Garden when the king of the NBA faced a genuine aspirant to the throne.

Outside of the boxing ring, no two players engaged in such a compelling, dramatic, lengthy, high-stakes rivalry than Bill Russell and Wilt Chamberlain. Russell revolutionized pro basketball upon his arrival on the Celtics roster in late 1956, making an already good team unbeatable. Chamberlain had been lurking in the background for years, waiting for his chance to show his stuff after an Overbrook High School career in Philadelphia that included a 90-point game and an All-American college career at Kansas.

Although he settled in Los Angeles after he retired, Chamberlain always had a soft spot for Philadelphia. When he returned to Overbrook for a special ceremony honoring him thirty-six years after he graduated, Chamberlain said his high school days represented the three happiest years of his life. He had tears in his eyes when he said it.

At 6-feet-9 and with his incredible quickness and leaping talent, Russell dominated the league's centers. Chamberlain, however, outweighed Russell by 50-plus pounds, depending on who was reading what scale, and was about four inches taller. Chamberlain admitted to being 7-foot-1 $^{1}/_{16}$ inches in height, but later many insisted he was taller, maybe even 7-3. Chamberlain stuck with the original measurement for the rest of his life. When the two players stood next to one another for the game's tip-off, Russell looked like a hungry refugee compared to the more muscular Chamberlain. Wilt could also jump, also had great timing, and was more of an offensive force than Russell.

Not football, not baseball, not hockey, nor any other sport with the exception of boxing, lends itself to such intimate confrontation, when bodies are pressed against one another, when arms tangle and the sweat of one man flying off his brow can land on the other man's shoulders. These players were also unique unto themselves. No one else in the game matched up with them in the paint. No one else possessed the same wide range of skills to give the other the supreme battle. Every great sportsman needs an equivalent rival to wring the best from his soul. Every great player needs a foil to raise his psyche to levels he did not know he could reach.

That was Bill Russell to Wilt Chamberlain and vice versa, during ten-year overlapping careers, during regular seasons and playoffs. That was Russell, the Celtics No. 6, and Chamberlain, the Philadelphia Warriors No. 13, scrapping for the same rebound, clawing for the same championship. They could both be great, but only one could be the champ in a single season. Either could earn the spoils of individual achievement, but only one at a time could capture the spoils of team accomplishment. Chamberlain won scoring titles and frequently outrebounded Russell, but Russell's Celtics won nine championships and Chamberlain one in their head-to-head years.

On that first night, Chamberlain scored 30 points and had 30 rebounds and Russell scored 22 points and had 35 rebounds. The Celtics, with better balance in the lineup (it was always thus), won the game. Afterward, Cousy called Chamberlain "the best rookie I've ever seen." But in a comment that would become a refrain throughout Chamberlain's career, Cousy said the big man could not win alone and must adapt more to team basketball.

Referee Earl Strom tossed the first jump ball in the first Russell-Chamberlain game, and many jump balls after that. He said Chamberlain always suffered in comparison to Russell because Russell had a better all-around team and Chamberlain had to score more for Philadelphia.

"There were so many close calls between Russell and Chamberlain," Strom said. ". . . Wilt was a master of direct intimidation. Russell's dominance was more subtle."

Russell was surrounded by future Hall of Famers. Chamberlain usually had a solid cast, but no better. Russell became known as the greatest winner in team sports. Chamberlain, who did win one title each with the Philadelphia 76ers and Los Angeles Lakers, was often regarded as an underachiever.

There was little mystery for Russell before his first showdown with Chamberlain. Chamberlain's debut was presented as the biggest splash in NBA history. He was more difficult to ignore than a tsunami. Chamberlain scored 43 points, collected 28 rebounds, and probably had a dozen blocked shots in his first game, though blocked shots weren't officially recorded by the league until years later.

The media hype for their first meeting was welcome. As long as people talked about basketball, Walter Brown was happy, and if that translated into big box office, he was ecstatic. Chamberlain-Russell was not quite Ali-Frazier in terms of worldwide impact, but it packed nearly the same punch whenever the teams were scheduled.

The newspaper comments after their first game were straightforward and heavy with respect. Russell said: "He's amazing." Wilt said: "The guy's terrific." They were both right.

In a sense, Russell and Chamberlain were dinosaurs, not because they were about to become extinct (on the contrary they were ahead of their time in athleticism), but because their size made the earth shake every time they met.

They also became giants in American society, two of the most prominent black men of their time. The silliest aspect of their rivalry, and one that drove them nuts, or amused them, depending on their mood, was that they were often mistaken for one another in public. Other than both being tall and black, Russell and Chamberlain did not look like each other. But the mistaken-identity thing happened often.

"I remember several times being a few steps away from Russell when people said to him, "Hi, Wilt,'" Chamberlain said. "This can grate on a guy. And it obviously grated on Russell."

From their beginnings in the league, both were outspoken about racial matters, attracted reporters as bees to honey—especially if they gave out sweet quotes—and always, always, were the focal point of description, performance, and results when they played each other. It was a built-in story line every time.

To fans and reporters of the time, Russell remained an enigma. He was set in his ways, not reacting particularly graciously at the arena when cheered, occasionally venting when he felt snubbed. He always brought his A-game to the court and no one could complain about his effort. If a fan booed Russell, it was more likely because he didn't like what he said, not because he didn't like what he did. Russell felt he was a man of principle and consistency. The pet peeve that probably inflamed the public against him the most was his refusal to sign autographs.

Whether it is children or adults, sports fans' limited connection to their sports heroes for decades has been significantly measured by the attitude adopted by ballplayers when approached for autographs. The fans consider it such a small thing to sign one's name. Fans feel players owe them that courtesy. Since they are ticket buyers who help pay players' salaries, they feel entitled to that small recompense when the situation arises. Sometimes players react badly, issuing insults rather than signing John Hancocks. When that happens, especially if it is the only direct interaction with the player during his career, fans form lifetime opinions, as in "He's a jerk." Russell was adamant about not signing. He more than once said he owed the public nothing except honest effort on the court. The stance did not help his popularity.

Russell often expended more effort to avoid signing an autograph than he would have in signing one. He resented being infringed upon in restaurants while eating and sometimes simply stared right through a fan requesting his signature. Sometimes he happily shook hands with an admirer and spoke to him, but still wouldn't sign. Once, Celtics players were eating together in a public place when a little old lady approached Russell for an autograph. He did not refuse, he did not say anything, he just ignored her. His teammates, pained by the situation, treated her with great solicitation, and signed autographs for her.

Tommy Heinsohn said during one of those old doubleheaders at Madison Square Garden in New York he was sitting in the stands with his uncle and young cousin watching the other teams play. He obtained Bill Sharman's and Bob Cousy's autographs for the boy, but when he asked Russell to help him out, Russell turned him down. Russell said, "If I sign for you, I'll have to sign for everybody else."

"Give me a break!" Heinsohn retorted.

Russell would not sign his name for Celtics sponsors, for Red Auerbach's friends, or for charities. When a ball was passed around the locker room, Heinsohn not only signed his name, he signed Russell's so as not to disappoint people. Russell never knew. And Heinsohn knew Russell would not approve. Heinsohn, who later in life became a successful painter, said his artistic skills were put to the test forging Russell's name. Who knows what sort of 1950s and 1960s memorabilia is floating around out there at sports shows or on fans' shelves featuring a fake Russell autograph?

Decades later, when the sports memorabilia market exploded, and Russell was in his sixties and seventies, far removed from his playing and coaching days, he began to sign autographs for money. He signed limited-edition photographs and basketballs for a fee. However, when he collaborated on a book, Russell made book-signing appearances where he signed autographs on the books for free. During those few-hour sessions he was unfailingly friendly and outgoing, offering glimpses of a hidden personality that assuredly would have been welcome in the past.

Cousy said he has teased Russell that his refusal to sign autographs as a player turned out to be an astute business move.

"Russ will sign if the bottom line is there," Cousy said. "He's the only athlete in the history of the country who gets $100,000 for a trade show or a card show, which is three or four hours of his time. A few years ago I remember saying to him, 'Russ, you SOB, you've been capitalizing on being a bastard all your life. You never would sign an autograph and as a result you're making all this money now.' And Russell laughed and cackled. "Yeah," Cousy added, "if whitey comes up with the right number on a piece of paper, that's one way that I think, other than earning an awful lot of money, [he has] of getting back at whitey. He thinks, well, whitey is paying him all this money for a lot of signatures."

Russell's ideology was established early. He saw blacks diminished by racism in the South. He watched his grandfather and father resist ridiculous pressures. And he vowed never to submit, never to back off from a position he thought was correct. He said when he took his two young sons to Monroe, Louisiana, to visit family on a vacation, locals gazed at his Lincoln convertible as if it were a spaceship. He knew he had outgrown this small corner of the world, but he also knew he would carry with him what he had learned from his older relatives and from that place. Cousy said that Russell already carried a "deep-seated" rage within by the time he came to the Celtics.

Announcer Johnny Most said he once had a confrontation with Russell when the player accused Most of not being able to understand him because he was white. Russell listened to Most, a Jewish man who said he had faced his own discrimination, talk about his own life and never again suggested such a thing. Later, when Russell referred to Boston as a racist community and Most called him out on the generalization, Most said Russell told him he knew that Most was not prejudiced.

Gradually growing into his basketball abilities, Russell was not completely self-confident when he enrolled at the University of San Francisco. He became friendly with K. C. Jones not as most people assume—on the basketball court—but because they were assigned as dormitory roommates. Russell said Jones was so shy that he didn't speak a single word to him for a month, but that soon Jones, who had a richer scholarship than he did, treated him to everything from shoes to meals to movie tickets.

K. C. said Russell was about as shy as he was at first, but when they opened up to one another they became inseparable pals. The young men talked about everything, but one of those things was the principles of basketball defense. Someone with a tape recorder should have been a fly on the wall for those chats, given that Jones became possibly the best defensive guard of all time and that Russell practically introduced defense to the NBA.

Jones is unequivocal in stating that Russell made the Celtics, was the core figure, from the moment he joined the team after the Olympics in Australia in 1956 until the moment he retired in 1969.

"And some people say, 'What made the Celtics champions?'" Jones said. "It was Russell. And that was it."

Russell was a rookie in classification only. Heck, between Russell's own manner and the veterans' instant admiration for his game, he was not even required to endure typical rookie abuse. Tommy Heinsohn was a rookie who had been with the team from training camp. He was ordered to tote the vets' bags, typical rookie hazing. When Russell showed up a few months later, Heinsohn logically assumed the new guy would take over. Not on your life. Russell was no bell man. Heinsohn was stuck with the job all season. He also said Russell gratuitously insulted him on occasion for unknown reasons.

"He's like a tough little kid who's always making it extremely difficult to test whether you love him or not," Heinsohn said once. "He did not let people get to know him. He did not let people get close." But Heinsohn also says Russell "was the best basketball player I ever saw."

By the time John Havlicek joined the Celtics in 1962, Russell had been in the league for nearly six years. Havlicek had never seen a player control the flow of the game with the force of his personality and agility the way Russell did. Havlicek said, "You could see the shooters just cringing any time they got within his range." The real issue was, What was Russell's range? He pounced so suddenly, came into the frame from the periphery of the picture so quickly, that shooters were astonished. They began hearing footsteps when there were none. That was part of Russell's psychology, scaring opposing players with his reputation, even when they had nothing to be scared of.

He didn't talk about it much in his years with the Celtics, but Russell later revealed he had hoped to be drafted by the Lakers, so he could stay on the West Coast and because in high school he had met the 6-foot-10 George Mikan, the NBA's first great big man, liked him, and was told by Mikan he could become a pro. Russell would have been tremendous anywhere, especially with a Laker team that added offensive weapons like Elgin Baylor and Jerry West a few years later. But he was perfect with the Celtics from the start.

Russell was always going to be Russell. Whenever he built up a reservoir of good will, something would happen that he felt compelled to comment on, or somebody would ask him a question and rather than deflect it or take the high road, he answered with a brutal frankness. In a December 1962 interview with New York sportswriter Milton Gross, Russell said of his basketball career, "Until today my life has been a waste. This [basketball career] is without depth. This is a very shallow thing."

The bite-the-hand-that-feeds-him description of the sport was not well received. Fans felt Russell didn't care about what he was doing. But even if Russell was doing more than making an off-the-cuff comment, he continued to give the fans their money's worth. In the days when Auerbach left him in for a full 48 minutes, Russell may have coasted a bit on offense. But the only time he regularly didn't put out was at practice. He annoyed his teammates by doing that, not the fans. Russell was probably one of the greatest practice loafers in NBA history. He despised practice. And the longer he played, with the more success he achieved, the shorter his behind-the-scenes attention span.

Cousy called it "a sticky area. To be blunt, Bill Russell was not a practice player." Cousy said near the end of his own career in 1963 sometimes players would just tell Russell to go sit in the stands and watch because his inertia was gumming up the practice.

It was a testament to such talented Celtics players' faith in Russell that he would always be there for them when it counted, that they didn't gripe more about this lazy streak. It was a testament too to Auerbach's wisdom in not placing inordinate pressure on Russell to shape up on the court when it didn't matter so much. Cousy said Russell played his best when the stakes were highest, getting better against Chamberlain each passing year, and practice was comparatively low-key.

Russell said there will always be tension on a team when so many competitive personalities are seeking to mesh into a cohesive unit to pursue a common goal, but that the job of the team that wants to win is to overcome the differences and put them on a back burner. He termed the Celtics "a group of people so diverse you can't imagine," but added, "one thing we've always had on the Celtics is mutual respect. And we think that's the most necessary ingredient for a winning combination. It never mattered who made the basket, as long as the basket was made."

Auerbach insisted he never broke his few team rules to accommodate Russell. But that was a fib. Auerbach relaxed his own rules all the time—if a player needed to do something important he granted permission. It was his sneaky way of managing men. He would play the benevolent dictator, but just would never let the guys take advantage of him.

Years later, Russell co-authored a book called *Russell Rules* about leadership. In it he did not exactly dwell on the suggestion that going to practice every day will make you great at what you do.

Russell demanded and commanded respect. Being shown respect, as a man and a player, may have been the most important thing to him. When Larry Bird, the Celtics great of the 1980s, first met Russell he called him "Mr. Russell." That had to please the older player.

Although the newspapers always juiced up Russell and Chamberlain's relationship as a hated rivalry, they were actually friends during the years they played against one another. They were more similar than dissimilar, with more in common than anyone else in the wide world. Early on they developed the habit of calling one another by their middle names. Russell called Chamberlain "Norman" and Chamberlain called Russell "Fenton." No one else around the NBA displayed such familiarity.

There was so much heat on the court that observers couldn't really comprehend how the duo could be friends outside the game. One way, Russell said, is that they hardly talked about basketball. They both loved jazz and good restaurants and were intelligent men conversant on the issues of the day.

In one of his books, *Second Wind*, Russell wrote, "Wilt Chamberlain and I carried on a friendship the entire time we played basketball together, even though the newspapers portrayed us as mortal enemies." The craziest thing of all, Russell said, was that he—the guy who made the establishment nervous and alienated his hometown fans—was portrayed as the Good Guy compared to Chamberlain's Bad Guy. Later in life, Chamberlain said he detested that characterization more than anything else.

Russell said he and Chamberlain laughed off the sensationalized build-ups to their games. Once, he said, Philadelphia owner Eddie Gottlieb took him aside, urging Russell to ignore the inflammatory remarks he was quoted as making that accused Russell of continuously committing goal-tending. Gottlieb told Russell that his newspaper diatribe was all about putting fannies in the seats. Meanwhile, Russell said, for about five years in a row when TV scheduled Boston and Philadelphia for Thanksgiving Day games in the City of Brotherly Love, Russell broke bread at holiday dinner with Chamberlain, Wilt's mother, and with Wilt's other relatives.

Still, there was always a sense of one-upmanship. Each coveted being seen as the best center. When Chamberlain commanded a $100,000 salary, Russell asked the Celtics to pay him $100,001. They did so. In his mind, Russell was at least a dollar better.

There was no doubt that Chamberlain was the superior scorer. His teams, the Philadelphia Warriors, the San Francisco Warriors, the Philadelphia 76ers (after they ceased being the Syracuse Nationals), and the Los Angeles Lakers, always needed more points from him than the Celtics needed from Russell.

Chamberlain was called by several nicknames, including "The Big Dipper," and "Wilt the Stilt" (which he hated), and had been in the basketball spotlight for years. He was recruited by at least one hundred colleges and chose Kansas to play under Phog Allen. In college, Chamberlain bristled at the amount of physical abuse he took on the court that he felt went uncalled. And he suffered racial verbal abuse at times, especially when the Jayhawks traveled to Texas.

Chamberlain spent a year playing with the Harlem Globetrotters instead of playing his senior year at Kansas and was paid about $40,000 as a rookie with Philadelphia, more than Cousy made in any single year of his career. Chamberlain was worth it to an NBA starved for publicity and that year he astounded fans with his numbers, averaging 37.6 points and 26 rebounds a game. Few realized that soon enough that statistical line would look like an off year.

Chamberlain made scoring look easy, but his life wasn't always easy off the court. In Lawrence, where Kansas University is located, he grew weary of integrating restaurants. It was a consciousness-raising experience though, and later Chamberlain marched with Dr. Martin Luther King Jr. Chamberlain also tired of being beaten up on the court because referees didn't protect him from the fouls of smaller men. That all contributed to his year-early departure from Kansas, an action that disappointed legendary coach Allen.

Under NBA rules at the time, however, Chamberlain could not join the league until his class graduated. Instead, he signed a sweet deal with the Harlem Globetrotters that paid him more than $50,000. Globetrotter owner Abe Saperstein had been after Wilt for several years. Even during his NBA career, Chamberlain joined the touring team for his off-seasons. Chamberlain enthralled Globetrotter audiences by sometimes playing point guard, dribbling the ball upcourt, and said his Globetrotter experience was the most fun he had playing basketball.

When Chamberlain came into the NBA in 1959, he discovered it still retained some elements of a backwater league.

"Conditions were terrible when I started out," Chamberlain said. "We played in dingy, poorly lit gyms. We had long, tiring road trips, and some of the hotels we stayed in weren't fit for dogs."

Before Chamberlain's debut, the NBA backboards belonged to Russell. Russell set single-game career marks for rebounding with totals of 49 and then 51. Chamberlain eclipsed those efforts with a still-standing record of 55 rebounds on November 24, 1960. Going into the 2006–07 season, the NBA official guide listed twenty-four performances where a player grabbed at least 40 rebounds. Nate Thurmond collected 42 rebounds in a game in 1965. Jerry Lucas collected 40 in a game in 1964. All the other top performances, decades after their retirement, belong to Chamberlain and Russell.

Similarly, entering the 2006–07 season, there had been ten NBA games when a player scored 70 points. Chamberlain accounted for six of them. It may be recalled that after his 71-point night, Elgin Baylor said it was entirely possible someone would some day score 100 points in a game.

That day arrived on March 2, 1962. The Philadelphia Warriors met the New York Knickerbockers in a game at the neutral site of Hershey, Pennsylvania. Almost no reporters traveled to cover the game. There is no film footage of the game. As the second game of a doubleheader that included the Harlem Globetrotters in the opener, the Warriors game did not even tip off until 9:30 P.M. eastern time. Chamberlain had spent part of the day playing cards with teammates and then pinball to kill time.

It was a game when Chamberlain's signature stuff, his finger-rolls and his fallaway jump shots, were unstoppable. Normally a horrible free-throw shooter, Chamberlain made 28 out of 32 attempts. He also hit 36 of 63 field goals. Chamberlain scored 41 points in the first half and added 28 points in the third quarter. As the clock ticked down, the Warriors realized Chamberlain had a chance to make history in the dingy, out-of-the-way gym. Teammates began feeding Chamberlain the ball every possession and he hit the 98-point mark with 1 minute, 19 seconds to play. Chamberlain missed two short shots, then forward Joe Ruklick fired a pass into the low post and Wilt jammed it through for his last two points of the night. There were 46 seconds left.

Only 4,124 fans paid admission (Lord knows in ensuing years how many people claimed to be present) in the chocolate capital of the universe, and it seemed as if they all abandoned their seats to flood the floor and celebrate Chamberlain's feat. Eventually, spectators were herded off the playing surface and the game concluded with Philadelphia victorious, 169–147.

When the game ended, famed Warriors publicist Harvey Pollack fashioned a homemade sign out of the only piece of paper he could find, scrawling "100" on it. Photographers snapped Chamberlain's picture holding the sign. The dearth of media coverage was unfortunate, but there were enough wide-eyed witnesses. Many Knicks were bitter at the way Philadelphia helped run up Chamberlain's total, especially when the Warriors fouled in the waning minutes to get the ball back. At the time, they may have felt scoring 100 could be an everyday occurrence for Wilt, and that he was making a mockery of their sport. But it was a once-in-a-lifetime night.

Point guard Guy Rodgers said, "There wasn't an easier way in the world to get assists tonight."

Humorously, there is a handwritten letter in the files of the library at the Naismith Basketball Hall of Fame in Springfield, Massachusetts, that alleges Chamberlain's 100-point game never happened, that it was all a hoax. The same letter-writer probably doesn't believe astronauts walked on the moon either.

The 1961–62 season was Chamberlain's greatest and the greatest ever compiled by an NBA player. He averaged a beyond-belief 50.4 points a game that season and played in all 80 games while sitting out only 8½ minutes of the season. A year later he averaged 44.8 points a game. Chamberlain was never shy about his prowess in any endeavor (witness his late-in-life claim that he bedded 20,000 women). He once talked of challenging for the heavyweight championship, was a professional volleyball player after retiring from basketball, and years into retirement said he could simply show up on the court on short notice and best the centers of the day.

By then, Chamberlain's résumé included two world titles from his fourteen-year career between 1959 and 1973, four Most Valuable Player awards (to Russell's five), seven scoring titles, and eleven rebounding titles. In a 1980 interview with the now-defunct magazine *Inside Sports*, Chamberlain said, "I'm forty-four now and I could come out of retirement right this minute and play guys like [Jack] Sikma, [Sam] Lacey, [Bill] Cartwright, and [Alvin] Adams in my sleep."

Johnny Kerr was not one of those guys. He kept Russell and Chamberlain wide awake with his own hustle between the 1954–55 season and his retirement after the 1965–66 season, averaging in double-figures in points and rebounds. Red Kerr was also 6-feet-9 and weighed 230 pounds, so he was not scared of them. He just wasn't as quick, so he knew he was always in for a tough night when the big men showed up.

"George Mikan invented the hook shot," Kerr once said, "and Bill Russell swatted it away. No man has ever blocked shots as well as Russell."

When Chamberlain said he could easily fit in with the NBA in his forties, it was taken as boastfulness. When Kerr said it about Chamberlain when The Big Dipper was in his fifties, fans blinked. Of course, Kerr added, at such an advanced age Chamberlain probably could only play fifteen minutes a game. Kerr said he thinks Chamberlain was at least 7-foot-2. Kerr also thinks Chamberlain could have been an even better player if he developed a hook shot for use in the lane and a mean streak. Kerr said Chamberlain was really too nice on the court, maybe too passive because everything came easily to him.

Kerr said against teams that were weak at center he knew he could score, but that when he played against Russell and Chamberlain, he couldn't count on a big night offensively and knew that he was going to get burned by Chamberlain defensively.

"Chamberlain had good scoring games against everybody," Kerr said. "And Russell was the best defensive player. He was absolutely something."

Not everyone around the league considered Chamberlain to be Mr. Nice Guy on the court. Although Chamberlain never fouled out of a game during his 1,045-game regular-season career or in his 160 playoff games, he knew how to use his body to move foes out of the paint. Sometimes they didn't like it. Chamberlain's matchups with Russell were as much chess games as basketball games. But sometimes Auerbach put Jim Loscutoff on Chamberlain to shake things up. Loscutoff was about seven inches shorter than Chamberlain and had to use his own strength to try to neutralize the big man. Occasionally, fireworks followed.

For a brief period during a 1962 playoff game, less than a month after Chamberlain's 100-point game, Loscutoff was covering Chamberlain and even outscored him 4–2. When asked how he did it, Loscutoff replied, "The idea is to give him that first shot instead of fouling him. But then block him off from getting the rebound if there is one."

A fight nearly broke out between Wilt and "Jungle Jim" during Loscutoff's second-quarter cameo.

"He pushed me and I pushed him back," Loscutoff said. "He beefed. 'Don't push me,' I told him, 'Then don't push me.' He's a prima donna out there. It's all right for him to push somebody else around, but you're not supposed to touch him."

Chamberlain did not exactly sound like a peacemaker.

"If Loscutoff wants a boxing match, he knows where he can get it," Chamberlain said. "I thought this was basketball. Well, I'm not going to take it next time."

The 6-foot-8 Gene Conley rarely got a chance to shine in limited minutes and when it was Russell against Chamberlain he could never count on seeing time in the pivot. But Russell was sidelined by an ankle injury for an October 1959 dust-up with Philadelphia and Conley started at center. He scored 24 points in 42 minutes, and when he fouled out Chamberlain strolled over to the Celtics' bench to shake his hand.

After years of winning championships, the phrase "Celtic Mystique" started to take hold. Oscar Robertson, like so many of the great stars of the day stymied by Boston's greatness, said the Celtic Mystique was not an aura, but attributable to one man—Bill Russell.

Heinsohn said Russell was "sensitive, but he played like a dock worker," particularly against Chamberlain. None of the seventeen top scoring games of Chamberlain's career came against Boston. Granted, his eighteenth-highest total of 62 points was recorded against the Celtics in the Boston Garden in 1962, but Russell always kept score by other means.

The Celtics beat the Warriors in the playoffs during Chamberlain's rookie year of 1959–60 and in the finals in 1964 after they moved to San Francisco. They beat the 76ers in 1965 after Chamberlain was traded back to the new team in Philadelphia, and in 1966 and 1968 as well, and they then knocked off the Lakers in 1969 after Chamberlain was traded west again.

"He was a supreme defensive player," Chamberlain said of Russell. "He was the best rebounder I played against. But I never had too many problems scoring against Russell. He simply couldn't cover me one-on-one. Russell had so much help it was unreal."

Chamberlain set a slew of records, but his sense of humor was working overtime when he was asked once how he wanted to be remembered by basketball fans.

"As the greatest free-throw shooter in the game's history," said Chamberlain, who was one of the worst.

Acerbic Boston sportswriter Clif Keane once said that Auerbach should have had fifty pictures on his Boston Garden office wall of Russell and kissed them every day because Russell "made" Auerbach's career. Auerbach has his own mountain-size ego and it was interesting to hear his reaction to the comment.

"In a way he did," Auerbach said. "What the hell. You got to be an idiot not to see that."

Chamberlain often said that if he played for the Celtics and Russell played for his teams, the head-to-head championship results would have been reversed. Bob Cousy doesn't buy that for a minute.

"Poor Wilt went to his grave saying, 'If I had been with the Celtics, we'd have won eleven out of thirteen championships,'" Cousy said. "It wouldn't have been close. We might have won once with Wilt, but our whole psyche was geared around the transition game. Wilt kind of played walk-the-ball-up-the-floor most of the time, with his team giving the ball to Wilt. As great an athlete as he was, he did not have the complementary skills close to what Russ did. Russ didn't need the ball every time he ran down the floor. Wilt's fadeaway shot was a rebuttal to Russ's defense. Every other center he would overpower and bring it to the basket. Russ was a student of the game. He beat him down court and didn't allow him to get into his favorite position, and then he'd push him out a little bit farther. In doing that he forced Wilt to take a dribble or two and being smaller and quicker, he stole it or knocked it away the minute Wilt put it on the floor.

"Wilt did develop that shot [the fadeaway] and he shot it very well. He had his moments of success against us, but never one that counted in my judgment. You've got the biggest, strongest man in the league and Russ forces him into taking a fallaway jump shot, which takes him out of any rebounding action. It was a great rivalry between the two."

It was. And a great friendship for a time. Russell and Chamberlain had a falling-out in 1969 at the end of Russell's last game when harsh words were said in the press. They didn't speak again for twenty-four years, but then, no doubt mellowing with time, they resumed a friendship in 1993 that lasted until Chamberlain's death from a heart attack in October 1999. The world was shocked that the big man passed away from an affliction that he kept quiet. Chamberlain's agent Sy Goldberg said Wilt had congestive heart failure, that his heart deteriorated for a month before he died, and that he lost between thirty and forty pounds during that period.

Bill Russell spoke at Wilt Chamberlain's memorial service in front of 800 people and admitted that the games they played, the little wars they shared, and the basketball accomplishments they recorded "bonded them for eternity."

So many years after retirement, there were no more Chamberlain-Russell basketball battles. There would be no more late-night telephone calls between Fenton and Norman either, and Bill Russell would mourn that.

16

CELTIC UNITY AMID AMERICAN DIVISIONS

The Boston Celtics became the NBA's most popular road attraction. They were the exemplars of the league and fans turned out in big numbers to see the world champions when they came to their town. But it was always a struggle to consistently fill the Boston Garden. Walter Brown dreamed up as many promotions as P. T. Barnum. Sometimes Ping-Pong players entertained at halftime with stunning smashes requiring the contestants to race around much of the basketball court.

Some ideas worked better than others. February 11, 1962, was Dollar Day, and still the Celtics drew only 9,024 fans for the bargain matinee to watch Tommy Heinsohn score 42 points in a 148–115 victory over the expansion Chicago Packers.

Big crowds or small crowds, the foundation of the championships was winning at home during the regular season. Some foes became phobic about playing in the Garden. Red Auerbach worked overtime to psych out visitors, and he was smart enough to do it. But the opponents helped too, constructing their own paranoia in coming to believe that Auerbach was the building manager as well as the coach. Opposing players carped about their tiny locker room, the temperature in the locker room, the temperature of the water in the showers, and the occasional rat they saw running under the stands. They made it sound as if they thought Auerbach had a trained rodent on the payroll.

Lakers coach Fred Schaus complained of finding the windows stuck in an open position during halftime of winter games so his players would freeze, of course overlooking that Auerbach was busy running a team in his own locker room. Philadelphia coach Alex Hannum once suggested that Auerbach had instructed the Celtics ball boys to give the 76ers only half-inflated balls for warm ups.

Visiting players discovered a towel shortage after games, leaving them the choice of drying off with toilet paper or putting their clothes on over damp bodies. Ultimately, announcer Johnny Most revealed that many of these locker room quirks were true, but arranged by equipment manager Walter Randall, not Auerbach. Auerbach could deny complicity with complete honesty.

Kenny Sailors remembers the Garden as "a palace," one of the nicest arenas around. Years into retirement, Bill Russell referred to the Garden as "a dump." Compared to modern-day arenas with their soft seats and better sight lines (with way fewer pillars), and locker rooms the size of townhouses, the Garden didn't stack up. Sometimes the late-season playoff games caught a late-spring hot spell and doors were opened to the outside.

"I vaguely remember playing the Lakers when there was no air-conditioning," Tommy Heinsohn said. "The idea of air-conditioning in the Boston Garden was that the ushers had fans. The Garden was not built for basketball. I mean half, or a third of the people, didn't see the whole court. The Bruins management got the best dates and they got the best locker room. Our locker room, you wouldn't believe how small it was. I'm sitting in a room right now, in my den, and it's as big as that locker room."

Celtics players of the era just chuckled at visitors' grumbling. They laughed harder when Auerbach wove stories about why the Garden gave the Celtics such a home-court advantage, like the one about the Celtics knowing where all the cracks and uneven places were on the parquet floor to avoid dribbling on them. In reality, the Celtics suffered their share of bad bounces and took their share of cold showers at the Garden.

Boston winning the NBA title every year, Boston winning the vast majority of games at home, and the fantasy image of Auerbach sticking pins into Syracuse Nationals or Philadelphia 76ers voodoo dolls all contributed to opposing teams hating to play the Celtics, hating the Celtics, hating Boston Garden, and wanting to punch out any leprechaun they ran across.

"They did hate us," John Havlicek said. "Some of my best friends were on other teams. Jack Marin [of the Baltimore Bullets], he used to hate playing us."

And it wasn't very much fun for Dolph Schayes either. Schayes was in his prime as a player when the Celtics began dominating the league. Then he coached the 76ers and couldn't beat the Celts in the playoffs over three years.

"One of the reasons I got fired was that we never could beat the Celtics," Schayes said. "We'd get to the Eastern Division finals and lose. At that time I wouldn't even speak to members of the Celtics if we were in the same place."

If you were a longtime opponent on a pretty good team, frustration mounted. You may have hated the Celtics because they were always in the way of where you wanted to go, but you had to admire them, too, because you knew how tough it was to win year after year.

"It was a credit to Red," Jack Twyman said. "He took advantage of all of their strengths and minimized their weaknesses. They had that big eraser Russell. The Celtics were unique in that they could gamble on defense. We [the Royals] were a normal team and couldn't overplay and gamble. Russell was always there to cover up for them, so they played a gambling, aggressive defense that other teams couldn't afford to play because they didn't have a Russell."

As a group, the Celtics were the biggest celebrities in the sport, but salaries of between $8,000 and $35,000 were the standard throughout the NBA, with the exception of superstars like Russell and Chamberlain. Tangible reward was limited, endorsements a rarity. K. C. Jones guffawed at the notion that he would have been hired to hype a product in the stone age of marketing.

"That wasn't that big at that time," K. C. said. "This was the time of black and white TV. We just floated through that right into Technicolor."

Ironically, one of the lesser-known Celtics may have reaped the largest dividends from product endorsement, albeit aided by Bill Russell.

Ronnie Watts was a 6-foot-6 backup forward, stuck so far down the bench that Red Auerbach needed a microphone to call him. Watts came out of Wake Forest to play the 1965–66 and 1966–67 seasons for Boston before heading off to Seattle in the expansion draft. He played one game his first year and appeared in twenty-seven his second year. His lifetime points per game with Boston is 1.4.

By acting in a catchy telephone company commercial with Russell, however, Watts raised his national profile 1,000 percent. The likening of a team to being a family has been an overworked sports concept in the twenty-first century, but some teams through the years exemplify that circumstance more than others. Red Auerbach used to say "once a Celtic, always a Celtic" and some players think he occasionally kept a guy around an additional year, even though he didn't play much, out of loyalty.

When Russell joined the Celtics a couple of months into the 1956–57 season, they already had a center. This is an obvious fact, but often overlooked. The incumbent was Arnie Risen, a 6-foot-9, 230-pounder out of Ohio State in the second of his three seasons with the Celtics. With all the hoopla over the drafting of Russell and the view of him as an instant savior, Risen knew his days were numbered as the starter. Indeed, he did become a backup—a valuable one averaging 8 points per game that season. Rather than sulking at what was lost, Risen played a role in what was gained by showing Russell the nuances of playing the pivot in the NBA, revealing tricks of the trade. Russell always praised Risen's generosity.

When Havlicek came out of college (also Ohio State) as the team's No. 1 draft pick in 1962, he arrived with a mental picture of the NBA as a dog-eat-dog world, where veterans anxious about their jobs froze out rookies. He exiled that image to the garbage can when he met Frank Ramsey. By then, Ramsey was an eight-year veteran, a hub of the Celtics' offense. Rather than worry about being shut out of the lineup by a talented newcomer, Ramsey embraced Havlicek.

"Frank Ramsey said, 'I'm really glad you're here,'" Havlicek recalled. "'You're going to add two years to my career.' I was stunned. But that was the way of Celtics thinking at the time. It was a winning attitude. That was all they were concerned about."

Another way coach Red Auerbach thought ahead of general wisdom was his emphasis on off-season conditioning. Not many players adopted summer workout programs remotely as challenging as those commonly employed by almost all professional athletes today. Auerbach required players to show up in shape for his training camps. The idea was to be ahead of teams starting the season and pile up some early wins while foes worked themselves into condition.

"To Red," Havlicek said, "the first game was as important as the last."

Bob Cousy said the four- to five-month break between the end of the championship rounds of the playoffs and the start of training camp was refreshing. It allowed the players to renew their energy and to stoke their hunger for another title run.

"We could come back, and God," he said, "the saliva would be dripping out of the corners of our mouths and we'd be saying, 'Kill! Kill!'"

Cousy developed a different type of relationship with Auerbach than most other players. Maybe because he was older. Maybe because he had been on the team the longest. But they also spent parts of their summer together.

Dorothy Auerbach, Red's wife, was about the only one beyond his childhood who called him Arnold. Cousy spent time with the couple and picked up the habit from her and while the rest of the world, whether they knew him or not, referred to Auerbach as Red, Cousy called Auerbach Arnold for the rest of his life.

For a period of about four years, Auerbach and Cousy traveled overseas and put on basketball clinics under the auspices of the U.S. Information Service and the State Department. They roomed together for six weeks at a time sometimes, and Cousy's use of the name Arnold just seemed more natural to him.

"So our relationship was just on another level," Cousy said.

Cousy said he used to tease Dorothy Auerbach about her unusual marriage, noting that Auerbach stayed in Boston for up to eight months of the year while she lived in Washington, D.C., and Cousy partnered with Auerbach overseas for about six weeks.

"So that leaves you with about six weeks or so with this guy," Cousy said to her. "'Do you think the marriage can survive? Can you put up with him that long?' And we'd all laugh about it, but there was a lot of truth to it because Arnold was a loner."

For Tommy Heinsohn, a fun-loving guy who also smoked cigarettes, training camp was the least enjoyable part of the season. He half-figured if he was going to run all of the time he might as well train for the Boston Marathon. As a rookie, Heinsohn said he tried to make an impression, dropping from 235 pounds at the end of his Holy Cross season to 216 pounds by training camp. It didn't help. He said on his third day of Auerbach's workouts, he could hardly stand because his body ached all over.

When he went to practice that day, Heinsohn realized everyone was in the same, sorry, hurting condition. Some fared much worse over the years. Forward Willie Naulls, the onetime UCLA star, was a veteran when he came over to the Celtics in 1963, fresh off a season split between the Warriors and Knicks averaging 12.9 points a game. In the afternoon session of Naulls's first Celtics two-a-days, first he threw up, then he passed out doing sit-ups. How much sympathy was there for Naulls? Did a trainer rush out to treat him? Was he sent to the hospital for observation? Auerbach had other players drag Naulls to the sidelines and resume practice.

Heinsohn's propensity to keep busy in the off-season with matters other than conditioning did not curry favor with Auerbach, who had ascertained early on that Heinsohn had a resilient personality. Auerbach was careful whom he chose as whipping boys and during the 1950s–1960s glory years he zeroed in on Jim Loscutoff and Heinsohn. It was nothing personal. Auerbach needed team foils to make examples of when something was amiss on the court and certain other players would not hold up well under his berating. Heinsohn understood the psychology of it all and shrugged off comments.

"He [Red] wasn't going to yell at Russell," Heinsohn said. "He wasn't going to yell at Cousy. If he yelled at Ramsey he would lose confidence and he never demeaned the black players. It ended up that I was the only starter left. Plus Loscutoff. But he didn't play as often."

The Celtics Dynasty began at the height of the country's dull 1950s complacency and carried through a period of youth rebellion nationwide. Elvis Presley topped the music bestsellers in the fifties, but the long-haired Beatles soon took command of the pop charts. Key Celtics were a little bit on the old side to gravitate to this new hip music—not that they disliked the Beatles, but their tastes were ingrained. Russell was a jazz aficionado. Cousy preferred jazz too. K. C. Jones liked ballads best, where the tunes were softer and the words told a story.

Somewhere along the line, blues-fan K. C., who enjoyed quartets doing their thing, developed a passion for Frank Sinatra songs. He loves the song "Georgia On My Mind." Jones likes all kinds of music. He called the Beatles "awesome", so he didn't exactly overlook the sixties, and he had a pleasing visit to the Rock and Roll Hall of Fame in Cleveland.

"I love the blues and I love rock and roll," Jones said, "and I don't know how I got into Sinatra. It's wild that it happened."

Even wilder, in 2007 as a once-a-week gig, K. C. fronted a small band at a restaurant-club in Connecticut, having fun covering Sinatra songs. Clearly, it wasn't just an infatuation.

Whether it was a by-product, or a revolutionary characteristic of the times, young people growing up in the sixties embraced rambunctious lyrics and harder rock, calling their parents' music "square" and too laid back. The 1960s were not tame in the United States. It was a time of social chaos, of examining all accepted precepts. The South seethed as blacks fought for their rights. The sexual revolution exploded with concepts of free love. Men's hairstyles might resemble cavemen's bird's nests, or long, flowing, down-the-back styles that conservatives derided for making guys look like girls. Political assassinations wounded hope for change. And there was a war going on half a world away in Vietnam that taught young people not to trust their own government anymore.

But one event from that time period gripped the nation like no other. Friday, November 22, 1963, was the beginning of one of the grimmest weekends in American history.

At approximately 12:30 P.M., Central Standard Time, while riding in an open-roofed limousine in a motorcade through Dallas, Texas, President

John F. Kennedy was assassinated. Three shots were fired from a sixth-floor window as the vehicles passed the Texas Book Depository.

The pink suit worn by distraught First Lady Jacqueline Kennedy was splattered with her husband's blood and brain matter. Through a tortuously long day in the motorcade, at Parkland Memorial Hospital, and accompanying the casket containing JFK's remains back to Washington, D.C., Mrs. Kennedy refused to change her clothes. She said she wanted the world to see what it had done to her husband.

Swiftly, a lone gunman, Lee Harvey Oswald, who had once lived in the Soviet Union and was a certified U.S. Army marksman, was apprehended and charged with the murder of the president through use of a high-powered rifle.

Vice President Lyndon Baines Johnson, after being safely rushed to Air Force One which was parked at a nearby airport in Dallas, was sworn in as the new president. As the frenzied news focus shifted back and forth from Texas to Washington, Americans were riveted to their television sets. The nation broke down in tears and was temporarily paralyzed for a long, numbing weekend. Two days after Kennedy was killed, Dallas strip-club owner Jack Ruby snuck into the basement of police headquarters and ambushed Oswald while he was in the company of law enforcement officials, shooting him in the stomach with a handgun. Jack Ruby was immediately taken into custody.

Almost immediately after Kennedy's assassination on Friday, November 22, the United States shut down. School children were sent home at mid-day. Businesses were shuttered. Networks broadcast nonstop news updates.

Amid this chaos leaders in the sports world had some tough calls to make. Three horse-racing tracks—Aqueduct in New York, Pimlico in Maryland, and Narragansett in Rhode Island—were among the first sporting-related entities to close down action.

In a decision that haunted him the rest of his life, National Football League commissioner Pete Rozelle decreed that his league would play its regularly scheduled games on Sunday. Rozelle's choice was not made with half-hearted thought. He somehow reached his old friend Pierre Salinger, JFK's press secretary, and Salinger said Kennedy would have wanted the games to be played. While the rival American Football League did cancel its games, the NFL played on and Rozelle issued a statement explaining why.

"It has been traditional in sports for athletes to perform in times of great personal tragedy," Rozelle said. "Football was Mr. Kennedy's game. He thrived on competition."

Going ahead with the business-as-usual schedule was denounced in most quarters and is seen as the biggest mistake Rozelle ever made in what was otherwise a greatly admired administrative career. Rozelle did order the cessation of halftime entertainment and no games were televised. A moment of silence was observed at the stadiums. The Dallas Cowboys were viciously booed throughout their game against the Cleveland Browns in Ohio.

Rozelle attended the New York Giants–St. Louis Cardinals game and said, "I brooded about my decision the entire game. If I'd had a chance I would probably have done it differently. The league took a lot of flak for that and it was a low period."

On the day of Kennedy's assassination, the National Hockey League had no games scheduled. There was one game played on Saturday in which the Toronto Maple Leafs defeated the Boston Bruins 4–1.

The NBA acted more aggressively. The league's first commissioner, Maurice Podoloff, had retired and new commissioner Walter Kennedy was just beginning his tenure in November 1963. The league had four games scheduled on the night Kennedy was murdered and cancelled them all. Four others were scheduled for the day after. Two were cancelled and two were played, because the visiting teams were already present. The New York Knickerbockers beat the Detroit Pistons 108–99, and the St. Louis Hawks beat the Cincinnati Royals 133–121.

No players quibbled with the decision to call off games, and players who played did not have their hearts in it. Wayne Embry, who joined the Celtics late in their Dynasty stretch, was then the Royals center and does not remember the game fondly.

"People criticized the fact that we played that game at all," Embry said. "We played the very next night after the assassination and there were those critical of us doing so. The reason why we did so was because the mayors in both cities [Cincinnati and Detroit] thought it would keep people off the streets."

Still, the NBA absorbed much less heat than the NFL. Playing basketball against the backdrop of this national tragedy produced limited rage and passed quickly. The black mark on the NFL stuck, but today virtually no fan can recall just what the NBA did during that demoralizing weekend. In a long season, with the swift resumption of games and the nation's attention turned to renewal in Washington, the NBA was quickly forgotten. The Celtics rolled on.

Some point to the assassination of John Fitzgerald Kennedy as the true start of the sixties, the beginning of a decade of American upheaval. The Vietnam War had been percolating beneath the consciousness of all but Southeast Asia scholars and foreign policy experts since the United States quasi-covertly ratcheted up its involvement following the abdication of the French at Dien Bien Phu in 1954.

During the height of the Cold War with the Soviet Union, President Dwight D. Eisenhower articulated U.S. policy for Vietnam. He subscribed to the Domino Theory, that if one country in the region fell under the sway of Communism, then other small neighboring countries would fall too. That was the prevailing belief, even after Eisenhower retired to play golf and Democratic successors planted their party flag in the White House.

It took several years of military expansion and frustration for Americans to grasp the scope of the hopelessness of the war, begin protests in the streets by the hundreds of thousands, and demand that U.S. troops be withdrawn. The debate rent the country.

Only two days after ascending to the presidency, President Johnson quietly met with top advisors and pledged not to lose Vietnam. In August 1964, Johnson took advantage of a report of U.S. destroyers being attacked in the Tonkin Gulf. LBJ rammed his Tonkin Gulf Resolution through Congress to gain legitimacy to fight a war and protect American interests without outright declaring a war. He committed forty-four divisions of U.S. soldiers to Vietnam in March of 1965. In 1968, on the eve of Tet, the Asian lunar New Year, the North Vietnamese launched a shocking military offensive and LBJ began troop buildups that deepened U.S. involvement in the morass.

Between 1965 and 1973, when the United States essentially gave up on Vietnam and turned the main thrust of war operations over to the South Vietnamese, Americans spent $120 billon, suffered with 58,000 troops killed or missing in action, and were complicit in the deaths of 4 million Vietnamese.

Unless you were living in an underground bunker for the sixties, it was impossible to avoid the war beamed into the living room and blazoned across the front page of newspapers. The Celtics were American citizens. Many had served in the military. But mostly they kept their thoughts on the conduct of the war to themselves.

Focused, motivated as always, the Celtics were a smooth-functioning unit more concerned with doing their jobs well than becoming political lightning rods. Just as they did with all other potential distractions, they blocked out the nation's most controversial issue while playing and winning. One exception was Bill Russell. Influenced by the strong stance of Boston's Cardinal Francis Spellman, Russell was opposed to the Vietnam War by 1963. Unlike Spellman, Russell was suspicious of Catholicism imposed on an Asian country and came to believe the war was motivated by racism.

In 1966, however, while conversing with a black officer who had been in Vietnam, Russell questioned some of his beliefs, wondering if an invasion of Chinese Communists would really take place and subjugate the natives if the U.S. pulled out. These were the ruminations of a thoughtful man and the tenets of the debate in U.S. society.

If American blacks were searching for things that would guide them in forming opinions about the war, they could point to two things to buttress antiwar sentiment. First, a disproportionate number of blacks to whites were fighting overseas. And Dr. Martin Luther King Jr., the foremost figure in the Civil Rights movement, weighed in and began denouncing the war.

King agonized about the rightness and wrongness of the war, and whether he should enter the fray when there was much still to be accomplished in the area of civil rights. On April 4, 1967, speaking at the Riverside Church in New York, he let his fury out.

"This business of burning human beings with napalm," King said, "of filling our nation's homes with orphans and widows, of injecting poisonous drugs into the veins of people normally humane, of sending men home from dark and bloody battlefields physically handicapped and mentally deranged, cannot be reconciled with wisdom, justice, and love."

Later in life, speaking out about the ills of the soul that create men who cheat without conscience and adopt a win-at-all costs attitude, Bob Cousy lumped the country's emphasis on success with the sensibilities of the officials who made the Vietnam War happen. He sarcastically described those government officials as "brilliant men."

Admitting that he had grown up with a killer instinct and played basketball with that outlook, Cousy said he could see where the same such hardcore win-at-all-costs attitude "had led the people who brought us Vietnam."

Wayne Embry, whose wife demonstrated for racial justice in the South, questioned the righteousness of the war during his playing career. He said he came to understand the necessity for World War II, but even upon close examination, "I still was not sure why we were sending our best and brightest to the battlefields of Vietnam."

If his 6-foot-8 height had not disqualified him from being drafted, Embry wondered if he would have been fighting in Vietnam. Instead, as he said, he was playing the comparatively insignificant game of basketball stateside, and attending the funerals of old friends returned from the distant war to their families in body bags.

17

COUSY RIDES INTO THE SUNSET

At the peak of the farewell ceremony that made Bob Cousy cry and lean his head on Red Auerbach's shoulder, there was temporary silence amid the 13,909 fans crammed into the Boston Garden on March 17, 1963. Suddenly, from the balcony, came a bellowing voice that summed up the moment, as well as the thirteen years Cousy had played guard for the Boston Celtics.

"We love ya, Cooz!" the man's voice shouted.

And they did. In the long history of Boston sports, from baseball to football, from hockey to basketball, Cousy might be the most popular athlete of them all. A pioneer at the position of point guard, team leader of the many-time world champions, and the NBA's first greatly admired star, yes Cousy was beloved. And as he choked up repeatedly on his day during the final season of his pro career, he loved everyone back.

The anonymous voice projecting such deep sentiment was discovered to belong to a man named Joe Dillon, then thirty-two, from South Boston, who worked for the Metropolitan District Commission water department.

Dillon managed to find the right words at the right time on the day of Cousy's last home regular-season game, when many eloquent, planned speeches groped for the same effect. The moment was unforgettable for those present who heard Dillon and the shout has gone down in Celtics lore commemorating Cousy's retirement better than other praise showered on him, or the gifts of a sterling silver cigarette case, a cigar humidor, congratulations from President John F. Kennedy, a sterling silver service set, a set of china, and paintings of his wife and daughters. Sought out later, Dillon was asked why he did it.

"I didn't even think about it," he said. "I just thought it was a good thing to say."

Cousy, the first cornerstone among Auerbach's building blocks, was just shy of thirty-five during the 1962–63 season, but he felt as if he had been around since the invention of the game. The Celtics were at the height of their glory, and Cousy had been present from the inception of Auerbach's vision. Boston had won five world titles and the team was on its way to a sixth. Enough time, enough effort, even enough winning, Cousy thought.

Cousy was still healthy. If there was slippage in his game it was so slight that few noticed. He could have played longer, gone on for another few years, and nobody was pushing him to retire. Cousy had actually thought about retirement the year before. Boston College's head basketball coaching job opened up, and it was offered to Cousy. He liked the idea, thought that was the right direction to take his career, but he wasn't ready. In a gesture of phenomenal respect that would be unheard of today, BC chose to play the 1962–63 season with an interim coach and keep the job open for Cousy for 1963–64. He was committed to the Eagles after the Celtics.

Cousy suffered from mental burnout far more than physical burnout. He was making a career-high salary of $35,000 and wondered about his future. Change, security, a new job, and the promise of a new long-term career motivated his retirement.

At the end of his career, Cousy was sick of road trips, he despised hotels, and he resented the time spent away from his wife and two daughters. He had poured so much of himself into the sport and his team that he was just plain tired. In the previous season's playoffs, Cousy hit a rough patch, committing 17 fouls in three games, and fouling out twice against the Lakers. That made him think he was slowing down. But he did not want to go out on what he considered a personally bad note, so he came back for one last ride.

Friendly with his teammates while traveling and in the locker room, Cousy became a self-described hermit in his final seasons, simply wanting to lock down in the hotel rooms he hated, waiting for the games to start. His last three seasons, Cousy said, he took most of his meals through room service and often turned down invitations to go out for dinner with Tommy Heinsohn.

"After you've hit the same cities over and over for thirteen years, the thrill is gone," Cousy said.

By announcing his retirement early, Cousy gave other teams not only a last chance to beat him on the court but also to honor his contributions to the game. On the Celtics' last road trips to each city that season, Cousy said he grew embarrassed from all the attention and affection shown him.

However, the feel-good stuff did not outweigh the aspects of the NBA that were aging him. Cousy said he was sick of being spit on by fans in Syracuse, Cincinnati, and St. Louis, felt an increasing urge to punch out hecklers, carried such pregame tension within that he constantly ran to the bathroom in the locker room and wondered what type of person he was becoming when he had to work up a hatred for individual foes like guards Frank Selvy and Dick Barnett.

A competitive hatred, Cousy called it. Not deep-seated hatred men might carry into war when their nations are enemies, but more like a boxer's hatred, where a man knows his job is to pummel another fighter whom he might very well hug the moment the event ends.

Near the end of his career, Cousy developed a tic in one eye from stress, said he was having nightmares—in French, the language of his youth—and more than once sleepwalked right out the door of his house, once running into a tree. Despite all those reasons, years later when Cousy reflected on the question of leaving basketball too soon rather than too late, he said he would have stuck around, maybe even for four more years, if NBA players got paid the millions of dollars they do now.

"Three or four years ago, the highest player in the league was Michael Jordan," Cousy said in 2006. "He was paid $36 million for one season. It's quite an escalation. I never would have got $36 million, but if I was paid a couple of hundred thousand, I'd have played longer. If I had been getting paid what Michael Jordan got paid, I'd have played till they carried me off.

"Given the money players have today, they get financial security after three or four years. I think it's a fair statement to say that they will fight every bit as hard as we did to get to the top of the hill, but in my judgment they will fight nowhere near as hard to stay on top of the hill."

Cousy averaged 18.5 points a game in his 917 regular-season NBA games, ranked third on the league's all-time scoring list at the time, played in thirteen All-Star games, and retired with a record 6,945 assists. But it was his sense of showmanship that dazzled, and by dribbling behind his back and throwing behind-the-back passes he demonstrated what the game could be, even in the context of playing "serious" basketball. He was the king of the fast break, leading the sprint downcourt ahead of defenders, pushing the pace and demoralizing foes.

When he watched Cousy play for Holy Cross, Auerbach figured he would be a cocky guy off the court and was surprised to find he wasn't. The more Auerbach watched Cousy make his fancy moves, he realized that they were not forced, but the result of impressive reading of the court.

"He didn't throw fancy passes just to throw fancy passes," Auerbach said. "He threw them because that was the best way to get the ball where it needed to go."

Most of John Havlicek's college experience was as a forward. But Auerbach used Havlicek as a swingman at first, and he had to work hard on his guard role. He said he was not a great ball handler and initially didn't have the confidence and know-how when asked to run the Celtics offense. Havlicek loved playing with Cousy in the backcourt and absorbing the lessons provided.

"They used to say that he hit rookies in the head with passes, but I was too fundamentally sound for that to happen to me," Havlicek said. ". . . there was nobody who could get the ball to you better than Cousy."

It was a tough ticket for Bob Cousy Day festivities. The Garden was sold out in advance. Celtics publicist Bill Mokray said the day's special program was expected to sell 6,500 copies, but 5,000 more were printed. Cousy, Mokray said, thought ahead, much as he did on the court, and expected he would be very emotional and did not want to ad lib, so he wrote out a speech planned to last seven minutes. Between Cousy's tears and crowd applause, it took twenty minutes to deliver. Later, Boston newspapers that were not around to cover the Boston Tea Party, labeled this the BOSTON TEAR PARTY.

Walter Brown, whose own days were numbered, made a self-deprecating joke: "I'm the guy who didn't want Bob Cousy. What a genius!"

Cousy's mother, Juliette, whom the son once said was "more French than Joan of Arc," recalled that when he was a little boy, about six, he grabbed his uncle's top hat and cane and announced, "Mama, I will be a big man some day."

He certainly was on this day.

Cousy began his speech by apologizing to the fans for using notes at all lest they think he was not sincere. He thanked sports editors and writers, the teams he played against, his wife, daughters, mother, father, teammates and Auerbach, the people who worked with him at his summer basket-ball camp, NBA officials, Walter Brown, "the fans of New England," Boston mayor John F. Collins—who had proclaimed it "Bob Cousy Week" in the city—and Massachusetts governor Endicott "Chub" Peabody. The address was too long to be an Academy Awards thank you. The network would have jumped to a commercial before Cousy finished.

"I just couldn't imagine playing anywhere but Boston," he said. "Everything I have materially, I owe to this fine organization and I always will be ready in the future to assist in its progress in any way."

By unofficial count, Cousy paused thirty times to cry. Cousy sometimes buried his head in a towel that he draped around his neck. At one point, daughter Marie Colette, twelve, walked onto the court and handed him a handkerchief. When Cousy finished speaking, fans rose and gave him a thunderous standing ovation lasting about 3½ minutes.

Cousy did not play much in the 125–116 win over the Syracuse Nationals, and afterward Auerbach teased him.

"Okay, Cousy," the coach deadpanned, "turn in your uniform."

Not quite yet. Cousy was a key figure in the playoffs once more. The tension within him only increased as the Celtics took a three-games-to-two lead in the NBA finals over the Los Angeles Lakers. The sixth game was played in Los Angeles on April 24.

The Celtics arrived early for the game and Cousy retreated to self-imposed, thirty-six-hour hotel-room jail. He walled off everything and everybody, using the time to think, to visualize the game, and devise his own game plan for matching up with Los Angeles guard Frank Selvy.

In the first quarter, Cousy took a long one-handed shot and knew it was in as the ball rolled off his fingers. His body and mind felt right. He was ready to go. So desperate to win the first title for L.A., the Lakers got off to a good start too, leading by 5 points. But the Celtics came back and took over, leading 66–52 at the half. Cousy said the Celts could smell the championship.

These were the Lakers of Elgin Baylor and Jerry West, however, and not a team that would wilt. Los Angeles fought back.

In the fourth quarter of his last game, Cousy was backpedaling on defense and responded to a sharp cut by L.A. guard Dick Barnett. Cousy twisted his left ankle violently and crashed to the hardwood. He agonized in intense pain.

Trainer Buddy LeRoux rushed out to attend to him, but Cousy had to be helped from the floor and half-carried as he leaned on LeRoux and Jim Loscutoff.

At the end of the bench, LeRoux iced Cousy's foot and then bandaged it tightly to hold the ankle in place. Sprained ankle was the preliminary diagnosis. On the court, the Lakers were mounting a run. Cousy was alarmed when he saw the scoreboard: Boston 100, Los Angeles 99. He walked upcourt and paused in front of Auerbach, who asked how he was.

"I think I can go," Cousy said.

Auerbach put him back in the game. Cousy had been sidelined for more than six minutes and limped when he returned for the last 4:43 of the 12-minute quarter. With 10 seconds to go, the Celtics led 112–107 and had the ball. Sam Jones passed to Cousy and he spontaneously heaved the ball toward the rafters, the clock running out while the ball descended from heaven.

Forgetting the injury, ignoring the pain, Cousy jumped up and down. One more championship. One last championship. Bill Russell retrieved the ball Cousy had carelessly discarded and handed it to the playmaker as a souvenir of his career. The last ball from the last game.

A sportswriter aware of Cousy's sob fest at the Boston Garden on his day asked if Cousy felt like crying again. Russell interrupted, saying, "I'd cry for you, but I'm too big and ugly to cry."

There was no champagne in the locker room, the staple of professional sports celebrations. Instead, it was awaiting the Celtics on their flight home. Cousy said he was unbelievably thirsty and desperate for a beer. He never found one.

"We didn't do too bad for a bunch of old men," Auerbach told reporters.

Back in Boston, the glow of the championship game still sustaining him, Cousy underwent fresh exams on his ankle. Torn ligaments, the doctors ruled. Cousy would not have been able to play a seventh game without tremendous pain, if at all. But the happy ending was already written. Bob Cousy limped off over the horizon.

18

HE SHOOTS, HE JOKES

He looks so young, so youthful in photographs of the time, fresh out of Holy Cross with a crew cut that in conjunction with his smile sometimes gave Tommy Heinsohn a he-knows-something-you-don't look. He was tall at 6-feet-7 and a slender 216 pounds. He had the body of a forward, but the skills of a guard.

Red Auerbach did not count on Heinsohn's rebounding so much as his scoring. On a team where everyone talked of Bob Cousy and Bill Russell as the leaders, Heinsohn was the third banana. Yet he often scored more than either of them (averaging 19.8 points a game for his career), made All-Star teams almost as often (six times), and was inducted into the Hall of Fame too. And in his nine seasons, the Boston Celtics won eight world championships.

Gene Conley roomed with Heinsohn for a year. One morning they were eating breakfast and reading Pulitzer Prize–winner Jim Murray's sports column in the newspaper discussing the previous evening's game against the Los Angeles Lakers. "Murray wrote about how Bob Cousy fooled everyone with his dribbling and how Bill Russell blocked shots and how great Bill Sharman's jumper was," Conley said.

And then they reached a point where Murray mentioned, oh by the way, Tommy Heinsohn scored 42 points and collected 15 rebounds. Heinsohn, said Conley, exclaimed, "'And finally. Hey, jeez.'"

When he departed from the Celtics, Heinsohn was just shy of his thirty-first birthday, young for retirement by any sport's standard, and it seemed he should have had many more years in a body that he admittedly did abuse with cigarettes. Red Auerbach harangued him about giving up smoking, but when Heinsohn did so temporarily he gained weight, which slowed him down. He was no workout maven either, at best grudgingly doing the push-ups and running Auerbach demanded.

Heinsohn has been asked repeatedly over the years why he retired so young, and he has always provided the same answer. His knees were going, he could barely jump, and within three years after retirement he could barely walk around a golf course. The hardwood of NBA courts is not user-friendly to the long-term health of basketball players' legs.

When 6-foot-10 George Mikan joined the Minneapolis Lakers in 1947, he introduced the hook shot as an offensive weapon that no defender could stop. The bespectacled Mikan towered over most players in the league and he was more talented than others of his height. He flipped his mini-hook shots over their heads from short distances. The hook shot became the big man's favorite in-close shot.

It was less common for perimeter players to employ the hook shot because they were stationed farther from the basket. It took audacity to toss up a hook from 15 feet or more. But Heinsohn was proficient at it. He was not a post player, but he was skilled at the postman's shot. There are old Celtics fans who will swear they saw Heinsohn throw up a hook shot from the corner, more than 20 feet from the basket, and saw it drop in. One habit that faked out defenders was shooting the hook from the baseline where the angle didn't allow for use of the backboard to bank it in. "Nobody was allowed to take them from 15 feet or 18 feet like I used to," Heinsohn said.

Sam Jones, who had the perfect jump shot form that coaches teach, said Heinsohn's hooks seemed odd, but worked.

"It looked silly, but what's silly when it goes in?" Jones said.

Red Auerbach would have had a conniption if Heinsohn heaved up hooks that were wild, but Heinsohn kept Auerbach's tendency to blow up under wraps because he made shots no one thought he should take. And they were more of a last resort than a first idea. The 24-second shot clock might be ticking down with teammates covered and Heinsohn holding the ball. So he did what he thought was best. "Those were bail-out shots," Heinsohn said with a little chuckle. "I had a reputation of being a gunner."

Heinsohn was as much a gunslinger as Billy The Kid. He was nicknamed Tommy Gun because he had the mentality and confidence of the no-conscience shooter. At other times, teammates called Heinsohn "Ack-Ack" for the sound of a machine gun being fired. No-conscience scorers know their best spots, know what they can do, and if someone is in the way, too bad. If the shot misses, boy, that's a shame, but he'll make it next time. You can't be a gunner and dwell on missed shots. If you are two for ten you know the next try is going down. If you start shaking your head, if your self-assuredness slips, you're doomed. If it happens too often, you're on the bench, or on a one-way trip to the waiver wire. Heinsohn's jumper did not conform to the picturesque image of the long-range shot. He shot a line drive.

"I had a tweener game," Heinsohn said. "Somewhat outside. I had the repertoire to shoot from the lane. My role was to be one of the scorers. I wasn't like Bill Sharman or Sam Jones, a great shooter per se. But I could get shots off. They were jump shooters who shot behind a pick. I could get a certain shot off in traffic. And I could play one on one and break the defender down, so when the offense bogged down, and we were going to lose the 24 seconds, then I shot."

No one ever accused Heinsohn of being too shy to shoot. One sportswriter of the time said, "Heinie lived for his next shot." Another wrote, "Tommy never found a spot he couldn't shoot from." Maybe Heinsohn really did know the undulations of the parquet floor. Jim Loscutoff said that once he and 1950s teammate Dick Hemric watched Heinsohn in an All-Star game and that of the twenty-three times he touched the ball, he shot twenty-one of them. Loscutoff implied that if it had been possible, Heinsohn would have shot the other two times as well. Heinsohn apparently quickly learned the All-Star show-off mentality that is so prevalent now. Some years later, Bob Cousy tweaked Heinsohn by noting, "Tommy never shot unless he had the ball."

Celtics championships began piling up. The titles were as much a rite of spring as the grass turning green after the snow melted. Heinsohn was present for the first championship his rookie year in 1957. Then came the big run, win after win, champs in 1959, 1960, 1961, 1962, 1963, 1964, and 1965. And Heinsohn was a key contributor to every crown. Celtics players never led the NBA in scoring. They spread the ball around too much for one man to score enough. And of course Wilt Chamberlain was in the way, so it was unlikely to happen anyhow. Heinsohn usually averaged near 20 points a game with a career best 22.1 in the 1961–62 season.

Heinsohn's career-high game was 45 points at Syracuse in 1961, but he also recorded games of 43 three times, 42, 41, and 40 once apiece.

To capture those titles, the Celtics beat the St. Louis Hawks, the Minneapolis Lakers, St. Louis Hawks, St. Louis Hawks, Los Angeles Lakers, Los Angeles Lakers, San Francisco Warriors, and Los Angeles Lakers in order. That was after blitzing the Syracuse Nationals and their successors, the Philadelphia 76ers, or the Cincinnati Royals in the Eastern Division. John Havlicek said that the Celtics were the New York Yankees of basketball, the winningest, proudest franchise. But a lot of other people thought it too.

The Celtics employed various mind games to motivate themselves in the real games. In the 1963 playoffs, it was a united pledge to win the title for the about-to-retire Cousy. The next year they wanted to prove they could win it without Cousy. And in 1965, they sought to win it to honor deceased owner Walter Brown.

Other NBA teams resented the repetitive performances. A legion of Celtics haters grew up. It was a club that never lacked for new members. Players on other teams did their best and came up short, discouraged enough to punch walls on their way to the locker rooms in a season ended by Boston. But some had mixed emotions.

"I never hated them," said Royals center Wayne Embry. "I felt respect for them because they were the team to beat. We had teams in Cincinnati, a couple of those years that were better than the Celtics. One year we won the season series in the regular season and lost to them in the playoffs. It was frustrating because the Celtics not only were good, but they had a degree of arrogance about them. It inspired me, but others didn't like them."

Heinsohn said he knows the Celtics' demeanor was viewed as arrogance, but he preferred to call it extreme self-confidence. He said he never felt the hatred that some players expressed when active and was surprised at the depth of it when various encounters after retirement with the Lakers' Elgin Baylor and Jerry West and the 76ers' Billy Cunningham indicated it was true.

Like so many of his teammates, Heinsohn said the Celtics did not see black and white in skin color. He thought if the entire country operated like the team, it would be better off. "We were like a lab of human relations," he said.

It is disputable if the Royals really ever had a team better than the Celtics. One thing that could never be contained by opponents was the opportunistic use of the fast break. The Celts were like piranhas at feeding time. Heinsohn said "The fast break can destroy the other team's will to win."

Celtic intangibles always entered the picture. They had quality and depth at all positions, but they also had chemistry, the difficult-to-define attribute that helps teams play well together. They were good at the little things, always knowing where the open man was. And they possessed the unselfishness to throw the pass to that man instead of taking their own shot.

"We were close together," Frank Ramsey said. "We all wanted to win and Red drafted by basketball ability, but he also drafted by personality. There were certain personalities that would never have fit with our team. He wanted you to be a winner, to come from a winning program."

When Ramsey talks about the players being close, he isn't exaggerating. Given their low pay, players shared in-season apartments if they didn't make their permanent home in the Boston area, and they carpooled as well.

The Celtics were so hard to beat because they had more good players than any other team. One team's starting unit might compare favorably with Boston, but when a starter needed a breather his backup might as well have been from a minor league. The other team's coach inserted a guy whom home fans might not have heard of. Auerbach sent in Ramsey or K. C. Jones. The fresh legs always got the other guys.

K. C. was not a great outside shooter. He had his moments, but his strong points were other aspects of the game. He drove teams cuckoo with his quick hands. But one night it was Jones's turn to shine on offense. He had the hot hand and his teammates realized it. For once they passed the ball to him more times than he passed it to them.

The Celtics beat the Hawks, 111–98, and the postgame emotions of St. Louis coach Harry "The Horse" Gallatin, a former Knicks top scorer, ranged somewhere between baffled and exasperated. "I can't figure this game at all," Gallatin said. "We concentrate on stopping Tommy Heinsohn and holding Sam Jones and what happens? K. C. Jones comes off the bench and murders us. You tell me what's going on around here."

Auerbach tried to do just that.

"I've been after him to shoot more and he finally took me serious," the coach said of K. C.

Someone relayed Gallatin's remarks to Jones and he didn't resent them. He understood them. "I can't say that I blame him that much," Jones said. "After all, I'm not noted for being much of a scorer."

That was the thing. Sure, the Celtics had their main point-getters, but someone always stepped up if a key shooter like Heinsohn or Sam Jones was off his game. The bench guys had their backs.

In 1964, on a trip Red Auerbach was asked to organize, Heinsohn joined other NBA stars visiting Egypt and the Soviet Union Communist satellite countries of Poland, Yugoslavia, and Romania to give basketball clinics under the auspices of the U.S. State Department. Camaraderie through sports. He wrote a diary from abroad about the trip for a Boston newspaper too. Some of the State Department no-no's: do not get mixed up with the black market and do not take pictures of military installations for the photo album. Another advance warning resonated with Heinsohn—many of the people were anti-German. It was understandable given the ruination visited upon them during World War II. Overseas, after he spoke to a female sportswriter, Heinsohn said he was told she thought he was a "nice fellow, even though he's German."

The first stop on the tour was Warsaw, Poland, and the flight took sixteen hours from the U.S. with intermediate stops in Western Europe. Must have been comfy for the big guys' long legs. The first clinic was conducted at the Palace of Culture, a typically grandiose Eastern European name.

Then the NBA stars, including Cousy, Russell, Oscar Robertson, and Jerry Lucas, played against a local Army team. Heinsohn was surprised how well the locals shot from outside, though the Americans won by about 20 points. Forty years before the world caught up to the U.S. in the American game at the world championships and Olympics, this was foreshadowing the interest in basketball worldwide.

During Cold War years, such gatherings and exchanges were always punctuated by a social event like a dinner or musical performance. Heinsohn said the hosts immersed themselves in the "Polish Twist." Calling K. C. Jones "the best dancer in pro basketball," the Americans prodded him into showing his stuff, and Jones dazzled on the dance floor.

As so often happened behind the Iron Curtain, social occasions led to toasts. From Moscow to Warsaw, the preferred beverage was vodka. Not wanting to seem impolite, Heinsohn said he freely indulged. And he liked the million-proof alcohol very much.

Auerbach chose the visit in Poland to play a practical joke on Heinsohn. One day, a knock came at the door of Heinsohn's hotel. Two trench coat–clad men stood in the hallway and ordered Heinsohn to join them for a ride to "headquarters." After Heinsohn grew nervous enough to start chain smoking, Auerbach told him the truth—the government "agents" were merely coaches with the Polish National Team.

In Egypt, Heinsohn made chit chat with the woman who was the local liaison for the visiting team, and speaking very slowly he informed her that her English was very good. She replied that it should be since she was from Toledo.

The overall journey left Heinsohn thinking that sports could be a link between cultures when politics and language were otherwise barriers. It figured that Heinsohn would appreciate such a convivial trip. He was the ringleader of Celtics extracurricular activities.

"Tommy Heinsohn was the social director, more or less," John Havlicek said. "He was the type of person who would set up the dinner spot after the game, or be the one to say, 'Let's do this' or 'Let's do that.'"

Bill Russell said that Heinsohn was always in the middle of pranks, either as prankster or the victim. Frank Ramsey, said Russell, used to bug Heinsohn in practice, pulling at his shorts, pinching him, or trash talking. Auerbach and Heinsohn had their exploding cigar exchange. Heinsohn got so exasperated by all of this, as well as Auerbach's riding him, that he once begged Red to ease up.

"You are getting on me so much, the rookies are stealing my socks," Heinsohn said. "So you know what he does? He goes into the locker room and says, 'Rookies, stop stealing Heinsohn's socks.'"

No respect. To illustrate how widely known Auerbach's penchant for loudly lecturing Heinsohn was, the *Christian Science Monitor's* Phil Elderkin wrote, "Red used to ride Heinsohn harder than Eddie Arcaro ever rode a horse."

Heinsohn persevered to have a good time anyway. Conley, the backup on three title teams, said, "He had a beer or two. Most of the guys did then. Tommy was his own man. What a ballplayer. He was our big scorer."

In 2006 a documentary was made about Heinsohn's decades with the Celtics as a player, a coach who led the team to two titles, and as a broadcaster. His Celtics longevity was second only to Auerbach's. Given that Heinsohn retired young, went into the insurance business, and even during his playing days took off to quiet locales to work on his oil paintings (which were so good that he surprised his teammates with his talent, and he was even able to sell them in galleries), Heinsohn seemed less likely than many of his contemporary Celtics to be the one so involved for so long.

Even Heinsohn said, "I wasn't totally submerged into basketball being my identity."

When Heinsohn retired, no one expected it because of his comparative youth. He did not want any part of the hoopla that surrounded Cousy's farewell tour and he did not want a Tommy Heinsohn Day at the Garden. When the season ended, he simply announced that he was not coming back for the 1965–66 season, and he did not.

19

CELTICS AGE,
BUT DON'T FADE AWAY

Sports teams are never static. Even if the entire roster is the same from one year to the next—and in 99 percent of cases it is not—no season is a mirror image. Another team might improve, one player might get injured who was healthy the year before, someone on another team who was injured might be healthy. A rookie may burst upon the scene.

Red Auerbach's eye for talent, his uncanny ability to pick up fresh players, allowed the Celtics to ease new men into the lineup. However, once Boston was at the top of the league, with Bob Cousy, Bill Russell, Bill Sharman, Frank Ramsey, Sam Jones, K. C. Jones, Tommy Heinsohn, and then John Havlicek on the roster, turnover was minimal. The old reliables were basically all on their way to the Hall of Fame, and for several years there was no lineup movement among the key guys.

Nothing lasts forever, however, even the Celtics. The first to depart from the core group after the 1961 season and four titles was Sharman, who, faster than a ball spinning on a guard's fingertip, shifted from being an active player to a head coach in the ill-fated American Basketball League.

It is one achievement to construct a championship team, another to guide it to a repeat and quite another to preside over a dynasty. A dynasty is about longevity. And with gradual turnover, the challenge is immense to keep a team at a high level of competition, never mind continuing to win titles year after year. As great as the individual components were, and as fantastically as they meshed, the real credit for the Dynasty must go to Red Auerbach. He had a brilliant knack for finding the right fill-in, the know-how to select the right player to replace a retiring player. He did it season after season. Sometimes it was by picking up another team's cast-off, talking a player contemplating retirement into sticking around another season, acquiring via trade somebody another team didn't consider so valuable any-more, or by selecting the useful college seniors in the draft despite always drafting last. "Red was the ultimate team builder," Wayne Embry said. "He understood chemistry. He would take players who failed elsewhere and make them winners by restoring their confidence. He never said a bad word about any of his players, regardless of ability. 'You never know when you might need him,' he would say."

Some players enhanced their reputations with the Celtics. Some joined up for the chance to win a title their teams couldn't win. All were thrilled to be coveted by the world-champion Boston Celtics.

Carl Braun was a top-flight guard with the New York Knicks. He played one year with the Celtics and earned a championship ring. Clyde Lovellette, the stalwart big man in the center of the St. Louis Hawks' formidable lineup during their best years, became a valuable backup to Russell for two sea-sons. Wayne Embry, frustrated by how the Celtics always beat his Cincin-nati Royals team, thrived with Boston for two years at the end of his career, stepping in when Lovellette retired. Slippery guard Emmette Bryant was acquired from the Phoenix Suns for a second-round draft choice. He played two seasons, including 1968–69, the final championship season in the run. And 6-foot-6 forward Don Nelson was targeted on the waiver wire in 1965. Tommy Heinsohn, who knew he was retiring, told Auerbach to grab Nelson as his replacement. Signed as a free agent, meaning the Celtics owed no pay-ment to any team, Nelson played eleven years for Boston.

Scrappy guard Larry Siegfried was another perfect Celtic. He played on five world-title teams while averaging in double figures. He was most proud of his defense, however, saying, "A loose ball was my ball." The epitome of a hard-nosed player, Siegfried was the kind of player Auerbach always coveted.

In 1964, the Celtics drafted Mel Counts, a 7-footer out of Oregon State; Ron Bonham, a sharpshooter out of Cincinnati; and John Thompson out of Providence, who later became a Hall of Fame coach for Georgetown University. In 1963 they made Bill Green out of Colorado State their No. 1 draft pick. Auerbach's Rocky Mountain contacts apparently were not as reliable as his bicoastal informants. Green never played a regular-season game and players said his undoing was fear of flying. He was a decade too late for train travel. No one's perfect, not even Auerbach.

Red's greatest rebuilding coup was the acquisition of 6-foot-7 forward Bailey Howell in 1966. He traded Counts to the Baltimore Bullets for the future Hall of Famer, whose lifetime scoring average was 18.7 ppg. Howell was one of Boston's highest scorers during his four years with the team.

"I was glad I was there," said Bryant, who was one of legendary coach Ray Meyer's favorites when he played at DePaul, "because in the sixties, it was everybody's dream to get to Boston. Then it was everybody's perception that they were old and probably wouldn't repeat. But the chances were that whenever you played for the Celtics, you would be on a championship team."

One reason Bryant said he was expendable in Phoenix after his quality New York Knicks career was his announcement that he was retiring over a contract dispute. Yet Bryant was staying active playing in the Catskills summer league. Auerbach, as always, was on hand, and he approached Bryant and asked if he would play for the Celtics if he could obtain his rights.

"I said yes," Bryant recalled. "I wanted to stay on the East Coast, at least because my first four years I was in New York. He gave them a first- or second-round draft pick [it was a second rounder], which really was nothing back in those days because they picked last all the time anyway, and the rest is history."

K. C. Jones had retired and the Celtics needed another playmaker and someone who could play tough defense. Auerbach was on the prowl and Bryant turned up. One thing Bryant discovered the hard way was how rugged Auerbach's preseason training camps were. Bryant thought he was in shape, like almost everyone who came along, and was surprised how Auerbach drilled the players. The veterans knew the score, but new guys didn't.

"You really got into condition," Bryant said. "You did more calisthenics and running than you did playing basketball. That was their trademark. They would get out of the gate fast [because they were in top shape]."

Wayne "The Wall" Embry was debating retirement, but he was energized when the Celtics plucked him from the Royals for cash and a draft choice in 1966. He knew he wasn't going to steal many minutes from Russell, but that wasn't the point. Embry was a star in Cincinnati, but he was after a ring in Boston.

"Anybody who competes at any level, the ultimate goal or reward is to win a championship," said Embry, who became the NBA's first black general manager with the Milwaukee Bucks. "Given the history of the Celtics, I thought the odds were pretty good."

As a longtime outsider, Embry had mulled over how the Celtics kept winning, but it was not until he became a Celtic that he actually comprehended the magic of their success. It was in the caliber of the players, for sure, but it was also in their heads.

"The Celtics just knew how to win," Embry said. "All of a sudden I'm in their team uniform. But I didn't really appreciate what made them until I got there and experienced the camaraderie at the Boston Garden and on the trips. It was just an aura around the team that you were the best. Not only did you declare yourself the best—and it provided inspiration—but in the case of the Celtics they rose to the occasion to prove they were the best."

In his two Boston seasons, Embry scored 5.2 points a game while appearing in almost every game. The 1966–67 season was the year of the Philadelphia 76ers though. It was the year that marked Wilt Chamberlain's first championship, and Chamberlain was finally surrounded by the super talent that he long felt was missing. The 76ers could score and they had depth, Celtic-quality depth, with Lucious Jackson, Billy Cunningham, Hal Greer, and Chet Walker, among others.

There were even a couple of holdovers from those old Syracuse teams in Larry Costello and Dave Gambee. Costello, a 6-foot-1 guard, was just about the last NBA player to live and die with a set shot. Costello then had a very successful coaching career, primarily with Milwaukee, and led the Bucks to their only title in 1971. Gambee was a forward who had the most unmistakable free-throw shooting style in NBA history. He stood at the foul line, kicked one leg back in the air with a balletlike move, and then tossed the ball underhand to the basket. If you saw it, you never forgot it. That was probably the only technique that Chamberlain, a horrible foul shooter who was more accurate from the field (.540) than the line (.511) during in his career, and who was always tinkering with his form, didn't try.

After winning eight straight titles, the Celtics lost to Philly in the Eastern Division finals, four games to one.

"My first year there, the 76ers had put together a very formidable team and we knew they were going to be competitive," Embry said.

Embry said what he learned with the Celtics was like earning a master's degree that combined psychology, sociology, management, finance, and history. When the NBA moved into Milwaukee in 1969, the Celtics lost Embry in the expansion draft. Embry was incredulous when a Bucks rookie asked him for an autograph.

One of the better drafts during the championship years in the sense of stocking backups rather than adding starters was 1964 when the Celtics added Mel Counts, Ron Bonham, and Thompson. They were drafted one, two, three that year.

Players did not have bargaining representatives then. Heck, when they first started to show up, Auerbach threw an agent out of his office. Counts and Bonham showed up at Auerbach's office together to negotiate their first contracts and the word "negotiate" was used loosely. Bonham arranged the scenario, perhaps foolishly thinking there was strength in numbers.

The top two from the draft walked into Auerbach's cozy office and there was the famous coach, leaning back in his chair, feet up on the desk, smoking a cigar.

"We sat down," Bonham said. "He had two pieces of paper and he threw them over to us. I think Mel and I signed for $17,500."

Counts said Bonham actually got $15,000 and he got $12,000. Either way they were not about to run down the block and invest in yachts or IBM stock. In minutes, they were out of the office, out of the building, wondering how it all happened so fast. They were in awe of Auerbach and they were in awe of the players. Counts called training camp boot camp, with too little emphasis on basketball.

When you are a high draft pick, teams have high hopes for you to make an impact if not immediately, then soon. Counts played center when Bill Russell didn't, his second season averaging 8.4 points a game. Despite his height, though, he was not a true post player. Counts routinely made jump shots from the corner instead.

It was all new to Counts and Bonham, becoming members of the best organization in basketball, and they still remember some oddities. Like Auerbach's pancake phobia. He banned the eating of pancakes because he thought they lay too heavily in players' stomachs and he didn't want them to be sluggish.

"He said, 'We don't do pancakes or carbohydrates,'" Counts recited.

The way the Celtics ran instead of walking the ball upcourt unsettled teams and enabled the Celts to get five-on-four or four-on-three defensive mismatches in a hurry, and they never got tired, either of running or winning.

"They were ahead of their time," Counts said. "Heart, passion, and fire, that's what the Celtics had. You talk about pressure. Everybody was out there trying to knock you off. I think it takes more than talent. A lot of people talk who do not give people proper credit, say they were arrogant. They were just darned good."

So was Bonham in high school in Indiana and in college at Cincinnati, just after Oscar Robertson departed. He was a fundamental, good-form, deadly jump shooter, a 6-foot-5 guard who came off the bench for two Celtics seasons before being lost to the Chicago Bulls in the expansion draft of 1966. Like so many other Celtics, Bonham was a role player. His task was to score in a hurry, provide spark, and shake up the defense. His rookie year he played in only thirty-seven games, averaging just 10 minutes per appearance but scoring 7.4 points a game. That's hurry-up shooting. His second season was similar, though his average dipped to 5.2 ppg. Two seasons, world championship rings, and a precious Celtics watch.

Bonham cherishes those prizes, but he never shows them off in public. "I've never worn them," he said. "They're all new in the box. I've had them on display."

Those are the gems of the basketball souvenir collection for a guy who saved everything from jewelry to yearbooks, and programs to photographs. Bonham roomed with John Havlicek, and not long ago while Bonham and his wife were moving around the memorabilia in their Muncie, Indiana, home, he came across some joke pictures. Havlicek posed for them on a road trip to San Francisco in one of those photo booths where the pictures come out in little strips.

"John was pulling his lips down, making faces; we were just playing around," Bonham said. "It brought back good memories."

For Bonham, the memories are as good as the tangible souvenirs. He knew he was truly a member of the Celtics tribe after he made the final cut. He was a Boston Celtic and the thing that solidified it, that made him feel like he belonged, was a team dinner. Bill Russell invited the entire team over to his house and fed the players a fine meal. Bonham still remembers the sweet potato pie. "It was like one big family," Bonham said.

One of the most important and surprising additions to that family was Bailey Howell, obtained for Counts. Howell was an established scorer, who had starred for the Detroit Pistons and Baltimore Bullets after a fabulous college career at Mississippi State, where he averaged 27.1 points a game.

Bailey Howell had played on his share of so-so teams in the NBA by the time he came to the Celtics and, boy, could he tell the difference between the first-class organization and some of his other experiences.

"It was the epitome of a team," he said. "I'd played on other clubs that hadn't been that successful and people had a tendency to go off on their own and look out for No. 1. They [the Celtics] were competitors and loved to win. They sacrificed and put the team ahead of everything."

Howell had paid his NBA dues and had enough time in to become weary of losing to Boston. It grew old, but he respected the Celtics, though he didn't quite know what to make of Auerbach firing up that victory cigar.

"They never rubbed it in on you when they beat you," Howell said. "I don't know what Red really thought or planned, or what statement he was trying to make with his cigar. Making a little light of you because 'we beat you.' But if you ever beat him, he'd make you pay the price. He'd put in his shock troops and they'd play really aggressive and bang you around. The guys who didn't play much."

No trash talking, the way Howell remembers it, the Celtics just beat his Pistons badly and walked off the court professionally.

The acquisition of Howell, who was then 30, was greeted with joy in Boston, and Howell said it was a great thing for him too. He had not shown any signs of slowing down, but sometimes teams overreact to birthdays. Howell, who shot one-handed jumpers in front of his face, was also a terrific garbage man who used his 220 pounds effectively under the hoop. Howell, elected to the Hall of Fame in 1997, averaged just under 10 rebounds a game, extraordinary for a forward.

From Tennessee to Mississippi, Howell was a Deep South product and one of those guys who wore a sign-of-the-times crew cut that would have fit in perfectly with Sergeant Rock and Easy Company. Howell's addition was invaluable. He averaged 20 points a game during his initial Boston season and in the 1968 playoffs played a critical role during one of the Celtics' most memorable comebacks that was also one of Wilt Chamberlain's most painful defeats—in more ways than one.

During the regular season, Philadelphia finished eight games ahead of Boston in the Eastern Division with 62 wins and compiled six more than St. Louis, the leader in the Western Division. The 76ers led the league in scoring average, with 122.6 points a game. Clearly, Philly thought it was its time and that the Celtics Dynasty was on the verge of toppling.

The 76ers bested the New York Knicks in the first round of the playoffs while the Celtics took out Detroit. That set up the showdown fans salivated over. The Celtics won the opener 127–118. Did that represent false hope? An angered Philadelphia, sick of years of losing to Boston, retaliated with three straight wins. Down 3–1 in a best-of-seven series, the Celtics were definitely in jeopardy. Philadelphia had proven itself stronger over the long haul of the regular season and made the Celtics seem old and slow in the playoffs.

Had time run out on Boston?

Things looked bleak, especially because Game 5 was scheduled for Philadelphia. Leading up to the contest, a sportswriter asked Howell if the Celtics had any chance.

"And I said, 'If we win down there, then they're going to start getting a little edgy about it because we're going back to Boston,'" Howell said. "And you should win your home games, of course."

The Celtics regrouped and won the game, 122–104. Still alive. Then they won Game 6, 114–106, setting up a deciding Game 7. Haunted by history, Philadelphia had to face its doubts. "It was just down to one game," Howell said.

The Celtics pulled it off, winning 100–96. Chamberlain did not take a shot in the fourth quarter, and that was one development analyzed to death. There was no mystery about it, according to Howell. "Any time he got the ball and was going to shoot, we just grabbed his arms and hacked him pretty good," he said. "That doesn't count as a shot attempted, so we put him at the foul line and it turned out to be good for us."

The victory put the Celtics into the finals once more. The Lakers were after blood, like Philadelphia believing Boston was vulnerable. L.A. was confident it was its turn to capture the crown. Yet the result was the same as it had been throughout the decade. Boston won four games to two.

"That's the biggest thrill I ever had in basketball," Howell said. "I played on a conference champion in high school and in college, but to win the world championship, talk about being on top of the world."

20

RED RETIRES

Midway through the 1965–66 season, Red Auerbach made an announcement that shook the foundation of the Boston Celtics organization. This, he said, would be his final season as head coach. Then he announced the decision to the world. Most people interpreted it as an act of arrogance based primarily on his here's-your-last-chance-to-beat-me statement. "I'm announcing it now," Auerbach said in January, "so no one can ever say I quit while I was ahead. I'm telling everyone right now—Los Angeles, Philadelphia, everyone—that this will be my last season, so you've got one more shot at Auerbach!"

From the moment Walter Brown hired Auerbach for the 1950–51 season, he was the cornerstone of the club. He was the coach, the talent evaluator, the mastermind behind trades and all player moves. More than anyone else, he was the public face of the team. Everyone who watched basketball knew who he was, everyone familiar with the NBA game knew about that danged cigar. In fact, Terry Cashman, who wrote the song "Talkin' Baseball," wrote a song called "Light It Up (Red Auerbach/Boston Celtics)."

Professional sports franchises have never argued that fans come to their stadiums and arenas to watch a coach coach. But the coach can be a lightning rod for opposing fans, someone who can distract opposing coaches into dwelling on the next game with the Celtics. If you were an NBA coach during the Auerbach reign, it was difficult not to think, "What is that SOB dreaming up next?" And if Auerbach heard such thoughts expressed out loud, he chortled.

The complications of running an NBA team had dramatically expanded since Auerbach came into the league and the offices were expanding to cope with the work demand. For some time, Auerbach had pretty much done all of the administration on his own as well as coach the team on the floor. By his final season, he was balder and grayer than ever, tired more easily, and worst of all, could not stoke the fire in his belly to care as intensely about the games. A guy who for years had been a human megaphone in referees' ears couldn't muster up the same enthusiasm anymore. It was time to go, not just call a time-out. Auerbach felt it was time to split the duties of supervising the team. So he let go of the game-time operation while retaining all the other responsibilities, first as general manager and then as president.

Auerbach won 938 regular-season games, a record not matched for years. The farewell year resulted in Boston's ninth title in ten years, but it was not easily achieved.

No doubt some coaches around the league wondered if Auerbach was faking it, just grandstanding to use the shock of the announcement to jump-start his sluggish team and remotivate them. Other organizations took his comments at face value. Auerbach was actually feted in some of the cities where he was ordinarily persona non grata. Showing an ironic and classy sense of humor in a tribute, the Cincinnati Royals passed out cigars to the first 5,000 fans at a Royals-Celtics game.

February 13, 1966, was proclaimed Red Auerbach Day at the Boston Garden. Tears flowed, cheers rang out at halftime, and Auerbach collected a technical foul in a loss to the Lakers. Maybe the passion wasn't diminishing after all. Bob Cousy, the already-retired Celtics favorite son, was involved in the presentation and speechmaking, and delivered the wryest observation of the evening, particularly given Auerbach's explosive tête-à-tête with the refs. "I sweated out the whole first half," Cousy said, "wondering what we'd do if you got kicked out early and couldn't come back to accept these gifts."

Auerbach had long been one step ahead of the rest of the league—make that three—but despite his smart draft picks and outstanding trades, he wondered if he was losing his footing. At the least, he felt he didn't have the stamina to keep up the pace necessary to rebuild the Celtics as one by one the old-timers retired. That was a full-time job, he knew. And so was coaching. "I had to stop coaching," Auerbach said. "If I hadn't I would have killed myself. I was completely worn out."

He had assumed even more responsibility for all things Celtics after Walter Brown died in 1965, a man with whom he had a special bond. For years, Auerbach never even had a formal contract with Brown. When each season ended, Brown cornered Auerbach in the Celtics' tiny offices. He suggested they adjourn to the men's room where no one would overhear them, and there the men dickered, if it could be called that, given the amiability of the sessions. Each year the Celtics won the world title Auerbach felt he deserved a 10 percent raise. He proposed that, Brown said okay, they shook hands on the deal, and that was it.

With Brown gone, contracts had to be formalized. With the league expanding, more scouting was needed. Players voiced more demands, agents were slipping into the picture. The NBA was on its way to the high-powered, glitzier league it is today. Auerbach reached the conclusion he could not be everywhere and shepherd his flock's needs.

Whether or not the timing of Auerbach's retirement declaration was a little bit Machiavellian, the Celtics players took it as a challenge. They did not want him to go out a loser. Although Bill Russell said Boston sometimes won championships on "general principles," there were a number of times the players were specifically charged up to win one for somebody. There was the title earned when Cousy retired and the victory recorded after Walter Brown died.

The aging Celtics (K. C. Jones retired the next year after twice being burned by a dribbler zooming past, who convinced him he was slowing down) were not the best regular-season team during the 1965–66 season. Philadelphia was on the move. Chamberlain was still Chamberlain, averaging 33.5 points a game. The 76ers finished 55-25, the Celtics 54-26. The Lakers were nearly ten games worse in the Western Division, but the breakthrough news was Philadelphia's finish. Any hint that the 76ers were catching the Celts was welcome in Philly. Topped by Sam Jones's 23.5 points a game, Boston put seven people in double figures for the season. The Celtics were hardly one-dimensional.

True to his philosophy, consistent with his outlook, and conforming with all Celtics statements since Brown drafted Chuck Cooper, when the time arrived that Auerbach thought it was in the best interests of his team and gave the Celtics the best chance to win, he started five African-American players.

It was a first in NBA history and it is regarded as a milestone. The best guys play, Auerbach always said. Over the years white players Bill Sharman, Bob Cousy, Frank Ramsey, and Tommy Heinsohn retired. It just so happened that as the 1965–66 season unfolded, Auerbach believed his five best players were black. Yes, K. C. Jones was nearing the end of the line and even he thought up-and-coming Larry Siegfried should play more. Siegfried, a 6-foot-3 guard out of Ohio State, where he was a teammate of John Havlicek's, averaged 13.7 points a game that year, his third year with the team.

A scrappy player who spent seven seasons with Boston, scoring in double figures from that year on, Siegfried would soon take over a starting position. But not yet.

Don Nelson, in his first Boston season, was coming on too, and would start. But not yet. Some of it was the mix of players and talents. Siegfried and Nelson, who averaged 10.2 points a game that season, could do damage off the bench. Both white men played extensively that year, but Auerbach preferred the lineup of Russell at center, Tom Sanders and Willie Naulls at forward, and Sam and K. C. Jones at guard to start games.

Five black starters. At the peak of the Civil Rights movement, the world noticed. This was a seminal moment at a time when blacks were battling for equal rights and seeking to knock down barriers placed in front of them for a couple of centuries. Obviously, Auerbach recognized it was an important moment too, but he never made a big deal out of it. To him, it was all about fairness, not being a pioneer. Neither Auerbach nor his NBA contemporaries had an inkling that by 2007 the league would be 80 percent black and the comparative curiosity would be a white starting player. Still, when

Auerbach died in 2006, *Boston Globe* sports columnist Bob Ryan wrote that it took "chutzpah" for Auerbach to start five blacks in the mid-1960s.

One reason Auerbach felt he had to move into the front office full-time was the self-imposed pressure to keep the Celtics Dynasty going. He was a man of his time, and later in life he never cared about using a computer to study NBA facts. He dealt with men, their personalities, their hopes, their likes and dislikes, and their motivations. He had run his little corner of the world as a fiefdom. As he aged, the image of Auerbach softened some. His laurels could be rested upon. Accolades came his way in flowery prose, effusive speech, and tangible plaques and the like.

Alan Cohen, a future Celtics owner, said of Auerbach in 1992: "I'm still a little in awe of Red. He never ceases to be someone who has incredible perception and sensitivity. Red could literally be president of the United States with his ability to understand what makes things happen."

Red Auerbach as president of the United States? Hmm. I'll trade you a secretary of state for a prime minister. But really, all Auerbach ever wanted to be was president of the Boston Celtics.

Being one of those five black starters, especially given the context of the era, is something K. C. Jones has remembered his whole life. When he retired, there was also a K. C. Jones Day at the Boston Garden. One of the gifts he received was a key to the city of Framingham, the community he and his family had lived in since 1961. Soon after, the Joneses decided they needed a bigger house. But when they shopped around and picked out a place they liked, the realtor told them no blacks lived in the neighborhood and they wouldn't be welcome there. Fat lot of good that key to the city did for them. It was a reminder that the Celtics practice of equality was not universal.

"I'd like to think this wouldn't happen today," Jones said about twenty years after the housing incident.

The drama was built in for the playoffs. Come and get me, Auerbach shouted, and good teams lined up to end his coaching career on a sour note. First came the Cincinnati Royals in the Eastern Division opening round. That was a best three-out-of-five series and the Celtics prevailed three games to two. There was no coasting. Oscar Robertson and Jerry Lucas were as potent a one-two combo as there was in the league and although they were aging, the Royals still had Wayne Embry and Jack Twyman too. Boston took the deciding game, 112–103. Sam Jones scored 34 points that day to break the Royals' morale.

"We failed as a team," Embry said, "losing to the same Celtics we were supposed to beat."

Supposed to? The Royals finished nine games behind the Celtics in the standings, though they did go 5-5 in the season series and they did take a 2-1 lead in the playoff series. No, it was the 76ers who were supposed to beat the Celtics that year. Unexpectedly, building on the momentum from the defeat of Cincinnati, the Celtics walked over the 76ers, four games to one. Boston won two, lost one, won two.

Wilt Chamberlain was stunned and depressed. But few felt very sorry for Chamberlain at that moment. He had written an ill-advised and ill-timed two-part series for *Sport Magazine* under the theme "My Life in the Bush Leagues." Although he poignantly lamented being considered a villain and treated as "Goliath," the stories generated more anger than sympathy.

One more round for the Celtics. No surprise who survived in the West. No one was more focused than the Lakers—not even Chamberlain—on killing off the Celtics to win a championship. It was a doozy of a high-scoring series (except for the last game) and the Celtics persevered to capture their last title under Auerbach's mentorship, four games to three.

The Lakers were looking ever more potent that season. Jerry West had surpassed Elgin Baylor, averaging 31.3 points a game. West was so competitive that a teammate recounted a story of the guard walking off the course at a celebrity golf tournament because he was so displeased with his play. But once again the Lakers were vanquished. No one interested in his personal safety wanted to go near a frustrated West soon. Whispers of "Nice game" or "Nice series" just didn't cut it anymore.

Boston took a 3-1 lead in the series. It was all but sewn up, all but clinched. Until the Lakers won two straight, forcing a seventh game at the Garden. A bit of suspense for Auerbach's final game. The 13,909 spectators howled all game long.

The Celtics led by 16 points at the beginning of the fourth quarter, and by 6 points with 16 seconds remaining when Auerbach allowed Massachusetts governor John Volpe to light the last victory cigar of his bench career. And wouldn't you know it, the Lakers rallied, cutting the lead to two points, almost before Auerbach could inhale. Uh-oh. The unbelievable was threatening. But Boston got the ball back, and K. C. Jones, a la Cousy, dribbled out the clock as the horn sounded.

It was over. Auerbach glowed as brightly as the lit tip of the cigar, sucking in the atmosphere of history, as well as the smoke from his favorite stogie. Fans rushed the court and lifted Auerbach on their shoulders. He shouted, "I feel drunk and I haven't even had a drink."

Center Bill Russell was astonishing that day, playing all 48 minutes while scoring 25 points and gathering a stupendous 32 rebounds. By then, Russell was in the news for more than his sterling play. In the middle of the series, Auerbach—sense of theater intact after all those years—called a press conference. While the Lakers were still taking their last crack at him, Auerbach announced his replacement.

It was a choice that exhilarated Boston fans and stunned the rest of the NBA. Beginning with the 1966–67 season, the new player-coach of the Boston Celtics would be Bill Russell. The player who more than any other had directed the storied franchise to its greatest moments of glory would have the fate of the team placed in his hands.

If anyone had previously pictured Russell as coaching material, it was probably only fleeting. People likely thought he wouldn't want to be burdened by the details. He had been outspoken, critical of fans in his club's city, and was regarded in some quarters as aloof and removed from the other players. And there was this: Never before had there been a black coach in any major American team sport. The first team to draft a black player, the first team to start five black players became the first team to hire a black coach.

Red was the pioneer once again. But not if you asked him. "The thought never crossed my mind, to tell you the truth," he said.

Russell and Auerbach had grown close. Theirs was a fascinating partnership, two men very different in upbringing and outlook with a shared passion for victory. Auerbach said he hired Russell because he was the best man for the job. Had Bob Cousy been available, Auerbach might have selected him, but Cousy was ensconced at Boston College. Tommy Heinsohn was

not then seen as coaching material—he fooled everyone with his championship success in the 1970s. If Red had gone out of the family, Russell probably would have retired.

Auerbach knew Celtics teammates admired Russell. He knew Russell
was the team leader on the court. And he knew as Russell aged, the challenging task of becoming a coach would motivate him. No one, Auerbach
figured, could motivate Russell better than Russell.

At the news conference, Russell said he had a tough act to follow given
all of Auerbach's championships. "He's got a pretty good record," Russell
said to laughter.

Longtime friend K. C. Jones, who shared so many thrills with Russell in
college, at the Olympics, and with the Celtics, approved of the move.

"He has such a brilliant mind and his intelligence is off the charts,"
Jones said. "It worked out. It was such a close relationship between the two
of them [Russell and Auerbach] from the time he joined the team. He was in
a place where he was very comfortable and becoming coach only increased
his tremendous determination."

Sounded good, but Albert Einstein was brilliant, so brilliance alone
doesn't make a coach. And unless Auerbach kept it under wraps, Russell
hadn't been a candidate during the search process. Could Russell coach? Was
Auerbach the indispensable cog in the Dynasty who couldn't be replaced?

One aspect of Auerbach's legacy is how he bred coaches. Certainly the
players he drafted were innately intelligent, but they learned from interaction with teammates and by watching Auerbach too. Among those Celtics
from the Dynasty years who coached were Bill Russell, Bob Cousy, Bill Sharman, K. C. Jones, Jim Loscutoff, and Tom Sanders, some in college only,
some in the pros, a few returning to guide the Celtics.

Bill Russell was the first of the group to lead the old team.

21

HAVLICEK STEALS THE BALL

The play that transformed John Havlicek from great Celtics player to great Celtics legend was dramatic, timely, and occurred at a moment when everything was at stake. And it didn't hurt that Johnny Most's vocal cords were working on all cylinders. "Havlicek stole the ball!" was a description and a summation, it became the title of a highlight record and a signature phrase, and in a single sentence it succinctly labeled the Dynasty.

It was a George Gipp, Chip Hilton, miraculous, stunning, seconds-long, frozen-in-place-on-videotape play that more than four decades after its occasion still provokes flushed-face, teary-eyed remembrances from Celtic fans of a certain age.

"Havlicek stole the ball!"

Yes, he did. To preserve the Dynasty. To demolish the 76ers' hopes.

In the seventh game of the Eastern Division finals near the end of the 1964–65 season, Boston had the ball and the lead with 5 seconds left. Once again Philadelphia was stymied. Once again Boston was heading on to the NBA finals to once again meet the Los Angeles Lakers.

All that Bill Russell had to do was safely and simply pass the ball to one of the Celtics' guards from his own end line next to the basket he was defending. A basic chore with the Celtics leading 110–109, a formality.

Only a minute earlier, the Celtics led 110–103, and coach Red Auerbach felt that was enough of a cushion to light his victory cigar. Then Philadelphia charged.

Russell demanded to be the man to put the ball into play. He loved his teammates, but he trusted himself the most in this kind of crucial situation. Under the rules, Russell had 5 seconds counted down by a referee to make a pass-in. He scanned the darting bodies, looking for a clear pass, and then threw the ball in play. Only it did not make it cleanly. The ball hit a wire extending out from the backboard, a guide wire. Under Boston Garden playing rules, the ball was immediately whistled dead. Russell was shocked. He grimaced at his gaffe, and dropping to his knees and shouted, "Oh, my God!" He asked his surprised but unshaken teammates "to bail me out." Tommy Heinsohn noted, "He had saved us so many times before." Later Russell said he was sure he was going to be haunted by the error, constantly hounded about why he made such a stupid mistake.

Official Earl Strom, who was working with a fresh cast on a broken thumb incurred the day before when he punched a fan, called the series one of the most dramatic he ever worked. Well versed in the house rules, Strom recognized instantly that when the ball hit the wire play had to be stopped.

A happy Boston crowd hushed and was now concerned. Philadelphia gained possession, with the action in its offensive end. Five seconds offered an eternity of a last chance to score. Strom handed the ball to 76ers guard Hal Greer for his own pass-in. Greer was 6-foot-2 to Russell's 6-9, so there was less chance an over-the-head pass from him would hit the wire, but Greer was probably more keenly aware of the obstacle than ever. The ideal Philadelphia play was to feed Wilt Chamberlain in the low post, but of course the Celtics knew that was the No. 1 option and protected against it. With Greer, a deadly jump shooter, standing out of bounds, the next best offensive option for a high-percentage shot was finding forward Chet Walker.

Havlicek covered Walker and when the pass from Greer was slightly short, he batted the ball away with two hands, much like a football defensive back swatting away a potential touchdown pass. The ball bounced to Sam Jones, who dribbled out the clock. Delirium. Most was losing his mind on the air, repeating "Havlicek stole the ball! It's all over. It's all over." Fans were wild in the stands. Then they rushed the court, seeking to touch, hug, or kiss Havlicek. No fool, Havlicek tried to sprint to safety in the Celtics locker room. He did not get there hands-free, however.

"They ripped my jersey," Havlicek said of his worshippers.

Film of the immediate postgame reaction shows Havlicek being swept along the court as if he was in the path of a tsunami, the thin shoulder straps of his uniform jersey being tugged out of shape, about to be torn in half.

"The crowd went crazy," said backup forward Ron Bonham, who was near Havlicek in the mob. "Everybody was just overwhelmed. My warm-up jacket was torn off. John and I both had welts on our backs."

Havlicek said his jersey went unwillingly, clawed to pieces, and he truly worried whether he would make it to the locker room before his shorts were stripped from him.

Havlicek created the moment, but Most supplied the background music. "Havlicek stole the ball!" became his most popular phrase. For years, Most was asked by fans in public to re-create the dramatic pronouncement. Once, Most said, he ended up with a crowd of about fifty people around him outside of a popular restaurant in the Boston suburb of Brookline. Eventually, a record was cut of Celtics highlights, and the featured selection was "Havlicek stole the ball!" It may not have become a gold record, but it represented the gold standard of Celtics play.

Meanwhile, Boston finished out the season by finishing off the Lakers for their seventh title in eight years.

Unlike other sports stand-alone highlights like Bo Belinsky's no-hitter, or an unassisted triple play by an unknown infielder, Havlicek's steal meshed with the flow of his career. He always made clutch plays. His lengthy, All-Pro career is remembered in many ways for many things, not just a single shining moment.

Similar to K. C. Jones's situation, Havlicek nearly turned to professional football instead of professional basketball. One of the standouts on a superb NCAA champion Ohio State team that featured Jerry Lucas and included a sixth man in Bob Knight who became slightly better known as a college coach, Havlicek was drafted by the Cleveland Browns. By then, Havlicek was already nicknamed "Hondo." Mel Nowell, another college hoops teammate who played in the NBA, gave him the moniker when the John Wayne movie of the same name was released.

The Browns thought that the onetime Ohio high school football star could make it as a receiver. So did Havlicek. He was 6-feet-5 and weighed 205 pounds. Jones decided he had a better chance to make a living playing basketball. Hondo was thinking more along the lines of two-sport pro Gene Conley when the Celtics drafted Havlicek No. 1 in 1962.

The NBA draft was not on television in those days. Havlicek was notified that the Celtics took him by a newspaper reporter, and he said, "Is that right? Never in my wildest dreams did I ever imagine I'd wind up with the Boston club. Never. You're not kidding me, are you?"

As impressed as Red Auerbach was with Havlicek, this was not a do-or-die draft situation the way it had been with Russell. In fact, Auerbach nearly chose Chet Walker, who also enjoyed a great NBA career. Auerbach said at the time that Walker had more offensive moves, but "what I like about Havlicek is his competitive spirit. He's a guy who can give you a hard-nosed brand of basketball and that's what I like. Of course he fits in our plans." Auerbach compared Havlicek to Ramsey as a supremely well-rounded player who could do just about anything on the court.

Still, if Havlicek had shelved basketball for football, the draft might have looked like one of Red's biggest mistakes.

"My original thought was to play both," Havlicek said. "It was all different back then. I think I only would have missed fourteen games with the Celtics. I probably would have had to make a decision between the sports over a period of time. But Cleveland felt familiar. It was only 130 miles from home. I wouldn't have been uprooting myself."

Havlicek's family has Czechoslovakian roots and they operated a grocery store when he was young. He often fished with his father Frank and among Havlicek's boyhood playmates were Phil Niekro, the Hall of Fame pitcher, and his brother, the late Joe Niekro. Always a sports fan, Havlicek was All-State in football and basketball for Bridgeport High. Among his suitors to play college football was the Buckeyes' legendary Woody Hayes.

Although Havlicek made his mark as a hoopster in college, the Browns still thought he had pro potential in football. Havlicek signed with his favorite football team for $15,000 and a new car. Havlicek started training camp with Cleveland, showed off his good hands, got clobbered trying to block Gene "Big Daddy" Lipscomb—then the most feared defensive player in the game—and got cut in late August.

When Walter Brown heard of Havlicek's exile from the Browns, he wanted to reach Havlicek swiftly and line up his basketball career. Only Brown couldn't touch base immediately. "I'm having trouble finding Hiram, Ohio, on the map," Brown said of the Cleveland Browns training camp location.

For Havlicek's next trick, he joined the Celtics and didn't leave until 1978 after playing in 1,270 games in sixteen seasons. Realizing they may have made an error, Havlicek said the Browns called him annually during his first five years in the NBA asking him to try football again. But Havlicek understood that joining the Celtics was something special. His college team won all the time and Havlicek was all about winning. What better place to be than on the roster of the perennial world champions?

"It was fun," Havlicek said. "I left one championship program and went to another."

It was easy to get used to winning, not as easy to get used to coming off the bench. The Celtics made him feel at home, but Havlicek was no different than most players who come into the NBA. They have been stars in high school and college, so they feel they should be starting right away in the pros. But Sam Jones sat. K. C. Jones sat. Frank Ramsey sat.

"We had six, seven, eight guys in double figures at different times," Havlicek recalled. "By sharing the ball the way we did, no one got to the point where they ever were bigger than the team. We had great depth."

It also meant that coach Red Auerbach could bring rookies along slowly, easing them into the lineup behind All-Stars. Havlicek was lucky that Ramsey was still there. Ramsey had been a college star too, and he had evolved into "the best sixth man in basketball" at a time when no one but Auerbach gave any thought to the value of a sixth man. Havlicek inherited the role when Ramsey retired. A player who could contribute at either guard or forward, Havlicek had the same ability to enter a game cold off the bench and change the tempo to give his team a boost. Besides, Auerbach always preached that it was more important who was on the floor at crunch time in the fourth quarter than who started the game.

Still, not starting nagged at Havlicek. He wound up playing more games as a Celtic than any of the other stars of the time, but he had to remind himself that he was performing a useful function. "'I don't think anyone can name the fourth and fifth starters,'" he said he told himself. "'Everyone will know who I am.' That was the mind game I played with myself.'"

There were always veterans around to put Havlicek in his place too. In typical rookie hazing, he was required to carry other players' luggage, and he remembers that for a neutral court game in Providence, Rhode Island, he was assigned the job of lugging in the 24-second clocks.

Overlapping with Ramsey helped Havlicek. He learned how to take offensive fouls from Ramsey. He learned how to cope with the sixth-man situation. Ramsey told him to sit near Auerbach on the bench as a reminder of his availability. Ramsey instructed Havlicek never to wear warm-up pants and to only drape his warm-up jacket over his shoulders, so he looked ready to check in. Over time Havlicek became a better player and became more and more important to the Celtics. Eventually, he became the captain of the team and led a new generation of Boston players to their own titles.

What impressed Havlicek's teammates from the start was his ability to run forever. The guy never got tired. He had the stamina of a marathoner. As veteran teammates retired one by one, Havlicek was relied on for longer and longer minutes. It reached the point that his playing time expanded to become Russell-like, with him almost never sitting down for an in-game breather.

Havlicek averaged 14.3 points a game as a rookie. It was a promising beginning. He showed he belonged and that he had raw talent that could be developed. Yet probably none would have envisioned Havlicek averaging 20.8 points a game for his career, or outscoring Larry Bird by 5,000 points on the Celtics' all-time list. K. C. Jones, who coached the Celtics before Havlicek retired, once said he has never seen a player grow steadily into greatness the way Havlicek did.

Guard Emmette Bryant, a latecomer in the Dynasty years, said Havlicek always kept the opposition off-balance. He might be in the game at forward, but he could run through a guard play that left bigger men backpedaling.

"They couldn't keep up with a guy like Havlicek," Bryant said. "He wasn't a graceful, beautiful player in terms of looking good on his shot. But man, was he effective, and he never stopped. He never quit. He kept moving all of the time, working hard."

Havlicek was thinking all the time too. Sitting next to Auerbach on the bench, Havlicek was amazed at how the coach seemed to substitute the right guy at the right time so consistently. He said Auerbach was brilliant at motivating players and his loyalty to his Celtics was a comfort that they wouldn't wake up one day and find out they had been traded to Syracuse.

If Auerbach was initially complimentary to Havlicek—as any coach would be about a first-round draft pick coming aboard—he gushed in the most uncommon of ways about the player after he played in thirteen All-Star games. "John Havlicek is what being a Celtic is all about," Auerbach said.

Former teammate Tom Sanders once described Havlicek as the link between three generations of Celtics, from the original Dynasty group, to the extension of the Dynasty, to the period beyond when the Celtics rebuilt. Once, Havlicek was asked directly if those Dynasty Celtics considered themselves unbeatable. The self-effacing answer would be to say, "Of course not." But that's not how Havlicek answered. The rugged winners he teamed with like Sanders, Tommy Heinsohn, and K. C. Jones took losing personally, as an affront, he said.

"We felt it was a mistake when we lost," Havlicek said.

Very few such mistakes were experienced during the Celtics Dynasty years. And Havlicek headed off one of those with his fabulous rescue stealing the ball against those pesky 76ers, a team just beginning to jell and one that would be after the Celtics with greater hunger in the coming years.

The joyous crowd that descended from the Boston Garden mezzanine to the floor to celebrate the biggest Boston theft outside of the Brinks robbery really did reduce Havlicek's jersey to shreds and threads. The hardcore pursuers, following underneath the stands, got a hold of the shorts too, though Havlicek managed to maintain some dignity before the locker room door slammed behind him.

The Boston Garden only held 13,909 fans, but Havlicek long ago lost count of how many people have said they were on the premises that night.

Far more have approached him bellowing, "Havlicek stole the ball!" instead of offering a simple hello. It is done in a friendly manner, however, by Celtics fans who cherish the moment. The phrase follows the man like an echo, sometimes to other cities. Once, in Philadelphia, an old 76ers fan sick of hearing "Havlicek stole the ball" told him, "Every time I hear that I want to strangle you."

Presumably, Chet Walker is not among those who go around repeating Johnny Most's famous play-by-play call. Walker was left empty-handed that night, the intended receiver of the pass that never got there. No, Walker said to a question phrased about the emotion attached to his memory, the play is not a bitter memory, but a nightmare. "I awaken a lot of nights thinking about that game," Walker said.

It never ends for Havlicek, day or night, with fans performing their Most imitations. How often does that happen?

"A lot," Havlicek said, laughing. "People do that all of the time. A million times. And every one of them thinks it's the first time someone has done it. And people still have pieces of it [the jersey]."

How does he know that? Simple. Because those people, who either liberated the jersey from his torso themselves, or inherited the souvenir cloth from a relative, come up to Havlicek and show the piece to him. The all-time champ is the woman who strolled up to Havlicek and flashed a jewelry brooch in his face, announcing, "This is part of your jersey."

Havlicek stole the ball, but she stole the jersey.

22

THE FIRST BLACK COACH AND MORE TITLES

Red Auerbach was weary, tired of the long hours and the longer days, burning out from burning the candle at both ends, so he gave up coaching. But he didn't give up the Celtics. Many of the Boston greats from the 1950s had retired. Others were aging alongside him.

The Celtics did not become the Celtics until Bill Russell joined them. Auerbach and Russell had a special rapport, and Auerbach did not see Russell easily adjusting to the authority of a new coach. As if sucking in the wisdom of his choice through the smoke of his cigar, Auerbach anointed Russell as his successor.

Brilliant selection, some thought. It will never work, others thought. For one reason, Russell was not retiring. The first black head coach of an American major sports team was going to be a player-coach. This only complicated his assignment. After all, Russell was used to playing nearly all 48 minutes a game. How could he watch the game and make suitable substitutes? How would he know if another player was tired? How could he be omniscient? Auerbach stepped back from the bench, but he did not step back from the team. He left Russell alone to do his job, but any time Russell

needed him, Auerbach was available. Auerbach was still the general manager, still Russell's boss.

Russell remained the team leader on the floor. He became the team
leader on the bench. During games the Celtics had always been a dictator-
ship, Auerbach ruling. Sure, there were the occasional recommendations
from a Bob Cousy or a Russell, but Auerbach was not a power-sharing coach.
By nature, Russell was confident, sure of himself, wary of taking orders, and
a possessor of so much pride he would definitely not tolerate team second-
guessing. But he had to rely on players' eyes and ears more than Auerbach
did. Russell was in the middle of the action, not a sideline observer of it.

Auerbach was sure he did the right thing. "What better way to motivate
Bill Russell the player?" he said with a grin on his face.

Perhaps the least surprised observer was K. C. Jones, Russell's old-
est friend on the team. Comparing Russell's connection with University of
San Francisco coach Phil Woolpert, Jones said Russell was always closer to
Auerbach. He said the relationship "was like a father-son kind of thing."

One of Russell's first acts as coach was to make John Havlicek captain.
In an era when the bench was still reserved for guys in uniforms more
than guys wearing suits, it made Havlicek a de facto assistant coach. Russell also bestowed upon Hondo the right to call timeouts. That was like
giving him power of attorney. But the team was a mature one anyway,
with Sam and K. C. Jones and Tom Sanders still in the mix, with Wayne
Embry as a Russell backup center, and high-scoring Bailey Howell joining
the frontcourt.

The Celtics made their draft choices. Auerbach made shrewd pickups
off the waiver wire, but in Russell's thirteen years as a player, Howell was
the only veteran player added to the roster by trade. A 20-point-per-game
scorer, Howell moved into the starting lineup for the 1966–67 season, scoring precisely that many points a game.

The league sat back to watch what unfolded in Boston. Auerbach was
no longer coach. Russell the great player was now being asked to coach as
well. And for the first time in several years, the Celtics were hearing footsteps in the Eastern Division. Footsteps as loud as a buffalo stampede on the
prairie. The Philadelphia 76ers, so fed up with losing, were loaded.

Wilt Chamberlain did not make a peep about his supporting cast. That season the 76ers had all the ingredients, from formidable 6-foot-9 forward Lucious Jackson to rebound alongside Wilt, to dashing second-year forward Billy Cunningham and high-scoring Chet Walker, accompanied by an all-around backcourt and seasoned veterans coming off the bench. Savvy Alex Hannum, a longtime Celtics victim, was the coach.

Russell guided Boston to a 60-21 record, not exactly chopped liver, especially for a rookie coach. But the 76ers finished 68-13, at the time the best single-season record in NBA history. Chamberlain led his team in scoring, rebounding, and assists. Boston actually won the season series, 5-4, but everyone knew the teams would meet in the eastern playoff finals after disposing of New York (Boston did so, 3-1) and Cincinnati (Philadelphia did so, 3-1).

The story line was simple. Could a hungry Philadelphia disrupt the Boston Dynasty? The Celtics seemed a step slow. Surely, it was Chamberlain's turn, wasn't it? Signs of a potential Celtics demise had been present before. Bill Sharman, Bob Cousy, Tommy Heinsohn, Frank Ramsey had all retired, and yet Boston won and won some more.

Not this time. The 76ers won the first three games of the series. There is no greater lock in American sports than a franchise leading a best-of-seven playoff series 3-0. The Celtics captured the fourth game and some wondered if this was a blip or if Boston's years-long stranglehold on Philadelphia's psyche was kicking in. On April 11, 1967, the 76ers crushed Boston, 140–116, in Philadelphia. The 76ers were kings of the East.

It was difficult to tell if Chamberlain was more happy or more relieved. "I've been chasing them a long time," he said.

For the first time since 1956, the NBA finals took place without Celtic participation. Delirious 76ers fans shouted, "The Celtics are dead! The Celtics are dead!" It certainly looked that way. Philadelphia topped the San Francisco Warriors, four games to two, and the descendants of the Syracuse Nationals gave Wilt Chamberlain his first NBA crown. For once, he got the best of Russell.

"They were definitely a great club," Bailey Howell said. "I believe Alex Hannum instilled in them a little bit more mental toughness than they had and they beat us. At that time everybody felt the Dynasty was over. All the players were kind of growing old together and Boston's 'dead.' We heard a lot of jeers and stuff."

Havlicek conceded it was certainly Philadelphia's year. "They just wiped us out," he said. "The crowd was never hungrier for Celtic blood than on that particular night [the final game]."

It was K. C. Jones's final game. He was retiring, another Celtic hanging up those trademark black sneakers. Russell put his arm around his old college roommate as they walked off the floor in Philadelphia.

After he showered and dressed, a flamboyant black cape on his shoulders, Russell trekked to the 76ers locker room to congratulate Chamberlain. It was a moment of supreme class, the appropriate gesture. He stood before Chamberlain, shook his hand, and said, "Great." That's all. "Great." Chamberlain said, "Right, baby."

The outside world figured the "fading" Celtics were toast and that the surging 76ers would take control of the league. After eight titles in a row, the Celtics could not get out of their own conference playoffs. For a moment, veterans like Bailey Howell and Wayne Embry, who had struggled so mightily to beat Boston for years, and had come over to the other side for their own chance at victory, must have thought they arrived too late.

"The Celtics always rose to the occasion to prove they were the best," Embry said, "but we knew the 76ers had put together a formidable team and we knew they were going to be competitive. They were all year and they did beat us."

Embry wondered what the Celtics postgame locker room would be like, honorable warriors, teammates and champions for so long, coping with defeat. "This was a new experience for the Celtics," he said, "and after the game, there wasn't a lot of remorse. There wasn't a lot of keeping your head down. The key players, Russell and Havlicek, those guys just said, 'They were better than us this year. We'll be better next year.'"

Auerbach said that he did not choose Russell as Celtics coach to make a statement about race relations. In fact, he said if he had mentioned that, Russell probably would have declined the job. But if Auerbach was colorblind, the rest of the world was not. Sportswriters did not always ask Russell the most intelligent questions that season. Although they just knew it was going to be fine for him because he was, after all, coaching many of his ex-teammates, how did he think white players elsewhere would respond to the authority of a black coach? Likely one of the worst questions asked of Russell was, if he as a Negro coach failed would it damage race relations?

An interesting dynamic that season was the roster addition of Howell, a white Mississippian, with the most extreme drawl this side of Scarlett O'Hara. Some wondered how a player of Howell's background would mesh with a black coach of Russell's characteristics. The short answer: Fine.

Wayne Embry said northern players sometimes made fun of Howell's accent, but said everyone—black and white—liked Howell. Howell liked to tease teammates, and that included the coach. Embry said Russell enjoyed the byplay. Embry also reported that one day Howell offered Russell a ride to his car parked far from the airport. With his wife and two daughters picking him up, Howell had a full car. When the little girl asked why she had to sit on a black man's lap, Howell was mortified. But Embry said Russell laughed about the matter.

If you are Bill Russell, you get used to near-perfection on a basketball court, but so much was asked of Russell during the 1966–67 season in replacing a legend on the bench that the task was nigh impossible. Russell made mistakes. Sometimes he sat a player too long. Sometimes he didn't bring a player in fast enough. Making the wrong move at the wrong time went to the heart of whether being the leader on the court and on the bench was too much for any man. Reporters covering the games logically took note of any error possibly leading to defeat. Sometimes newspaper headlines pounded home the point.

Russell was not only under great pressure to perform as a player and coach, but he also had the added challenge of treating friends and teammates appropriately, of pulling back from them because he was now their boss. Similarly, some teammates judged his inaugural season just as they would have another coach's.

A little more than a month after the end of the season, guard Sam Jones's name turned up in a newspaper story in which he said he didn't think Russell could play and coach effectively. Jones said he "didn't feel [Russell] can be a player of his caliber where he has to play 48 minutes per game and coach a ball team." Jones did not "think it can be done."

Maybe, maybe not, but neither Russell nor Auerbach were giving up on the deal. When the 1967–68 season began, the Boston Celtics were not favored to win their own division. The mighty 76ers, with all key players back from the championship club, seemed capable of starting their own dynasty.

The Celtics did not do a lot of talking outside of their own locker room at the time, but it rankled them that many so-called experts leapt on the 76ers bandwagon. No, they were not upset about anybody regarding Philadelphia as the best in the league the previous season. The 76ers had proven themselves. The Celtics had their chance and they lost. Fair enough. What the Celtics seethed about, from Auerbach to the last man on the bench, was a sudden groundswell of opinion suggesting the 1966–67 76ers might be the greatest team of all time. Yes, the 76ers won more games in a single season than any other squad. But hello? How about eight world titles in a row? Call us back in a decade, was the Celts' attitude. Even today mention of the 76ers in the same paragraph evaluating great teams can irk a Celtic of the period.

"I say to people today, I'm proud of a lot of things we were involved in with the Celtics," Bob Cousy said, "and I know legends are made to be broken, but one that will stand forever in my judgment is eleven championships in thirteen years."

The 1967–68 season began with a 25-7 Celtics burst, showing they were going to be around. But the 76ers gradually pulled away to win the Eastern Division with a 62-20 record, eight games better than Boston.

Havlicek, Howell, and Sam Jones all averaged around 20 points a game and the Celtics had four additional players averaging in double figures. Russell still patrolled the middle. Tom Sanders remained a key man. And guard Larry Siegfried and forward Don Nelson pushed themselves into the mix. More of a spot player in his first Boston season, Nelson was relied on more heavily, appearing in every game.

It was counterintuitive to believe that Boston was of championship mettle again. Losing the previous season was evidence their time was past.

Once a team seems to be past its prime the only trajectory is downward. The Celtics stayed on top longer than any other professional basketball team, but it took blind belief to think they could reverse the one-year slide. It was not simply the issue of age, but of having a peaking power in their own division. There was no way to dodge the 76ers.

The 1967–68 season was also probably the greatest test of the Celtics' concentration. Besides still adjusting to Russell as coach and seeking to rebound from the first season in nearly a decade to end with a loss, the Celtics lived in a country in turmoil because of the war in Vietnam and the continuing struggles of American blacks fighting a Civil Rights war on the home front. That also was the season the fledgling American Basketball Association declared war on the National Basketball Association.

The NBA had brushed aside the brief challenge of the American Basketball League earlier in the 1960s. Although NBA owners could not have known, this time a new rebel league had staying power and would reorder the established league's way of doing business. The ABA introduced a red, white, and blue basketball. While a nod to patriotism and a flashy piece of equipment, the ball never crossed over to the NBA. But the three-point shot did. The new arc around the foul lane, offering a bonus point for a long-distance shot, took over the game at every level.

There were fly-by-night ABA franchises that failed early, and there were entertaining franchises seeking a foothold. The Miami Floridians played in an old airplane hangar and featured bikini-clad courtside dancers. (They were ahead of their time.) The ABA gave Connie Hawkins, unjustly banned from the NBA, a stage. The ABA stole Zelmo Beatty from the Hawks with a lucrative deal. The ABA introduced George "Iceman" Gervin, George McGinnis, Moses Malone, and above all, "Dr. J." Julius Erving and his trapeze act, to the world of pro basketball.

Determined and deep-pocketed ABA owners offered outrageous sums of money to established NBA stars to jump leagues. They even swooped down and carried off some of the most prominent referees, including Earl Strom, who had been on the scene for so many famous NBA moments. Strom said his pay and benefits package was $150,000 for three years, double what he was making across the street.

Red Auerbach, who believed in loyalty as one of the ten commandments, could not imagine any of his players defecting. But it was early in the game. The offers would increase, the battle for draft choices intensify, and soon players content with salaries of $40,000 would be making $400,000. Auerbach would live to see professional basketball paychecks jump to $4 million—and more.

The Celtics were not raided that season, but the pursuit of quality players was just beginning. It was just another backstory during the Dynasty that had the capability of preoccupying players, of shaking up team chemistry, but another development that was never allowed to interfere.

Throughout the 1960s, the nation's jittery focus alternated between the war in Southeast Asia that was brought into living rooms by television and the front-yard confrontations in the South, where red-faced sheriffs brutalized black-faced Americans. By the middle of the decade, Dr. Martin Luther King Jr. was probably the second-best-known American next to President Lyndon B. Johnson.

In 1964, King was presented the Nobel Peace Prize, the world's most prestigious award, and one that not only gave added legitimacy to the black cause internationally, but also added to King's stature with the American politicians he sought to influence. The fight on American soil for Americans born and raised there seemed never-ending, defying the bounds of logic. How could Americans live peaceably in the knowledge that so many millions of them were routinely disenfranchised?

With an impatient constituency, an ever angrier populace no longer willing to wait out an impassive Congress, King was under siege from some of his natural allies. King preached nonviolence, but increasing numbers of black Americans felt there would be no progress without it. But winning the Nobel Peace Prize represented endorsement of his methods. The world was watching, the world approved of the struggle, and the world approved of King's tactics.

But hate would not take a holiday. And neither the assurances of his compatriots, nor the umbrella shield of the prize swayed King from ever-present thoughts of his own premature death. He witnessed too much violence and killing, read too many ugly messages of loathing on racists' faces to relax.

A preacher first, King delivered his message of God and righteousness, of man and rights, at a borrowed pulpit in Memphis, Tennessee, on April 4, 1968. Some hours later, in the midst of dressing for dinner at the Lorraine Hotel, Martin Luther King Jr. stepped out of his room onto the second-floor balcony for some air, Southern Christian Leadership Conference partner Reverend Ralph Abernathy at his side.

The assassin's rifle shot pierced the calm, ripped through King's jaw and neck, and dropped him to the ground. As the blood spread on his white shirt, King died in Abernathy's arms and a nation went berserk. Rising up to riot in protest, hope stolen by the death of a revered leader, agonized and enraged Americans trashed their cities. The leader of a movement embracing nonviolence was murdered and a country's conscience was stained, a country's belief in justice was diminished.

The Boston Celtics and Philadelphia 76ers were poised for a rematch of their own private little playoff war when King was gunned down. The teams each had polished off an Eastern Division first-round opponent April 1. The next round—against each other—was scheduled to start April 5, the day after the King assassination. What a grisly thing to gain experience in, but following the assassination of President John F. Kennedy, the United States' sports leagues should have grown wiser about showing respect in such situations. Apparently, sensitivity training was still necessary. The NBA plunged into the series as scheduled.

Many members of each team were black. None had the appetite to play. Hal Greer, the 76ers star guard, immediately told his wife that there was no way the scheduled game would go on. Sportswriters suggested it was inappropriate to play and wrote that sports meant little in the big picture with the death of the great man.

Wilt Chamberlain publicized his feelings: The game should be postponed. "I would personally like to see the whole day taken off as some kind of memorial to Dr. King," Chamberlain said.

About three hours before tip-off, Bill Russell reached Chamberlain on the phone. They agreed the game should not be played, but thought it was too late to stop it since fans were already on their way to the Spectrum. At the arena, the 76ers (who had six black players on the team) held a meeting and took a vote on whether or not to play. The vote was 7–2, with only Chamberlain and guard Wally Jones voting not to play. A distraught Chet Walker abstained during the vote. There was fear fans might riot inside if the game was called off. Red Auerbach had called a team meeting of the Celtics (who had seven black players) in the afternoon, but there was not enough sentiment to urge boycotting the game.

The Celtics won the game, 127–118, but never was so meaningless an important game contested. "No one was in any mood to play," Wayne Embry said.

Russell talked about his feelings afterward, saying, "I've been in a state of shock. I didn't sleep last night."

President Johnson, noting blazes in the streets, announced that Sunday, April 7, two days later, would be a day of national mourning for King. So the NBA announced that no games would be played that day. Chamberlain and Russell attended King's funeral in Atlanta on April 9 and the Celtics-76ers series resumed April 10. Still, depression over the murder permeated many players' thoughts. Walker seemed deeply affected. Embry thought there should have been a longer break.

Yet the games resumed and the series began playing out exactly as expected—the 76ers jumped ahead 3-1. The same fans who chanted gleefully about Boston's basketball death the year before were ready for another round of drinks. Even Boston sports writers said the situation was hopeless.

Some Celtics thought otherwise. Captain John Havlicek and Embry, who said he was sort of captain of the backups, exhorted their teammates. They wrote inspirational messages on the locker room blackboard like PRIDE. DETERMINATION. And oh yes, these being professionals, they punctuated the words with a small dollar sign.

No telling what worked, but the Celtics handled Philly, 122–104, in the fifth game, won the sixth game 114–106, and set up a seventh game. This was the game Russell chose to employ Embry on Chamberlain in a defensive switch. At courtside, just before the game, a Philadelphia fan holding a banana approached Embry, and said, "Here, this is for apes." Embry said he was rearing his fist back to punch the guy out, but Auerbach intervened. Embry said he always prayed for a clean game during the National Anthem, but at that turbulent time began adding a prayer that the Lord make Martin Luther King Jr.'s dream of equality come true.

After the Celtics overcame the 3-1 deficit to win the last game, 100–96, Johnny Most said "Celtic Pride" forevermore would be the team rallying cry.

The championship was Boston's tenth since 1957 and the first on Bill Russell's watch. Later in 1968, Russell signed a new $200,000 contract. Maybe the guy could coach after all.

23

RUSSELL GOES AND
SO DOES THE DYNASTY

Where had the time gone? Bill Russell was in his thirteenth professional basketball season and before the 1968–69 season ended he turned thirty-five. Basketball players age faster than dogs. Sprinting up and down that hardwood does it to them, wearing down the ligaments and muscles in their legs prematurely. One day they just can't jump as high or run as fast, and usually they sense it before the coach can notice it.

In his third season as head coach, Russell's lithe form was aching. He played in 77 of the team's 82 games, but he was not always in top form. The iron man player who routinely played 48 minutes most of his career, listened to the advice of his former coach, Red Auerbach, and sat down more frequently. This is one time, with the two jobs now held by one man, that there was no fooling the coach.

Russell averaged only 9.9 points a game that season, the lowest of his career, the only time he did not average double figures. The Celtics, who thrived on the fast break, were definitely a step slower. The rest of the league thought Boston was running on empty, and finishing fourth with a 48-34 record in the Eastern Division fed ammunition to critics and skeptics.

Never one to confide his innermost thoughts to teammates, Russell could not hide his nagging injuries in the locker room.. He sought to nurse himself through the regular season in the hope that minor, bothersome aches would heal, or that he would just be able to shunt them aside and ignore them at money time.

"Russell was hurting," Havlicek said of the Celtics' pivotal player many years later. "But he told us, 'I can get the job done in the playoffs.'" Havlicek said Russell missed his handful of games at the end of the season, something Havlicek termed "a blessing" because it enabled the big guy to start the playoffs refreshed.

Yet, anyone who thought Russell was running on fumes was sadly misjudging the situation. He played 3,291 minutes that season—still 117 minutes more than Havlicek, another guy who seemed never to rest. They were twin peaks of stamina. Red Auerbach had long before uttered his belief that it didn't matter who started a game, but rather who finished. Russell and Havlicek were present and accounted for at both ends, for the opening tip and the closing buzzer.

The Baltimore Bullets, the Philadelphia 76ers, and the New York Knicks all finished ahead of Boston during the regular season. The dying embers of the Dynasty set off only the faintest of glows. Observers believed the Celtics' last hurrah had come in the spring of 1968 when they upset Philly. Now they were just hanging on and the standings supported the notion.

During the trying season Russell also lugged around a secret. He had decided to retire after the playoffs. But he wanted to avoid the farewell salutes bestowed on Bob Cousy and he did not relish giving other teams additional motivation to knock him off as Auerbach had. This decision was between Russell the coach and Russell the player. Sterling guard Sam Jones had also committed to retirement, though he announced it. Jones would turn thirty-six immediately after the playoffs. It was time, he thought.

Jones's teammates knew he was gone after the playoffs. But guard Emmette Bryant, in his first year with the club, has at best a hazy memory of Russell even hinting to the guys about his plans. Much later, Russell said the only one he told was Oscar Robertson, the final time they met on the court. Russell said he had long graded his own performances and during the season realized his marks were slipping. Once a straight-A student Russell felt he was in danger of dropping off the honor roll. That's when he decided to retire.

A team that had been so remarkable in winning one for Walter Brown, winning one for Bob Cousy, and winning a good-bye title for Red Auerbach, made no such public pronouncements that it was going to win one for Sam Jones.. Maybe it would have seemed presumptuous after finishing only fourth in the East and with only the equal fifth-best record in the NBA that year, even if the Celtics wanted to give Jones a going-away present.

There was no super team in the East since Wilt Chamberlain had been traded to the Lakers. Now L.A. had the makings of an unbeatable club with Chamberlain, Elgin Baylor, and Jerry West in the same lineup. Boston had done well enough during the regular season against Philadelphia, but the Celts had not fared well against the Knicks. Bailey Howell said the Celtics weren't favored against anybody in the postseason.

What the Celtics counted on was their playoff experience, the desire of veterans to win one more ring, and their ability to adapt and adjust in a short series against a younger, but less savvy opponent. Boston bested Philadelphia 4-1 in its opening series. An improving Knicks team surprisingly demolished regular-season division-champ Baltimore, 4-0.

These were the Knicks of Willis Reed, Dick Barnett, Walt Frazier, Bill Bradley, Cazzie Russell, and Dave DeBusschere, a jelling core of talented, unselfish players a year away from a title. That was the thing—the Knicks were still a year away. The young legs didn't overtake the old legs in 1969 and Boston triumphed in the series 4-2.

New York still probably can't figure out how it lost that round. ". . . we could make the plays and do the things we needed to do to win," Howell said.

Celtic Mystique was a magic spell by then, and one aspect of Boston's consistent greatness during the Dynasty was its ability to win the seventh game of a playoff series. Usually, by virtue of a first-place regular-season finish, that seventh game was at the Boston Garden. This time the Celtics had home-court advantage over nobody.

Not even the smartest of money in Las Vegas would have bet on the Boston Celtics still having a pulse by the time the NBA Finals rolled around in 1969. Gone were the Bullets, toast were the 76ers, devastated were the Knicks. Out of the mix in the Western Division were the Atlanta Hawks and their 48 victories. The last men standing, so appropriately, were the Boston Celtics from the East and the Los Angeles Lakers from the West. Again. History, it seems, has a sense of irony.

Never were the Lakers more determined. Never were the Lakers more convinced they had the weapons. Grim-faced, jaws set, they were ready for high noon. Chamberlain, Baylor, and West. No one had ever put such firepower on the floor at once. And to boot, the Lakers had the seventh-game home-court advantage, if the series even lasted that long. The last game would be in Los Angeles, in beach weather, in the Fabulous Forum, not in that rat-infested relic of a Boston Garden. In the Finals for the sixth time in eight years, the Lakers were certain they had the Celtics just where they wanted them.

The series opened in L.A. A Boston win might have crushed the Lakers' spirit, sent a message that this playoff series would be no different than all of the others. Instead, L.A. took everything Boston could muster and survived, 120–118. West was phenomenal with 53 points.

Somewhat humorously in retrospect, West bumped into Russell at the arena and told him that he was incredibly tired and felt as if the season had "been two years long." West played 46 minutes that night. Call it a second wind.

When teams expect a long series, the visitor always tries to "steal" one of the other team's home games right away. Heading home 1-1 is so much more uplifting than trailing 0-2. L.A. took Game 2, 118–112, and this time West pumped in 41 points with Baylor adding 32 points. The Celtics were respected for their defense, but they were being shredded. Two games in Los Angeles, two games in the L.A. win column.

"They beat us good the first two games," Bryant said. "And then looking at the big picture you think now Boston has to win four out of five. When you put it like that it doesn't sound very good. But we didn't approach it like that. We thought, 'Okay, they won their two and now we're going home. Let's get ready for the next game.' We always thought about the next game. We were not going to look down the road. One at a time."

In the Boston Garden, the Celtics bested the Lakers, 111–105. The fourth game was critical. If Los Angeles won the lead would be 3-1, a margin rarely surmounted. If Boston won, the series would be knotted, 2-2, and the outlook from both sides of the fence would be completely different.

Jerry West scored 40 points, but it didn't matter. Boston won, 89–88, though by less than a clean knockout. A controversial call claiming that Baylor had dribbled out of bounds gave the ball to the Celtics trailing by one point with seconds left. The odds of pulling it off? Don't ask. The method by which things played out? Ridiculous.

Earlier in the year in practice, realizing his team needed a buzzer-beating play, Russell let the players draw one up. John Havlicek and Larry Siegfried, teammates at Ohio State, remembered a play from college. They named it "Ohio" and although it had never before been used, this was the play the Celtics called. It almost didn't work. Sam Jones, Boston's best sharpshooter, ended up with the ball, but he slipped as he shot. From 22 feet away, the ball left Jones's right hand, hit the front rim, bounced off the backboard, off the back rim, and went through the hoop with one second left.

"I was lucky," Jones said afterward. "Kiss the Blarney Stone," *Los Angeles Times* sports writer Mal Graham wrote. Some fans even thought the Celtics' impish leprechaun mascot guided the ball into the basket.

Back and forth the series went, by jet plane between coasts, in victories between home arenas. The Lakers captured the fifth game, 117–104, with West pouring in 39 more points and Chamberlain seizing 31 rebounds. Boston captured the sixth game, 99–90 after Chamberlain was poked in the eye by Bryant and suffered from blurred vision. Three games all. The seventh game was set for May 5, 1969, in Los Angeles.

It was the last game of the NBA season. Few knew it was to be the last game of Bill Russell's career. For the Celtics there would be one more glorious, glowing sunset, or a dark night of Lakers retribution.

In what might have been one of the worst, premature celebratory strategies in the history of sport, Lakers owner Jack Kent Cooke, anticipating that his three-point favorite team would notch its first NBA title, made elaborate plans to fete his team.

This was not some hurried, scratched-out-on-a-napkin plan. This was not a proposal for a parade through Hollywood a couple of days hence. Nope. Cooke envisioned an on-the-spot party in the arena after the buzzer. Instant New Year's Eve. The celebration was scripted in more detail than a presidential candidate's visit. Cooke even had his public relations staff draw up a press release revealing the commemoration's blow by blow. Sheets of paper with all the details were left on fans' seats. Thousands of balloons, a rainbow of round rubber, were tied to the rafters of the forum in fishermen's nets, just waiting to be freed and dropped on the crowd. The University of Southern California band was scheduled to play "Happy Days Are Here Again."

In his autobiography, broadcaster Johnny Most recounted the scene as he read the schedule in the presence of famed Lakers announcer Chick Hearn. "What's all this?" Most asked. Hearn, apparently more aware of Celtics-Lakers history than the owner, replied, "It's dumb, that's what it is. I can imagine what Russell is going to say to his team about this nonsense."

There is a certain fuzziness in the memory of Celtics about just which one of them saw the plans first. Might have been Sam Jones. Might have been Russell. Don Nelson remembers Red Auerbach frowning about the balloons and making sure the Celts knew they were up there, multicolored stars cluttering the Forum sky. Make no mistake, the Celtics were incensed at the gaudiness of the plan and what it represented—that the Lakers were taking them for granted. That sheet of paper—read aloud from top to bottom in the locker room—is seared in the minds of the 1968–69 Celtics. They bristled at the lack of respect. As if they needed more motivation. As if.

"They had champagne back there on ice too, you know," Bryant said. "We made note of it."

Made note of it? A Celtic or two might have been pleased to make the bottles' close personal acquaintance with a sledgehammer. And a Celtic or two might have enjoyed popping a few balloons by firing a BB gun at the ceiling. Instead, the Celtics did what they had done best for thirteen years. They ran, shot, and passed with exquisite crispness and going into the fourth quarter, led the Lakers 91–76.

There came a moment when West, who produced one of the greatest playoff performances of all time, was standing at the foul line with just under 8½ minutes remaining. He missed the free throw and made a motion as if to punch the ball with his right hand. Frustration.

In the late going, Havlicek picked up his fifth foul and so did Chamberlain. Sam Jones, in the final game of his career, fouled out. West was dribbling and Jones reached, then quickly retracted both hands to his shoulders before dropping them to his sides too late. He was given a standing ovation by Los Angeles fans and retreated to the bench. Jones tied a white towel around his head and resembled a Bedouin as he anxiously waited for time to run out.

In a development that remained controversial years later, Chamberlain left the game with 5:55 on the clock after landing awkwardly under the Celtics' basket and coming up with a limp. He had 18 points and 27 rebounds. Wilt sat on the bench with his head tilted back, face registering obvious pain. A trainer worked on his knee and a few minutes later Chamberlain said he clamored to return to the floor. However, coach Bill van Breda Kolff left him there stewing, refusing to reinsert Chamberlain into the lineup. In future years, Chamberlain expressed fury over the exile. Russell was angry too, feeling Chamberlain had taken himself out despite not suffering a serious injury.

Frustrated or not, West wasn't finished. Shooting that picturesque jumper, West carried the Lakers. The Celtics lead evaporated. With about 3 minutes to go, Mel Counts, the onetime 7-foot Russell backup, hit a jump shot in the lane for the Lakers, narrowing the score to 103–102 Boston.

The frenzied next possessions produced ill-timed fouls, poorly taken foul shots, and off-target passes on both sides. The basketball ricocheted off players like a pinball. Laker Keith Erickson made a bad pass. Havlicek stole the ball underneath the Celtics' basket. But the ball was batted to Don Nelson inside the foul line. Nelson, whose best offensive weapon was an awkward-looking one-handed push shot, released his favorite shot. The ball hit the front rim, bounced high in the air, and fell through the basket, giving Boston a critical 105–102 lead.

"That was the luckiest shot I ever made in my life," Nelson said, while admitting that it might be the only shot from his playing career he checks out when it appears in a TV highlight.

Nearly two minutes remained, but Nelson's was the back-breaking basket, on a shot so ugly that at best it emulated a goose flying with one healthy wing. The final score was 108–106. Auerbach, who grinned and puffed on a cigar, wondered what the Lakers were going to do with all of those balloons.

"They were still there when we left," Bryant joked years later.

The 17,560 fans went silent. Jerry West, who scored 42 points and won the series Most Valuable Player award despite playing on the losing team, went limp. Sam Jones admitted West was unstoppable this series.

"I had to say a little prayer every time he got the ball," Jones said.

As a team the Celtics averaged thirty-two years of age. The old guys had done it one more time. The locker room was wild. Interviewed by Jack Twyman for television, the retiring Jones, who scored 24 points in his last game, savored the moment. "This is the one that's the greatest," he said.

Russell was emotional on camera, choking up, laughing, shedding tears. They were characteristics of relief, of having reached the summit one last time, and of privately knowing it was the last time.

"This is such a great bunch of guys," Russell said. "It's so fabulous the way they played for me."

Fabulous is the way the Boston Celtics had played for thirteen seasons. In the basketball lifespan of Bill Russell, Boston won eleven titles. Russell packed a green and white uniform in his suitcase for the last time in Los Angeles. Others, unaware Russell was retiring, recognized that this was at least the twilight of the gods.

In fact, the Dynasty was over. A group of men so talented, so diverse, striving with a single purpose, crossed paths with history for a time and put their stamp on it. Neither their aging bodies, nor their magnificent unity could last forever. But what they accomplished has. Celtic Pride remains intact and pure.

EPILOGUE: CELTIC PRIDE

The highlights of men's lives happen when they choose to, not conjured up on command or by the wish of the men. Not to say there will never be other highlights, with spouses, children, unrelated achievements, but the pinnacle of team sport is capturing a championship, and the players who made it to the mountaintop treat the mementoes of the climb with reverence and fondness.

Maturity and the passage of time help them understand even better than the joy of the moment what was achieved, what was shared. For teammates in that championship season, the journey and its culmination usually serve as a lifetime connection. Winning a single championship—the World Series, the Stanley Cup, the National Football League title, or National Basketball Association trophy—is special. The Boston Celtics Dynasty transcended that glory, piling accomplishment upon accomplishment in winning eleven world titles in thirteen years.

Only Bill Russell was present for all eleven. But several Celtics collected championship rings as if they were as easy to gather as butterflies. Some Celtics contributed to just one triumph, and if anything they treasure the victory that brought a single ring as much as the men who won five, six, seven or eight. The onetime champion player is as much a part of the Celtics family as many-time winners such as Russell, Bob Cousy, or Tommy Heinsohn. That player did his part, and when the buzzer sounded for a final time in his magnificent season, he knew that season he was a member of the best team.

Emmette Bryant played two years with the Celtics and was on the last Dynasty champion only. Nearly forty years have passed, but beating the Lakers, being part of Russell's final season, is as vivid to him now as it was then. "I think back to it all the time," Bryant said.

There are always reminders. Some old Celtics sign autographs at sports memorabilia shows. Some return for reunions at the Celtics current home arena, the TD Banknorth Garden.

The Boston Celtics pioneered one more now-commonplace facet of professional sports. Hanging from the rafters, first at the Boston Garden, then at the Fleet Center, now at the renamed home arena, are banners that shout out the team's glorious history. The green-trimmed, white banners are sentinels of the past, listing each championship season. The Celtics introduced the practice and other teams, in basketball, football, hockey, in pro ball, college ball, and at high schools, emulated them. Celtics banners show off about world championships. Other teams advertise division titles or conference championships won.

Additional banners in the TD Banknorth Garden feature retired numbers, the numbers worn by the greats who made it all happen, who brought honor to the franchise, some of whom graduated to the Basketball Hall of Fame. No basketball team has been as enthusiastic about retiring numbers as the Celtics. Current-day players are lucky their numbers aren't all something like 64 or 87.

No. 1 was retired for Walter Brown. No. 2 was retired for Red Auerbach in 1985. From the Dynasty era, Bill Russell's No. 6 went up, as did Bob Cousy's 14, Tommy Heinsohn's 15, Tom Sanders' 16, John Havlicek's 17, Don Nelson's 19, Bill Sharman's 21, Frank Ramsey's 23, Sam Jones's 24, and K. C. Jones's 25. The Celtics also retired Jim Loscutoff's nickname, "Loscy" since his No. 18 was later used and retired for Dave Cowens.

Russell avoided Boston after he retired, a payback of sorts for his resentment over the racism he experienced. When No. 2 was retired for Auerbach in January of 1985, Russell appeared in public and along with Dorothy Auerbach helped raise the number to the rafters. When Russell was asked why he came back this time, he said, "Red Auerbach is my friend."

Brown, Auerbach, Cousy, Russell, Sharman, Ramsey, Havlicek, Sam Jones, K. C. Jones, Bailey Howell, Lovellette (primarily for his seasons with the Hawks) and Wayne Embry (as a contributor as the first black general manager) are all in the Hall of Fame. John Thompson, who played briefly as a backup to Russell, was selected for his college-coaching excellence at Georgetown. Johnny Most is in there too, for his creative work behind the microphone. He was, after all, the voice of the Dynasty.

The Celtics Dynasty stretched from 1957 to 1969 and counted eleven world championships. Under Auerbach the administrator, the Celtics rebuilt twice. The 1973–74 and the 1975–76 teams won world championships with Heinsohn as coach. The 1980–81 team tutored by Bill Fitch (and with K. C. Jones as assistant coach) won the first title of the Larry Bird–Kevin McHale–Robert Parish era. That core group of Celtics won again in 1983–84 and 1985–86 with K. C. as head coach. Despite a drought since 1986, the Celtics have won sixteen NBA crowns.

John Havlicek, who arrived during the heart of the Dynasty, persevered through the second batch of titles. "The 1974 and 1976 teams were special," Havlicek said. "They sort of became my teams."

Havlicek stayed with the Celtics long enough to be offered a contract with the upstart American Basketball Association. He turned it down.

After leaving the bench, Auerbach stayed in the front office, associated with the Celtics in one capacity or another, from general manager to president, from elder statesman to legend, until he died at age eighty-nine in October 2006 after more than a year of failing health.

Frank Ramsey tried to stay in touch with Auerbach in Washington, D.C., by telephone from Kentucky.

"To me, he was a heck of a guy," Ramsey said some weeks after Auerbach's death. "I always called him on his birthday and this past year when I called he was down because he was having to go through kidney dialysis. He was always into fitness and he was dependent on people to take him around. Anyway, he was one of a kind. They broke the mold when we lost him."

After Bill Russell retired as player and coach of the Celtics in 1969, he took a break from basketball. But he returned twice to coach, first with the

Seattle Supersonics and then the Sacramento Kings, though with considerably less success than he had with Boston. Comments were made that his teams didn't win because he didn't have Bill Russell at center. Russell also spent time as an NBA television commentator.

Bob Cousy went straight from the Celtics to Boston College. When he tired of the recruiting grind and what he felt were hypocritical NCAA rules, he returned to the NBA and coached the Cincinnati Royals. He spent time as a Celtics broadcaster too.

Tommy Heinsohn's first splashy return to "active" Celtics duty was as coach. In the mod 1970s his hair was much longer than it was in the 1950s and 1960s, and he was occasionally spied in a plaid sport coat. Heinsohn's artwork flourished and he sold more paintings. He also returned to Boston yet again as a TV broadcaster, and his partnership with Mike Gorman has spanned more than a quarter of a century.

Before K. C. Jones coached the Celtics to fresh glory, he coached at little Brandeis University and in the ABA. Besides Boston, K. C. coached the Washington NBA franchise and Seattle. During the 2006–07 season, he worked as a radio color commentator on University of Hartford men's games.

By comparison, Sam Jones has mostly stayed out of the limelight. He has lived in North Carolina and Florida and occasionally appears at sports memorabilia shows for autograph signings.

Tom Sanders coached Harvard University between 1973 and 1977 and also got his chance to coach the Celtics briefly in 1978 before working extensively for the NBA over a period of years.

Jim Loscutoff kept his summer basketball camp going for decades in Massachusetts, and his son still runs it. Jungle Jim lives in Florida year-round now.

So does Gene Conley, who stays on the go between Celtics-related events and Braves-related events. His wife wrote a book about Conley's unusual professional sports life.

After retiring from pro basketball, Bailey Howell returned to his college roots and settled down in Starkville, Mississippi.

Don Nelson, the great Auerbach pickup at forward, is still coaching in the NBA. In 2007 he guided his eighth-seeded Golden State Warriors to a shocking first-round playoff upset of the top-seeded Dallas Mavericks.

Bill Sharman went directly into professional coaching and ultimately was elected to the Hall of Fame as both a player and a coach. He won an NBA title as boss of the Lakers, then moved to the front office. More than forty-five years after his retirement as an active player, Sharman was still affiliated with Los Angeles as a consultant.

Wayne Embry was a barrier breaker as general manager of the Milwaukee Bucks and built winning teams for the Cleveland Cavaliers. After sampling retirement, Embry joined the Toronto Raptors as a consultant and enjoyed the team's return to the NBA playoffs in 2007.

Ramsey became a successful businessman in Kentucky and resides in a more sophisticated version of Madisonville, where he grew up. A storm ruined his home, but one of the items salvaged from the destruction was an original painting of him from the early 1960s that was used that season on some game programs. It is a prized possession. And Ramsey's Celtics tenure is a prized experience.

"That whole group has been successful after basketball," Ramsey said. "As you get older you appreciate it more. It sure was a great time."

The Celtics of the Dynasty years were just about all successful at whatever they tried in the years that followed. Forty and more years after they last played or won a title, they have collected AARP cards and have persevered into silver-haired senior citizenship. The only one gone is the leader, Red Auerbach.

For Auerbach's sixty-eighth birthday in September 1985, in appreciation for what he had done and who he was, Boston officials erected a statue of the old coach at Faneuil Hall. Auerbach's bronze figure sits on a bench smoking a cigar and holding a rolled-up program (some thought it should have been a Chinese menu). Red took a close-up look at himself frozen in one of his most popular poses, and said, "It makes you humble, you know, like you keep asking yourself, 'Did I do enough to deserve this?'"

Over the following twenty years, with the passage of time and the perspective of distance, hopefully Red Auerbach took a moment to reflect. His once ragamuffin team became a synonym for greatness. His blindly liberal racial outlook practiced as much as preached equality. The phrases "Celtic Pride" and "Celtic Mystique" have become ingrained in the lexicon.

Perhaps for just a few minutes in one of his final years, Auerbach sat back in repose and inhaled a favorite cigar, and while staring through the haze of smoke that he always considered akin to the clouds of heaven, exhaled with the certainty that he had indeed done quite enough.

SOURCES

BOOKS

Auerbach, Red and Feinstein, John. *Let Me Tell You A Story: A Lifetime in the Game*. Little Brown and Company, 2004.

Bishop, Jim. *The Day Kennedy Was Shot*. Toronto: HarperPerennial, 1992.

Carey, Mike and McClelland, Michael D. *Boston Celtics: Where Have You Gone?* Champaign, Illinois: Sports Publishing, 2005.

Carey, Mike and Most, Jamie. *High Above Courtside: The Lost Memoirs of Johnny Most*. Champaign, Illinois: Sports Publishing, 2003.

Cherry, Robert. *Wilt: Larger Than Life*. Chicago: Triumph Books, 2004.

Conley, Kathryn R. *One of A Kind: The Gene Conley Story*. Advantage Biography, 2004.

Cousy, Bob and Devaney, John. *The Killer Instinct*. New York: Random House, 1975.

Cousy, Bob and Linn, Edward. *The Last Loud Roar*. Englewood Cliffs, New Jersey: Prentice-Hall, Inc., 1964.

Cousy, Bob and Ryan, Bob. *Cousy on the Celtic Mystique*. New York: Zebra Books, 1988.

Egan, John. *The Vern Mikkelsen Story*. Minneapolis: Nodin Press, 2006.

Embry, Wayne and Boyer, Mary Schmitt. *The Inside Game: Race, Power, and Politics in the NBA*. Akron, Ohio: The University of Akron Press, 2004.

Fortunato, John A. *Commissioner: The Legacy of Pete Rozelle*. Lanham, Maryland: Taylor Trade Publishing, 2006.

Garrow, David J. *Bearing the Cross: Martin Luther King Jr. and the Southern Christian Leadership Conference*. New York: Perennial Classics, 2004.

Grenier, Mike. *The Champion Celtics*. Danvers, Massachusetts: Book Productions Services, 1974.

Havlicek, John and Ryan, Bob. *Hondo: Celtic Man in Motion*. Englewood Cliffs, New Jersey: Prentice-Hall, Inc., 1977.

Heinsohn, Tommy and Fitzgerald, Joe. *Give 'Em The Hook*. New York: Pocket Books, 1988.

Johnson, Richard A. and Johnson, Robert Hamilton. *The Celtics in Black and White*. Charleston, South Carolina: Arcadia Publishing, 2006.

Jones, K. C. and Warner, Jack. *Rebound*. Boston: Quinlan Press, 1986.

Karnow, Stanley. *Vietnam: A History*. New York: Penguin Books, 1994.

Kasher, Steven. *The Civil Rights Movement: A Photographic History, 1954-68*. New York: Abbeville Press, 1996.

Kerr, Johnny and Pluto, Terry. *Bull Session*. Chicago: Bonus Books, 1989.

May, Peter. *The Big Three*. New York: Simon & Schuster, 1994.

May, Peter. *The Last Banner*. New York: Simon & Schuster, 1996.

McCallum, Jack. *Unfinished Business*. New York: Summit Books, 1992.

Reynolds, Bill. *Cousy: His Life, Career and the Birth of Big-Time Basketball*. New York: Simon & Schuster, 2005.

Robertson, Oscar. *The Big O: My Life, My Times, My Game*. Emmaus, Pennsylvania: Rodale, 2003.

Russell, Bill and Branch, Taylor. *Second Wind: The Memoirs of an Opinionated Man*. New York: Random House, 1979.

Russell, Bill and Falkner, David. *Russell Rules: 11 Lessons on Leadership From the Twentieth Century's Greatest Winner*. New York: Dutton, 2001.

Shaughnessy, Dan. *Ever Green*. New York: St. Martin's Press, 1990.

Shaughnessy, Dan. *Seeing Red: The Red Auerbach Story*. New York: Crown Publishers, 1994.

Strom, Earl and Johnson, Blaine. *Calling the Shots: My Five Decades in the NBA*. New York: A Fireside Book, 1992.

Sullivan, George. *The Boston Celtics: A Championship Tradition*. Del Mar, California: Tehabi Books, 1996.

Taylor, John. *The Rivalry: Bill Russell, Wilt Chamberlain, and the Golden Age of Basketball*. New York: Random House, 2005.

Thomas, Ron. *They Cleared the Lane: The NBA's Black Pioneers*. Lincoln, Nebraska: University of Nebraska Press, 2002.

PERSONAL INTERVIEWS
Emmette Bryant

Ron Bonham

Gene Conley

Mel Counts

Bob Cousy

Wayne Embry

John Havlicek

Tommy Heinsohn

Bailey Howell

K. C. Jones

Johnny Kerr

Jim Loscutoff

Bob Petit

Frank Ramsey

Kenny Sailors

Tom Sanders

Dolph Schayes

Bill Sharman

Jack Twyman

CONVERSATIONS AT PUBLIC FORUMS
Sam Jones

Bill Russell

FILM AND VIDEO
NBA Dynasty Series: Boston Celtics, The Complete History. 2004 NBA Properties.

Tommy: Forever Green. Fox Sports Network television documentary of Tommy Heinsohn, 2006.

REFERENCE BOOKS
Sporting News Official NBA Register, 2006-07.

Sporting News Official NBA Guide, 2006-07.

Official National Basketball Association Guide, 1963-64.

Boston Celtics Media Guide, 2005-06.

WEBSITES
NBA.com/NBAEncyclopedia

Wikipedia, The Free Encyclopedia

MAGAZINES
Boston Garden: Banner Years, 1928-1995, A Lifetime of Memories

Inside Sports, November 30, 1980.

Sports Illustrated, November 6, 2006.

NEWSPAPERS
Associated Press, October 14, 1999.

Atlanta Constitution, Associated Press, April 6, 1975.

Boston Globe, November 1, 1957.

Boston Globe, January 20, 1958.

Boston Globe, November 26, 1958.

Boston Globe, January 4, 1959.

Boston Globe, January 17, 1959.

Boston Globe, January 18, 1959.

Boston Globe, February 2, 1959.

Boston Globe, February 27, 1959.

Boston Globe, March 7, 1959.

Boston Globe, April 8, 1959.

Boston Globe, September 14, 1959.

Boston Globe, December 15, 1959.

Boston Globe, December 27, 1959.

Boston Globe, January 10, 1960.

Boston Globe, October 18, 1960.

Boston Globe, October 18, 1961.

Boston Globe, December 26, 1961.

Boston Globe, December 27, 1961.

Boston Globe, March 28, 1962.

Boston Globe, April 1, 1962.

Boston Globe, April 7, 1962.

Boston Globe, April 13, 1962.

Boston Globe, April 19, 1962.

Boston Globe, August 23, 1962.

Boston Globe, March 18, 1963.

Boston Globe, March 24, 1966.

Boston Globe, September 24, 1968.

Boston Globe, March 20, 1981.

Boston Globe, January 5, 1985.

Boston Globe, September 18, 1985.

Boston Globe, November 4, 1999.

Boston Globe, October 29, 2006.

Boston Globe, October 30, 2006.

Boston Globe, October 31, 2006.

Boston Globe, November 1, 2006.

Boston Herald, November 15, 1957.

Boston Herald, December 20, 1957.

Boston Herald, December 25, 1957.

Boston Herald, January 28, 1958.

Boston Herald, February 25, 1958.

Boston Herald, October 23, 1958.

Boston Herald, January 8, 1959.

Boston Herald, January 28, 1959.

Boston Herald, February 17, 1959.

Boston Herald, September 21, 1959.

Boston Herald, November 7, 1959.

Boston Herald, November 13, 1960.

Boston Herald, December 7, 1961.

Boston Herald, February 11, 1962.

Boston Herald, December 12, 1962.

Boston Herald, January 2, 1963.

Boston Herald, March 18, 1963.

Boston Herald-American, January 4, 1985.

Boston Record-American, December 18, 1972.

Boston Traveler, March 26, 1962.

Boston Traveler, October 16, 1962.

Christian Science Monitor, November 17, 1959.

Christian Science Monitor, October 26, 1963.

Christian Science Monitor, January 31, 1964.

Cincinnati Enquirer, May 2, 1983.

New York Post, November 15, 1960.

New York Post, November 20, 1960.

New York Post, *December* 13, 1962.

New York Times, April 27, 1980.

Philadelphia Inquirer, March 18, 1991.

Springfield Daily News (Massachusetts), May 31, 1967.

INDEX

ABOUT THE AUTHOR

Lew Freedman grew up in the Boston area as a Celtics fan. An author of thirty books, Freedman currently works in the sports department of the *Chicago Tribune*. He is a graduate of Boston University's School of Public Communications. Formerly on staff at the *Anchorage Daily News* and *Philadelphia Inquirer*, he has won more than 250 journalism awards. He is looking forward to the next Celtics championship parade through downtown Boston.